GATHERINGS

A collection of highly entertaining menus by the Junior League of Milwaukee.

**Editor &
Food Stylist**
F. Lynn Nelson

**Art Direction
& Design**
Rachel J. Stephens

Photography
Scott Lanza

*This book represents the efforts and dedication
of the members of the Junior League of Milwaukee, Inc.*

To order additional copies of GATHERINGS send for a
brochure: Junior League of Milwaukee, Inc., 626 North
Broadway, Milwaukee, WI 53202, or call (414) 276-6613.

Published 1987. Second Edition 1987.
92 90 89 88   9 8 7 6

Library of Congress Catalog Card Number: 87-81395
ISBN 0-9618294-0-0

The Junior League of Milwaukee is an organization of
women committed to promoting voluntarism and to
improving the community through the effective action
and leadership of trained volunteers.

Proceeds from the sale of GATHERINGS will be returned
to the community through support of the Junior League
of Milwaukee's projects.

Photographs

Ghivetch, recipe 155
Herbed Salmon Steaks, recipe 92
Asparagus Romano on Tomato Fettucini, recipe 92
Guacamole Shrimp Tortilla Chips, recipe 137
Cranberry Shortcakes, recipe 16

TABLE OF CONTENTS

GATHERINGS.
In the language of the Potawatomi Indians native to our
region, "Milwaukee" means "gathering place by the waters."

Thus, GATHERINGS—the best recipes gathered from
our Great Lakes community and arranged into ten chapters
of complete menus. Chapters create a mood to fit every dining
occasion. Menus present a mélange of contemporary
yet classic Midwest cooking which forms the foundation
of heartland cuisine. Boldfaced recipes are featured
with accompanying serving suggestions.

All of this is designed to conserve every cook's most
precious commodity—time.

The editors selected recipes which highlight Wisconsin
products. "America's Dairyland" ingredients include
products such as cream, butter, cheese and frozen custard.
Wisconsin also stars in the roles of producer of
wild rice, cranberries and mushrooms; grower of fresh fruits
and vegetables; supplier of bountiful freshwater fish;
provider of prime veal, ham, lamb, pork and sausages; and
brewer of Old World beverages like beer, malt and ale.

GATHERINGS represents nearly two years of
work by dedicated groups of Junior League of Milwaukee
volunteers, community advisors and culinary
professionals. They gathered and triple-tested the book's 400
recipes, transforming them into this 200-page menu
showcase illustrated with 31 poster-quality color pages.

Experience the joy of your own special GATHERINGS
with this classic cookbook presented by the
Junior League of Milwaukee.

Quiet Gatherings
easy elegance for family or friends

*California Red
Zinfandel*

•

*On a balmy summer
evening, vaguely
reminiscent of
Mediterranean nights, use
red geraniums,
Milwaukee's official
flower, as the centerpiece on
top of a green & white
striped or checked cloth.*
❦

Poulet Provençale

•

4 boneless, skinless chicken breast
  halves, pounded thin
2 tablespoons flour
1 tablespoon fines herbs
  salt & pepper
2 tablespoons butter
2 tablespoons olive oil
1 clove garlic, minced
1 small onion, chopped
3 plum tomatoes, peeled, seeded
  & chopped
½ cup red wine
½ cup pitted, chopped Niçoise or
  Kalamata olives

Combine flour, herbs, salt & pepper.
Lightly dredge chicken in flour to
coat both sides. Heat butter & oil in
large skillet. Sauté chicken 3 minutes each side. Remove to a plate.
Sauté garlic & onion 3 minutes.
Add tomatoes & wine. Return
chicken to pan. Spoon sauce over
chicken. Lower heat. Simmer until
sauce is slightly thickened. Garnish
with olives.

4 servings

Baked Onions

•

5 tablespoons butter, divided
½ pound fresh mushrooms, sliced
1 tablespoon flour
1 teaspoon balsamic vinegar
¾ cup light cream
1½ pounds sweet onions, sliced
  ¼-inch thick, separated into rings
¼ teaspoon pepper
½ pound Swiss or Gruyère cheese,
  grated
6-8 French bread slices, ½-inch thick
  soft butter

Preheat oven to 350°F. Butter a
13x9-inch baking dish.

Melt 3 tablespoons butter in saucepan. Add mushrooms. Sprinkle
with flour. Cook over medium heat,
stirring occasionally 8-10 minutes.
Add vinegar. Slowly stir in cream.
Cook & stir until mixture thickens.
Add pepper. Set aside.

Sauté onion rings with 2 tablespoons
butter in a large skillet 10-15 minutes. Arrange onions in baking dish.
Sprinkle cheese over onions. Top
with mushroom sauce. Butter bread
slices on both sides. Arrange on top.
Bake 30 minutes.

6-8 servings

Lentil Garden Salad

•

8-ounces dried lentils
2 teaspoons salt, divided
½ cup red wine vinegar
¼ teaspoon freshly ground pepper
1 clove garlic, minced
½ cup olive oil
4 cups assorted vegetables:
    chopped cauliflower
    cucumber
    broccoli
    celery
    scallions
1 cup julienned ham, optional
½ cup crumbled feta or blue cheese,
  optional

Wash lentils. Cook in boiling water
to cover with 1 teaspoon salt until
tender, not overcooked, 10 minutes.
Drain.

Combine vinegar, pepper, garlic &
1 teaspoon salt. Stir in oil. Marinate
lentils & vegetables in dressing overnight in refrigerator. Add ham &
cheese, if desired, at serving time. Be
creative in your choice of vegetables
to make it as appetizing & eye appeal-
ing as possible. Use Egyptian lentils
for colorful orange-yellow pzzaz.

8-10 servings

MENU

Grilled
Strip Sirloin
Steaks

**Italian
Mushroom
Salad**

**Pasta
with
Gorgonzola Sauce**

**Raspberry
Tart**

*Chianti
Riserva*

•

*Wind surfing, sailing,
water skiing, swimming,
sunning & water
volleyball have filled your
day. Come home, light
the coals & toss the
salad. Serve!!!*
❦

Italian Mushroom Salad

•

½ pound mushrooms, sliced
2 cups sliced zucchini
1 cup halved cherry tomatoes
1 cup pitted ripe olives
⅓ cup olive oil
⅓ cup red wine vinegar
2 tablespoons capers
1 clove garlic, minced
¼ teaspoon rosemary, crumbled
¼ teaspoon oregano, crumbled

Combine mushrooms, zucchini & tomatoes. Arrange in large glass dish or pan. Combine remaining ingredients. Pour over vegetables. Cover & refrigerate.

6 servings

Pasta with Gorgonzola Sauce

•

3 tablespoons butter
3 cups heavy cream
¼ cup freshly grated Parmesan
½ pound Gorgonzola cheese
  white pepper
¾ pound rotelle or spiral
  shaped pasta, cooked & drained
  freshly grated Parmesan
  freshly ground black pepper

Melt butter. Add cream. Simmer about 5 minutes until thickened slightly. Add Parmesan, Gorgonzola & white pepper. Cook, stirring until cheeses melt. Toss with pasta. Serve with additional grated Parmesan & black pepper.

4 servings

Raspberry Tart

•

½ cup butter, softened
2½ tablespoons sugar
½ cup finely chopped walnuts
1 egg, beaten
1⅓ cups flour
¾ cup chocolate chips
2 egg yolks
2½ tablespoons sugar
2 tablespoons cornstarch
1 teaspoon vanilla
⅔ cup milk
3 tablespoons butter, softened
3 cups sweetened raspberries,
  reserve juice
3 tablespoons cornstarch
  whipped cream

Preheat oven to 350°F. Butter an 11-inch tart pan.

Cream butter & sugar. Add walnuts, egg & flour. Press onto bottom & sides of pan. Refrigerate 30 minutes.

Bake 15-20 minutes. Immediately sprinkle with chocolate chips. When softened, spread chocolate over crust.

In a bowl, beat egg yolks, sugar, cornstarch & vanilla until pale & thick. Heat milk in heavy saucepan. Combine milk with yolk-mixture. Return mixture to saucepan. Whisk over medium heat until very thick. Pour mixture into bowl. Beat 5 minutes. Add butter, one tablespoon at a time. Cool filling.

In a small saucepan, combine cornstarch with reserved raspberry juice. Cook until thick. Add raspberries stirring until coated.

Spread custard mixture on chocolate crust. Top with raspberry sauce. Refrigerate at least 2 hours.

Top with whipped cream if desired.

8-10 servings

MENU

**Beth's
Sherried Wild Rice
Soup**

**Cranberry
Pork Chops**

Scalloped
Potatoes

**Zucchini
with
Toasted Walnuts**

Crème de Menthe
Parfaits

*California
Gewürztraminier*

•

*Return after an evening
of cross-country skiing to
the smells of pork chops
& scalloped potatoes
filling the house. Light a
fire in the fireplace
& relax!!!*
❦

Beth's
Sherried Wild Rice
Soup

•

2 tablespoons butter
1 tablespoon minced onion
¼ cup flour
4 cups chicken stock
½ teaspoon salt
1 cup light cream
¼ cup dry sherry
½ cup wild rice, cook according to
    package directions
    minced parsley or chives

Melt butter in saucepan. Add onion.
Cook to light golden. Blend in flour,
broth & salt, stirring constantly
until thickened. Simmer 5 minutes.
Blend in cream & sherry. Simmer
until heated through.

To serve, place ⅓ cup wild rice in
bottom of soup bowl. Ladle soup
over rice. Garnish with parsley or
chives.

6 servings

Pictured page 58.

Cranberry
Pork Chops

•

6 pork chops
   salt & pepper
1 cup whole berry cranberry sauce
½ cup crushed pineapple
¼ cup fresh orange juice
1 teaspoon grated orange peel

Trim fat from chops. Place fat in
skillet. Sauté fat until crispy. Reserve.
Season chops with salt & pepper.
Brown on both sides. Remove to a
buttered baking dish. Combine
remaining ingredients. Pour over
chops. Cover & bake at 325°F. 45-60
minutes. Sprinkle with cracklings.

4-6 servings

Zucchini
with
Toasted Walnuts

•

6 medium zucchini, sliced
   ½-inch thick
2 tablespoons butter
1 teaspoon salt
½ teaspoon pepper
1 cup chopped, toasted walnuts

Sauté zucchini in butter until tender
but still firm. Season with salt &
pepper. Toss walnuts with zucchini.
Serve.

4 servings

*California
Sonoma
Chardonnay*

•

*Stay out of the kitchen heat
in summer with this
quickly prepared menu.
Enjoy the summer's
evening with friends &
a chilled glass of wine.*
❧

Veal in Madeira & Cream Sauce

•

  1 pound veal round steak
  ¼ cup flour
  2 tablespoons butter
  1 tablespoon vegetable oil
    salt & pepper
  ⅓ cup Madeira
  ½ cup heavy cream
  ¼ teaspoon salt

Cut veal into serving pieces. Dredge in flour. In a skillet large enough to hold the veal in one layer, heat butter & oil. Brown veal over medium-high heat 3-4 minutes on each side until golden. Remove from pan. Season with salt & pepper.

Add Madeira to pan. Reduce heat to medium, stirring up brown bits on bottom of pan. When wine begins to boil, stir in cream & salt. Boil until thickened. Season to taste. Return veal to pan. Simmer, covered, 20 minutes.

2-3 servings

Feather Biscuits

•

  1 package yeast
  ¼ cup water
  2½ cups flour
  1 teaspoon baking powder
  1 teaspoon salt
  ¼ cup sugar
  ½ cup shortening
  1 cup buttermilk

Preheat oven to 400°F.

In small bowl, dissolve yeast in warm water. Set aside.

Mix dry ingredients. Cut in shortening. Stir in buttermilk & yeast mixture. Blend thoroughly. Dough may be covered in a lightly oiled bowl in refrigerator at this point.

Turn out dough onto a floured surface. Knead lightly. Roll out ½-inch thick. Cut with a biscuit cutter. Place on buttered baking sheet. Let biscuits rise 40 minutes. Bake 10 minutes until lightly browned.

18-24 biscuits

Chilled Tangerine Soufflé

•

  2 cups heavy cream
  1 teaspoon vanilla
  3 egg yolks
  ¾ cup superfine sugar
  ½ cup tangerine juice
  ¼ cup grated tangerine peel, divided
  ¼ cup cold water
  1 package gelatin
  ¼ cup hot water
  4 egg whites

Whip cream. Add vanilla. Chill.

Beat yolks. Add sugar, tangerine juice & 3 tablespoons grated peel.

Add cold water to gelatin. When soft, add hot water & dissolve completely over very low heat. Add tangerine mixture to gelatin.

Beat egg whites until stiff. Fold into mixture. Fold in cream. Pile into soufflé dish or bowl. Top with reserved tangerine peel. Chill at least 6 hours. Can be frozen. Any citrus fruit may be substituted for tangerine.

8 servings

MENU

**Spinach
Melon
Salad**

Sourdough
Rolls

**Oriental
Roast Pork
Tenderloin**

**Parmesan
Onions**

Hot Fudge
Sundaes

*Spanish
Pink Cordornieu*

•

*How about a bridge party
in front of the fire? Serve
buffet-style on black
plates!*

Spinach Melon Salad

•

¼ cup vegetable oil
1 tablespoon vinegar
¼ teaspoon salt
¼ teaspoon celery seed
¼ teaspoon Dijon-style mustard
4 cups torn spinach
2 cups cantaloupe balls
1 cup quartered, thinly sliced
   zucchini
2 tablespoons chopped scallions

Combine oil, vinegar, salt, celery seed
& mustard in a cruet. Cover &
shake. Refrigerate.

Combine spinach, cantaloupe,
zucchini & onion in a bowl. Toss
with dressing prior to serving.

6 servings

Oriental Roast Pork Tenderloin

•

Marinade:
1 cup chicken stock
¼ cup soy sauce
¼ cup honey
2 tablespoons sherry
1 tablespoon lemon juice
1 clove garlic, crushed
1 teaspoon cinnamon
¼ teaspoon fresh grated ginger

3 pork tenderloins
2 tablespoons cornstarch

Combine marinade ingredients.
Marinate pork 2 hours, turning frequently. Drain meat, reserve
marinade. Coat meat with cornstarch. Place in a shallow roasting
pan. Bake at 325°F. 45 minutes,
basting frequently with reserved
marinade.

8 servings

Parmesan Onions

•

1 large onion per person
1 tablespoon butter
3 tablespoons freshly grated
   Parmesan cheese

Peel & quarter onion. Place on a
square of aluminum foil. Place butter & cheese on top. Fold up foil,
securing edges & ends well. Place
packages on grill or in 350°F. oven
1 hour.

1 serving

MENU

**Shasti's
Navarin**

**Sautéed
Mushrooms
& Tomatoes**

**Roquefort-Stuffed
Potatoes**

Cheesecake
with
Fresh Fruit

*Spanish
Red Rioja*

•

*A wonderful winter's meal
after a night of ice
skating. Serve hot
toddies while you are
warming up & the
dinner is being
prepared.*

Shasti's
Navarin

•

4 slices bacon
1 medium onion, chopped
1 pound lean lamb cubes or
   leftover lamb
1 tablespoon flour
1 tablespoon sugar
   salt & pepper
2 cups beef stock
3-4 tablespoons tomato paste

Crisp-cook bacon in skillet. Remove
bacon & crumble. Set aside.

Brown onions in bacon fat. Reserve.
Brown lamb. Return crumbled
bacon & onions to pan. Blend in
flour, sugar, salt & pepper. Cook
mixture over medium-low heat 7
minutes. Blend stock & tomato
paste. Slowly stir into pan. Cover &
simmer on low heat 1 hour. Add
liquid if needed. Stir.

4 servings

Sautéed
Mushrooms
& Tomatoes

•

1½ pounds mushrooms, quartered
2 tablespoons chopped onions
2 cloves garlic, minced
4 tablespoons butter
2 tablespoon olive oil
4 tomatoes, peeled, wedged
1½ teaspoons salt
¼ teaspoon pepper
1 teaspoon sugar
¼-½ teaspoon marjoram

Sauté mushrooms with onion & garlic in butter & oil 10 minutes. Add
tomatoes. Stir in salt, pepper, sugar
& marjoram. Cook, uncovered,
until liquid is evaporated.

4-6 servings

Roquefort-Stuffed
Potatoes

•

6 large baking potatoes
¼ cup butter
3 tablespoons warm milk
1 cup sour cream
4-5 ounces crumbled Roquefort
   cheese
2 tablespoons minced chives
1 teaspoon salt
   freshly ground pepper

Preheat oven to 450°F.

Wash & dry potatoes. Rub skins with
vegetable oil. Bake until tender,
about 45 minutes. Cut in half &
scoop out pulp, being careful not
to puncture skins. Mash potatoes. Beat
in butter, warm milk & sour cream
until mixture is light & fluffy. Stir in
cheese. Add chives, salt & pepper.
Put into shells, mounding slightly.
Return to oven 8-10 minutes to
heat through.

12 servings

15

Four Cheese Puffs

•

1 pound loaf unsliced white bread
½ cup butter
¼ cup grated mozzarella cheese
¼ cup grated sharp cheddar cheese
¼ cup grated Swiss cheese
1 package (3 ounces) cream cheese, softened
½ teaspoon dry mustard
⅛ teaspoon cayenne
 pinch salt
2 egg whites

Trim & discard crusts from top, bottom & sides of loaf. Cut bread into 1-inch cubes. Set aside.

In saucepan, combine butter & cheeses. Stir over moderate heat until melted. Add mustard, cayenne & salt. Remove from heat.

Beat egg whites until stiff. Fold into cheese mixture. Using a fondue fork or skewer, spear bread cubes one at a time & dip into mixture until well coated.

Arrange cubes on a baking sheet. Freeze immediately until firm, preferably overnight. Remove puffs from baking sheet. Store in plastic bags in freezer until ready to use.

At serving time, place frozen cubes on baking sheet. Bake at 400°F. 10 minutes, until nicely browned.

50 puffs

Split Pea & Pepper Soup

•

1 pound dried split peas
6 cups chicken stock
2 meaty ham bones
3 celery stalks with leaves, chopped
1 bay leaf
1 teaspoon thyme
2 tablespoons butter
3 sweet peppers (green, yellow, red), chopped
1 large onion, chopped
½ cup dry white wine
½ teaspoon grated nutmeg
 salt & pepper
 sour cream
 popcorn

In a large pan combine peas, stock, ham bones, celery, bay & thyme. Bring to boil. Reduce heat. Simmer 45 minutes. Remove bay leaf. Purée 1 cup celery & peas in blender. Return to pan. Stir to blend.

In skillet, over medium heat, melt butter. Sauté peppers & onions 5 minutes. Add wine & nutmeg. Simmer 3 minutes. Season to taste. Pour into soup mixture. Serve garnished with a dollop of sour cream & popcorn.

6 servings

Cranberry Shortcakes

•

1 cup sugar
3 tablespoons butter
1½ cups flour
1½ teaspoons baking powder
½ teaspoon salt
¾ cup milk
2 cups halved cranberries

Glaze:
½ cup butter
½ cup light cream
½ cup brown sugar
½ cup white sugar

Cream butter & sugar. Add dry ingredients. Stir in milk. Add cranberries. Stir just to mix. Pour into 9-inch square pan. Bake 375°F. 40-45 minutes. When nearly cool, cut into squares. For glaze, boil butter, cream, brown sugar & white sugar over low heat 15 minutes. Serve hot over warm shortcakes.

8-12 servings

Pictured page 8.

MENU

**Mom Terschan's
Beef Goulash**

Buttered
Brussels Sprouts

**Lois'
Pilaf**

Bibb Lettuce
with
Lemon Vinaigrette

**Savory
Topped
Rolls**

Cherries Jubilee
over
Vanilla Custard Ice Cream

*French
Rhône Tavel*

•

*This meal is one to be made
the day before. Finish
watching that all-
important football
game. Then put together
the last minute items
& serve.*

❧

Mom Terschan's
Beef Goulash

•

5 tablespoons vegetable oil, divided
6 medium onions, sliced &
   separated into rings
3 pounds beef chuck, cut into
   1½-2-inch cubes
2 teaspoons paprika
1 teaspoon salt
1 tablespoon vinegar
1 tablespoon tomato paste
½ teaspoon caraway seed,
   finely ground
1 clove garlic, minced
1½ cups beef stock
2 teaspoons flour

Heat 2 tablespoons oil. Sauté onion
rings until transparent. Remove
onions, reserve. Add remaining oil.
Brown meat over medium-high
heat. Add paprika & salt. Stir. Return
onions. Add vinegar & tomato
paste. Add caraway seed, garlic &
1 cup stock. Simmer until meat is
tender, about 2 hours. Mix flour &
remaining stock. Add to pan. Blend
well. Simmer a few minutes. Serve.
Best if made the day before!

5-6 servings

Lois'
Pilaf

•

1½ cups fine noodles
½ cup butter
1 cup rice
1 small onion, chopped
2 cups chicken stock
1½ cups water
½ teaspoon salt or other herbs
   pepper

Brown noodles in butter. Add
remaining ingredients. Bring to
boil. Immediately turn down heat.
Simmer covered, 25 minutes. Pilaf
can be held for a long time if serving
is delayed.

6-8 servings

Savory
Topped
Rolls

•

½ cup mayonnaise
½ cup Parmesan cheese
¼ cup finely chopped red onion
5 dinner rolls

In a small bowl, mix mayonnaise,
cheese & onion. Break rolls in half.
Spread broken surfaces of roll with
cheese mixture. Toast under broiler
until brown. Serve immediately.

5 servings

•

*Remember that luncheon
you have been wanting
to give? Here's the
perfect menu. Set your
table with white lace &
yellow daffodils galore.*
❧

Seafood
Gratiné

•

1 pound cooked shrimp, split
    lengthwise
1 cup cooked, flaked crab meat
½-¾ cup chopped green pepper
¼ cup finely chopped onions
1 cup thinly sliced celery
1 cup mayonnaise
1 teaspoon white wine-
    Worcestershire sauce
½ teaspoon salt
¼ teaspoon pepper
1 cup fresh bread crumbs
1 tablespoon butter

In a medium bowl, combine shrimp,
crab, green pepper, onion, celery,
mayonnaise & seasonings. Spread
mixture in 13x9-inch casserole. Top
with bread crumbs & butter. Bake in
350°F. oven 30 minutes, until lightly
browned.

8-10 servings

Florentine
Tomatoes

•

4 medium tomatoes, hollowed
2 cups packed, cooked, chopped
    spinach, well drained
1 cup sour cream
2 tablespoons minced onion
½ teaspoon seasoned salt
    chopped parsley

Combine spinach, sour cream, onion
& seasoned salt. Fill tomatoes &
bake, uncovered, in muffin tin 30
minutes at 325°F. Decorate tops with
chopped parsley if desired.

4 servings

Julie's
Wheat Bread

•

3 cups warm water
3 packages yeast
3 cups whole wheat flour
½ cup honey
2 teaspoons salt
¼ cup vegetable oil
3-4 cups flour
    milk

Combine water, yeast & whole wheat
flour. Cover. Let rest 15 minutes.
Add honey, salt & oil. Mix well. Add
3-4 cups flour. Knead on floured
surface 5-10 minutes, adding flour if
needed.

Place in oiled bowl, turning dough
to coat. Cover, let rise one hour
until doubled.

Preheat oven to 450°F. Butter 2,
9x5-inch loaf pans.

Punch dough down. Divide into two
loaves. Place in loaf pans. Cover, let
rise one hour. Place in oven. Immediately reduce heat to 375°F. Bake
35-45 minutes. Remove from pans.
Brush with milk & cover with towels
a few minutes until crust is soft.

2 loaves

*Fill a Chinese lantern with
a string of small white
Christmas lights. Hang
from the ceiling or outdoors
in the trees & plug in.
Use bright colored
tablecloths & dishes.
Of course use
chop sticks only.*
❧

Chinese Spareribs

•

4 pounds pork spareribs
2 cups water
½ cup liquid from braising
½ cup honey
¼ cup soy sauce
½ cup ketchup

Braise spareribs & 2 cups water at
350°F. 1 hour & 20 minutes.

Place spareribs in a large pan.
Combine braising liquid, honey, soy
& ketchup. Warm this mixture, pour
over ribs. Allow meat to marinate
in refrigerator at least overnight.
Broil, or roast meat at 450°F.
½ hour, until crispy & brown.

4 servings

Broccoli with Lemon Mustard Cream Sauce

•

1½-2 pounds broccoli
½ cup mayonnaise
2 tablespoons lemon juice
1 tablespoon Dijon-style mustard
⅓ cup heavy cream, whipped

Steam broccoli until just tender.

Whisk together mayonnaise, lemon
juice & mustard. Fold in whipped
cream. Pour sauce over hot broccoli
& serve.

4-6 servings

Mocha Ice Cream Dessert

•

24 cream-filled chocolate cookies
⅓ cup butter, melted
½ gallon coffee ice cream, softened
3-ounces unsweetened chocolate
2 tablespoons butter
1 cup sugar
   pinch salt
1 can (11 ounces) evaporated milk
½ teaspoon vanilla
1½ cups heavy cream, whipped
1½-ounces coffee-flavored liqueur
   powdered sugar to taste
¾ cup chopped pecans

Crush cookies in blender or food
processor. Combine crumbs with
butter. Press into a buttered 13x9-
inch pan. Chill. Spoon softened
ice cream on chilled crust & freeze.

Melt chocolate & butter. Add sugar,
salt & milk. Bring mixture to boil.
Stir until thickened. Remove from
heat. Add vanilla. Chill. Spread on
top of ice cream & freeze.

Add powdered sugar & liqueur to
whipped cream. Spread over chocolate layer. Sprinkle with chopped
nuts. Freeze.

25 servings

A
Veil
Caper

•

MENU

**A
Veal
Caper**

Buttered Spinach Noodles
with
Poppy Seeds

**Cabbage
&
Grapes**

**Cranberry
Crisp**

California Pinot Noir

•

*The combination of colors
in this menu is a delight
to the eye. Serve on
yellow or white plates
with pale green linens.
Rave reviews!*
❧

2 pounds veal stew meat
2 stalks celery, cut into 2-inch
  lengths
1 small whole onion
1½ cups chicken stock
6 peppercorns
2 tablespoons butter
2 tablespoons flour
2 tablespoons lemon juice
2 teaspoons capers
  salt & white pepper

Preheat oven to 350°F.

Place meat, celery, onion, stock &
peppercorns in 2-quart covered casserole. Bake 1-1½ hours until meat is
fork tender. Discard celery, onion
& peppercorns. Reserve pan juices.

In small saucepan, melt butter. Add
flour. Mix well. Add juice from
meat. Cook until thick & smooth.
Add lemon juice, capers & meat.
Season with salt & white pepper.
Serve over rice or noodles.

4 servings

Cabbage
&
Grapes

•

1 small head red cabbage
½ cup seasoned, toasted bread
  crumbs
2 tablespoons butter, divided
1 cup seedless grapes, halved
1 tablespoon flour
1 cup milk
¼ teaspoon salt
¼ teaspoon pepper
¼ teaspoon curry powder
  pinch cayenne pepper
½ pound Gruyère cheese, grated
1 tablespoon white wine

Preheat oven to 300°F. Butter a
13x9-inch baking dish.

Chop cabbage into bite-size pieces
or wedges. Boil in salted water 5-6
minutes. Drain.

Sauté bread crumbs with 1 tablespoon of butter. Set aside. Melt 1
tablespoon butter in medium saucepan. Add flour & cook 2 minutes.
Add milk, salt, pepper, curry powder
& cayenne pepper. Stir until thickened. Add cheese to mixture, stirring
until melted. Add white wine.
Combine cabbage, grapes & white
sauce. Place in baking dish. Top
with crumbs. Bake 15-20 minutes.
Try red cabbage with green grapes,
green cabbage with red grapes.

8-10 servings

Pictured page 174.

Cranberry
Crisp

•

1 pound fresh cranberries
¾ cup sugar, divided
¼ cup chopped nuts
1 egg, beaten
½ cup flour
¼ cup butter, melted
  whipped cream

Preheat oven to 325°F. Butter an
8-inch pie pan.

Cover bottom of pan with cranberries. Sprinkle cranberries with ¼
cup sugar & nuts. Add remaining
sugar to beaten egg. Add flour &
melted butter. Pour over cranberries.
Bake 45 minutes. Serve warm with
fresh whipped cream.

6-8 servings

Orange Roughie Dijonnaise

•

Sauce:
2 tablespoons butter
1 small onion, chopped
2 tablespoons flour
⅓ cup dry white wine
¼ cup water
   salt & pepper
1 tablespoon Dijon-style mustard
⅓ cup milk or light cream
⅓ cup grated mozzarella cheese
1 peeled, seeded & chopped tomato

2 pounds orange roughie fillets
2 tablespoons butter, melted
2 tablespoons fresh lemon juice
   salt & pepper

For the sauce, melt butter in saucepan over medium heat. Sauté onion 3-5 minutes. Add flour. Cook 2 minutes. Add wine, water, salt, pepper & mustard. Stir & cook until thickened. Add milk & cheese. When cheese melts add tomato. Remove from heat. Cover & keep warm.

Preheat broiler. Arrange fillets on broiler pan, turning under thin ends. Brush with melted butter. Sprinkle with lemon, salt & pepper. Broil 4-inches from heat 8-10 minutes until fish flakes with a fork. Cover fillets with sauce. Return to broiler until sauce is lightly browned, 2-3 minutes.

4 servings

Beets Romaine

•

French Dressing:
½ cup vegetable oil
⅛ cup red wine vinegar
1 tablespoon water
1 tablespoon tomato paste
1 clove garlic, minced
   pinch salt, pepper & sugar

2 cups cooked, julienned beets
1 tablespoon prepared horseradish
1 tablespoon grated onion
1 head romaine lettuce, torn into
   bite-size pieces

Combine ingredients for dressing. Toss beets with horseradish, onion & ½ the dressing. Refrigerate several hours. Toss romaine with remaining dressing. Arrange on flat serving platter. Arrange beets in center.

4 servings

Velvet Pound Cake

•

1½ cups butter, softened
1 teaspoon almond extract
1 pound powdered sugar
6 extra large eggs
3 cups cake flour

Preheat oven to 350°F. Butter & flour a 10-inch tube pan.

Beat butter & extract until very light & fluffy. Add sugar, a little at a time. Add eggs alternately with flour, beating well after each addition. Bake 1 hour 10 minutes. Cool 10 minutes. Remove from pan. Cool on wire rack. Will stay fresh tightly covered 5 days or frozen 1-2 months. Serve with berries or sliced fruits.

12-15 servings

MENU

Orange Roughie Dijonnaise

Ancini di Pepe
Pasta

Beets Romaine

Velvet Pound Cake

Sliced Nectarines

French White Burgundy Mâcon-Villages

•

The menu tastes as outstanding as it looks. Served to family or guests, anyone would feel particularly special.

MENU

**Flank Steak
with Red Wine
& Shallot Sauce**

Corn-on-the-Cob
with
Blue Cheese Butter

**Garlic
Primavera**

**Brown Bag
Apple Pie**

*French Red Bordeaux
Saint Émilion*

•

*Treat yourselves on a
Sunday afternoon of
cleaning the garage or
basement to a repast
instead of supper. Grill
the Steak if you like.*
❧

Flank Steak with Red Wine & Shallot Sauce

•

1½-2 pounds flank steak
    soy sauce
    freshly ground pepper
  1 teaspoon dried thyme
1¼ cups chopped shallots
1½ cups red Bordeaux or
    Burgundy wine
 ½ cup butter
  2 tablespoons finely chopped
    parsley

Heat broiler or prepare grill.

Brush both sides of steak with soy sauce, twice. Sprinkle with pepper & thyme. Broil or grill 3-4 minutes each side.

In saucepan, bring shallots & wine to boil. Cook 10 minutes. Off heat, add butter & several grinds pepper. Stir until butter melts. Add parsley.

To serve, slice steak very thinly on diagonal. Ladle sauce over steak on serving platter.

4 servings

Garlic Primavera

•

 ½ pound vermicelli, cooked &
    drained
1½ cups mayonnaise
  2 teaspoons mashed garlic
    pepper
  1 tablespoon vinegar
  4 asparagus spears, cut in 1-inch
    lengths
  2 cups sliced zucchini
 ½ cup peas
  1 cup broccoli flowerets
 ¼ pound mushrooms, sliced
  2 tomatoes, sliced
 ¼ cup chopped parsley
  3 tablespoons chopped fresh basil

Rinse pasta with cold running water. Drain.

Blend mayonnaise, garlic, vinegar & pepper. Set aside.

Blanch asparagus, zucchini, peas & broccoli 1-2 minutes. Rinse in ice cold water. Drain well. Toss blanched vegetables, spaghetti, mushrooms, tomatoes, dressing, parsley & basil in large bowl. Chill until served.

8-10 servings

Brown Bag Apple Pie

•

  1 unbaked 9-inch pie crust, pierced
    with fork
  4 cups sliced MacIntosh or Granny
    Smith apples
  2 tablespoons lemon juice
  1 cup sugar, divided
 ½ cup plus 2 tablespoons flour
 ½ teaspoon nutmeg
 ½ cup butter
    whipped cream garnish

Preheat oven to 425°F.

Toss apples with lemon juice in bowl. Arrange on pastry. In small bowl, combine ½ cup sugar, 2 tablespoons flour & nutmeg. Mix well. Sprinkle over apples.

Combine remaining sugar & flour. Cut butter into mixture to make coarse crumbs. Sprinkle over apples.

Slide pie into large brown paper bag. Fold end over twice & secure with paper clips. Put on baking sheet. Bake 1 hour. Garnish with whipped cream.

6-8 servings

Casual Gatherings
informal, picnics & grilled foods

A portable Soup & Sandwich supper can be hearty & extremely appetizing. Serve the soup at your next tailgate party in mugs topped off with sour cream or croutons. The Drambuie Cake can be made into muffins for individual servings. Everything tastes better if made in advance!

Carrot Soup

•

2 slices bacon, chopped
½ cup chopped onion
1 clove garlic, minced
3 cups chicken stock
2 cups chopped carrots
1 cup peeled, seeded & chopped tomatoes
1 cup diced potatoes
1 teaspoon salt
   white pepper
   Seasonings to taste: ginger, cinnamon & lemon juice; or, dill & paprika; or, coriander & ginger
   sour cream

Cook bacon, onion & garlic in large saucepan until bacon is crisp. Drain fat. Add stock, carrots, tomatoes, potatoes, salt & pepper. Heat to boiling. Reduce heat. Add your choice of seasonings. Cover & simmer 20 minutes until carrots are tender. Blend smooth in blender or processor. Best to make 1 day in advance. Reheat to boiling. Serve hot garnished with sour cream.

4 servings

Hot Mustard Sauce

•

4-ounces dry mustard
½ cup tarragon vinegar
1 egg, slightly beaten
½ cup sugar

Put mustard & vinegar in top of double boiler. Let stand overnight. Heat over boiling water. Add beaten egg & sugar. Cook until thick & smooth. Stir often. Remove from heat. Beat with mixer until steam is gone. Mustard steam will smart your eyes.

1 pint

Horseradish Sauce

•

2 egg yolks
2 tablespoons prepared horseradish
1 tablespoon water
1 tablespoon butter
½ teaspoon sugar
   pinch salt
1 cup heavy cream, whipped

In top of double boiler, combine yolks, horseradish, water, butter, sugar & salt. Blend well. Cook over low heat until thick, stirring constantly. Cool completely. Fold cream into cooled mixture. Chill overnight. Prepare 1 day before serving.

1½ cups

Drambuie Cake

•

2½ cups unbleached flour
   pinch salt
1 teaspoon baking powder
1 teaspoon baking soda
1 cup butter, softened
1 cup sugar, divided
3 eggs, separated
1 tablespoon grated orange peel
1¼ cups sour cream
2 tablespoons Drambuie liqueur

Sauce:
½ cup sugar
½ cup orange juice
¼ cup Drambuie liqueur

Preheat oven to 325°F.

Sift flour, salt, baking powder & soda.

Cream butter & ⅔ cup sugar until light & fluffy. Add yolks, one at a time, beating one minute after each addition. Add orange rind. Add Drambuie. Alternately add dry ingredients & sour cream.

In small bowl, beat egg whites until soft peaks form. Gradually add remaining ⅓ cup sugar, beating until stiff & glossy. Gently fold into batter. Pour into a 10-inch tube or bundt pan. Bake 1 hour 20 minutes.

For the sauce, combine sugar & orange juice in small saucepan. Cook mixture until sugar dissolves & mixture boils 1-2 minutes. Remove from heat. Add Drambuie. Pour over hot cake. Poke holes in cake to absorb sauce. When cool to the touch, turn out cake onto plate. Chill.

20 servings

*French Red
Bordeaux Côte de Bourg*

•

*Invite the Grandparents
over for a Sunday
afternoon of storytelling
with the grandchildren,
"What it was like
when you were young?"*
❧

Marinated
Chuck Roast

•

4 pounds chuck roast
1 clove garlic

Marinade:
½ cup soy sauce
½ cup water
1 tablespoon sugar
3 tablespoons wine vinegar

Rub meat with garlic clove on both sides. Let stand ½ hour. Pierce meat thoroughly with fork. Combine marinade ingredients. Marinate four hours. Broil or grill 12-15 minutes on each side, 4-inches from heat. Warm leftover marinade to use as au jus.

6 servings

Potatoes
&
Beer

•

4 medium potatoes, thinly sliced
1 large onion, thinly sliced
4-5 tablespoons butter
    salt & pepper
2 cups beer
1 cup heavy cream

Preheat oven to 525°F.

Overlap potatoes & onions in 11x9-inch pan. Dot with butter. Salt & pepper to taste. Pour beer over potatoes. Bake 10 minutes. Reduce heat to 375°F. Continue baking 40 minutes. Add cream. Bake an additional 10 minutes.

4 servings

Milwaukee's
Country
French Bread

•

2¼ cups water
¾ cup beer
1½ packages active dry yeast
1 tablespoon salt
7 cups flour
1 egg white, lightly beaten

Preheat oven to 375°F.

In a large bowl, combine water, beer, yeast, salt & 3 cups flour to make a pancake-type batter. Allow to rest at least one hour in a covered bowl. Turn out onto a floured surface. Add enough additional flour to make a smooth ball. Knead 10-15 minutes. Form into a large round loaf, or two small loaves. Place on buttered baking sheet to let rise, covered, one hour. Brush with egg white or sprinkle with water to make crusty. Bake one hour.

1 large loaf or 2 small loaves

MENU

Yellow Cherry Tomatoes
Stuffed with
Herbed Goat Cheese

Grilled
Swordfish
Steaks

Rice
&
Green Chilies

Strawberry
Muffins

*California
Chardonnay*

•

*This is a beautiful menu
when presented on white
plates with white
napkins on a white
tablecloth surrounded
with crystal vases
filled with white Lilies of
the Valley. Use crystal
oil-burning candles to
give a soft sheen
to the whole meal.*

Grilled
Swordfish
Steaks

•

6 swordfish steaks, 1-inch thick
½ cup olive oil
1 cup dry white wine
1 small onion, chopped
 juice of 1 lemon
2 teaspoons salt
2 teaspoons oregano
1 clove garlic, minced
 mayonnaise

Place steaks in shallow baking dish.
Mix oil, wine, onion, lemon juice,
salt, oregano & garlic. Pour over
steaks & let stand one hour at room
temperature. Drain. Baste steaks with
mayonnaise. Grill 4-inches from
coals, 6-8 minutes each side, basting
several times with mayonnaise.

6 servings

Rice
&
Green Chilies

•

1 cup uncooked rice
½ pound Monterey Jack cheese,
 coarsely grated
1 can (4 ounces) chopped green
 chilies
2 cups sour cream
2 tablespoons butter

Cook rice according to package
directions. Add cheese to hot rice.
Add green chilies & sour cream. Mix
well. Put in buttered casserole dish.
Dot with butter. Bake 350°F. 30 minutes until bubbly.

4 servings

Strawberry
Muffins

•

2 cups strawberries
1¼ cups sugar, divided
1½ cups flour
½ teaspoon baking soda
1 teaspoon cinnamon
½ teaspoon nutmeg
2 eggs, beaten
¾ cup vegetable oil
1 teaspoon vanilla
¾ cup chopped walnuts

Preheat oven to 350°F. Butter a
muffin pan.

Clean, hull & chop strawberries.
Combine with ¼ cup sugar. Let
stand one hour. Combine flour, soda,
cinnamon & nutmeg. Set aside. Mix
eggs & oil. Add one cup sugar. Stir
until well blended. Add vanilla &
strawberry mixture. Blend together.
Add nuts. Fold into dry ingredients.
Mix only until moistened. Fill 12
muffin tins ¾-full. Bake 25 minutes.

12 muffins

MENU

**Italian
Sausages**

**Blue Cheese
Potato Salad**

Cucumbers
&
Yellow Tomatoes

**Poppy Seed
Cookies**

*Italian
Red Vino
Nobile di Montepulciano*

•

*Going to the Brewers
baseball game? Make
Sausages the night before
& reheat before
departing. Take along
plenty of napkins.*

Italian
Sausages

•

12 Italian sausages
3 medium onions, sliced
2 cans (12 ounces each) tomato paste
3 cups water
2 tablespoons sweet basil
2 tablespoons oregano
1 teaspoon parsley
2-3 bay leaves
salt & pepper
3 large sweet green peppers, sliced

In a 3-quart saucepan, brown sausage. Remove to plate. Sauté onions. Add tomato paste, water, basil, oregano, parsley, bay leaves, salt & pepper. Heat thoroughly. Add sausage & simmer one hour. Cover & refrigerate overnight. Before serving, add green peppers. Simmer one hour. Serve in Italian sausage buns.

6 servings

Blue Cheese
Potato Salad

•

8 to 10 new potatoes, unpeeled
½ cup blue cheese, crumbled
1 cup chopped celery
2 tablespoons chopped chives
2 tablespoons sliced scallions
¾ cup sour cream
¾ cup mayonnaise
3 tablespoons vinegar
½ teaspoon salt
¼ teaspoon pepper

Wash potatoes. Cook in boiling water until tender. Slice with skins. Combine with blue cheese, celery, chives, & scallions. In a separate bowl, combine sour cream, mayonnaise, vinegar, salt & pepper. Stir until blended. Fold into potatoes. Chill thoroughly.

6-8 servings

Poppy Seed
Cookies

•

1 cup butter
½ cup sugar
2 egg yolks
1 teaspoon vanilla
2 cups flour
¼ teaspoon salt
3 tablespoons poppy seed
sugar

juice glass

Preheat oven to 375°F. Butter a baking sheet.

Cream butter, sugar & egg yolks. Add remaining ingredients. Mix well. Chill 1 hour. Roll 1 teaspoon dough into a ball. Place on baking sheet. Fill sheet with dough balls. Dip bottom of juice glass into sugar & press dough balls flat. Bake 10 minutes. Cool 2 minutes. Remove from pan to cooling rack.

4 dozen

MENU

Marinated
Vegetables
on Skewers

**Jack Birchhill's
Beef Barbeque**

Sliced Goat Cheddar
& Colby

Grilled
Corn-on-the-Cob

**Cucumber-Pimiento
Salad**

**Mrs. Repetti's
Cupcakes**

Homemade
Ice Cream

*Spanish
Red Rioja*

•

*Picnic supper before the
4th of July neighborhood
fireworks display.
Serve cupcakes & ice cream
after the walk back to
the house.*
❧

Jack Birchhill's
Beef Barbeque

•

6 pounds beef chuck roast
1 cup chopped celery
1 large onion, chopped
1 large green pepper, chopped
1 bottle (10 ounces) ketchup
3 tablespoons barbeque sauce
3 tablespoons vinegar
1½ cups water
1 teaspoon hot pepper sauce
2 tablespoons chili powder
2 teaspoons salt
1 teaspoon pepper

Cut meat into large pieces. Place in roaster or dutch oven. Combine remaining ingredients. Pour over meat. Cover. Bake 6 hours at 300°F. Stir several times during cooking. Shred meat with 2 forks. Discard fat. Continue cooking 15 minutes, uncovered. Serve in assorted hard rolls.

2½-3 dozen

Cucumber-Pimiento
Salad

•

3 cucumbers
5 tablespoons lemon juice
2 tablespoons honey
¾ teaspoon salt
¼ teaspoon white pepper
1 small onion, chopped
½ cup sour cream
¼ cup mayonnaise
1 jar (4 ounces) chopped pimientos
leaf lettuce

Score cucumbers. Cut in half lengthwise. Remove seeds. Slice thin. Pat dry. Combine lemon juice, honey, salt, pepper & onion. Toss with cucumbers. Cover & refrigerate 1-2 hours, stirring occasionally. Combine sour cream, mayonnaise & pimientos. Cover & chill 1-2 hours. Drain cucumbers, reserving 3 tablespoons marinade. Whisk marinade into sour cream mixture. Add to cucumbers. Serve in bowl lined with leafy lettuce.

4-6 servings

Mrs. Repetti's
Cupcakes

•

1 package (8 ounces) cream cheese, softened
1 egg
⅓ cup sugar
⅛ teaspoon salt
1 cup semi-sweet mini chocolate chips
1½ cups flour
1 cup sugar
¼ cup cocoa
1 teaspoon baking soda
⅛ teaspoon salt
1 cup water
⅓ cup vegetable oil
1 teaspoon vinegar
1 teaspoon vanilla
powdered sugar

Preheat oven to 350°F. Butter 18 muffin cups.

In a small bowl, beat cream cheese, egg, sugar & salt. Stir in chocolate chips. Set aside.

In a large bowl combine flour, sugar, cocoa, soda & salt. Add water, oil, vinegar & vanilla. Fill muffin cups ½-full with cocoa batter. Top each with 1 heaping teaspoon cream cheese mixture. Sprinkle with powdered sugar. Bake 30-35 minutes. Can also be made in 13x9-inch pan. Drop cream cheese mixture evenly over top of cake. Bake 40-45 minutes.

18 servings

•

*A meal for a night on the
deck when the lake
is quiet, the moon is just
coming up over the
horizon as the sun sets
in a multitude of
harmonious colors . . .*

Martini Sole
on the
Grill

•

  2 tablespoons butter
  1 teaspoon chopped shallots
  4 fillets of sole
    pinch seasoned salt
⅓ cup dry vermouth
  1 teaspoon cornstarch
  1 tablespoon gin
  2 teaspoons chopped parsley
    sliced green olives

Warm butter & shallots in flat pan
inside covered grill. Sprinkle sole
on both sides with seasoned salt.
Arrange in pan with shallots & butter. Mix vermouth, cornstarch & gin.
Pour over fish. Grill 5-6 minutes.
Sprinkle with parsley. Baste fish with
the pan juices. Cook another 5 minutes. Serve with a few sliced green
olives.

4 servings

Pictured page 60.

Cashew Rice
with
Scallions

•

  2 cups long grain rice
3½ cups cold water
  1 teaspoon salt
¼ cup chopped scallions
½ cup cashew halves
  2 tablespoons honey

Place rice, water & salt in medium
saucepan. Bring to a boil. Boil 4
minutes. Cover & cook on low heat
15-20 minutes, until liquid is
absorbed. Remove from heat. Let rest
10 minutes. Fluff rice & add green
onions, cashews & honey.

8-10 servings

Sauce
for a
Summer Sundae

•

½ cup raspberry jelly
1½ tablespoons cornstarch
  1 cup orange juice
    pinch salt
  2 tablespoons orange-flavored
    liqueur
  1 cup sliced, unpeeled nectarines
½ cup raspberries
½ cup blueberries

Melt jelly in small pan over low heat.
Mix cornstarch, orange juice & salt.
Stir into melted jelly. Cook, stirring
constantly. Boil mixture gently until
sauce is clear. Add orange liqueur &
fruit. Chill. Serve over vanilla or
lemon custard ice cream.

3 cups

*A wonderful weekend at
the cabin with friends.
Take a short walk while
the appetizers are baking.*

Green
Chili
Bites

•

8-ounces whole green chilies
10-ounces sharp cheddar
   cheese, grated
3 eggs, beaten
1 tablespoon prepared mustard
   dash Worcestershire sauce
   dash hot pepper sauce
   paprika

Preheat oven to 350°F. Butter a
9x9-inch pan.

Remove seeds from green chilies,
rinse & drain well. Mix cheese, eggs,
mustard, Worcestershire & hot pepper sauce. Mixture will be thick.
Line pan with green chilies. Spread
cheese mixture over the top. Sprinkle with paprika. Bake 25 minutes.
Cut into small squares & serve hot.

8 servings

Flank Steak
with
Asparagus & Broccoli

•

¾-pound flank steak
1 can (12 ounces) beer
½ cup soy sauce
½ teaspoon ground coriander
¾ pound fresh asparagus, sliced
   diagonally
1 bunch broccoli, cut into flowerets
1 red pepper, thinly sliced

Dressing:
⅓ cup soy sauce
¼ cup white vinegar
3 tablespoons sesame oil
1½ tablespoons grated fresh
   ginger root
1 teaspoon sugar
   freshly ground pepper

Marinate flank steak in beer, soy
sauce & coriander 4 hours or overnight. Remove from marinade, grill
or broil to desired doneness. Slice
thinly. Blanch asparagus, broccoli &
peppers in salted water for 30 seconds. Drain & cool. Set aside.
Combine ingredients for dressing.
When ready to serve, combine steak,
vegetables & dressing. Serve at room
temperature. 8-ounces water chestnuts & 2-ounces pimiento may be
substituted for asparagus when not
in season.

4 servings

Sour Cream
Potato Salad

•

⅓ cup vinaigrette dressing
7 medium pototoes, cooked,
   peeled & sliced
¾ cup celery
⅓ cup sliced scallions, including tops
4 hard-cooked eggs
1 cup mayonnaise
½ cup sour cream
1 tablespoon prepared horseradish
   salt & pepper
1 cucumber, peeled & diced,
   optional

Pour dressing over warm potatoes.
Chill at least two hours. Chop egg
whites. Add to potatoes with celery
& scallions. Sieve egg yolks & mix
with mayonnaise, sour cream &
horseradish. Gently fold mixture
into salad. Add salt & pepper to taste.
Chill 2 hours longer. Garnish with
cucumbers.

8 servings

Spanish Red Rioja

•

*Take a break from snow
shoveling or cleaning the
basement & enjoy this
hearty meal. Use all the
chunks & pieces of cheese
in the refrigerator for
the Sandwich.*
❦

Ultimate Grilled Cheese Sandwich

•

1 small loaf French bread, halved
  lengthwise
2 tablespoons prepared mustard
½ pound cheese, grated, preferably
  more than 1 type
¼ cup butter, softened
½ teaspoon Worcestershire sauce
1 egg
4 slices crisp-cooked bacon,
  crumbled
2 scallions, chopped

Spread cut sides of bread with mustard. Mix cheeses, butter, Worcestershire, egg, bacon & scallions in mixer
or food processor. Spread mixture
on bread. Place on baking sheet.
Broil until puffed & lightly
browned, 5 minutes. Serve immediately. Can be cut into one inch strips
& served as appetizers too!!!

4 servings

Creole Onion Soup

•

8 cups heavy cream
1 cup chicken stock
9 tablespoons unsalted butter,
  divided
4 medium onions, shaved
2 tablespoon flour
1-2 tablespoons Curry Mix,
  recipe follows
  freshly ground white pepper

Curry Mix:
1½ teaspoons cumin seed
1 teaspoon coriander seed
1 teaspoon whole black pepper
1 teaspoon turmeric
1 teaspoon dried chili pepper
½ teaspoon ground ginger
½ teaspoon hot pepper
¼-½ teaspoon cinnamon

Scald cream & chicken stock in a heavy
saucepan over low heat. Remove
from heat. Set aside. Melt 6 tablespoons butter in heavy saucepan over
medium heat. Add onions. Sauté
until onions are soft, 6-7 minutes.
Remove onions with a slotted spoon
to a small bowl. Reserve. Add remaining 3 tablespoons butter to saucepan. Stir in flour. Cook, stirring often,
3-4 minutes. Add curry mix. Cook,
stirring constantly, 2 minutes. Add
hot cream mixture in a steady
stream, whisking constantly. Cook
until smooth & begins to thicken.
Heat to boiling. Reduce heat to low.
Simmer 15-20 minutes. Add
reserved onions to soup. Season with
salt & white pepper. Thin soup with
additional stock if desired.

For curry mix, grind ingredients in
a mortar or electric grinder until
powdered. Put ingredients through
sieve.

8 servings

Chocolate Chocolate-Chip Cookies

•

1 cup butter, softened
1½ cups sugar
2 eggs
1 teaspoon vanilla
1 tablespoon coffee-flavored
  liqueur
2 cups flour
⅔ cup cocoa
¼ teaspoon baking soda
½ teaspoon salt
2 cups chocolate chips

Preheat oven to 350°F.

Cream butter, sugar, eggs, vanilla &
liqueur. Combine flour, cocoa, baking soda & salt. Blend into creamed
mixture. Add chips. Drop by teaspoonfuls 2-inches apart on baking
sheets. Bake 8 minutes. Leave on
sheets to cool 2 minutes before
removing.

4 dozen

ENTREE

VEGETABLE

DESSERT

Our Best
Barbecued
Ribs

•

Harvest
Corn
Relish

•

Sour Cream
Apple Squares

•

1½ cups ketchup
1 cup sour mash whiskey
¾ cup chili sauce
½ cup vinegar
⅓ cup Worcestershire sauce
⅓ cup firmly packed brown sugar
3 tablespoons fresh lemon juice
1 tablespoon paprika
2 teaspoons salt
1 clove garlic, crushed
¼ teaspoon hot pepper sauce
5 pounds pork back ribs
  salt & pepper
  thin slices onion
  thin slices lemon

Preheat oven to 450°F.

Combine ketchup, whiskey, chili sauce, vinegar, Worcestershire, brown sugar, lemon juice, paprika, salt, garlic & hot pepper sauce in large sauce pan. Heat to boiling. Reduce heat. Simmer 30-45 minutes until sauce is slightly thickened.

Cut meat into 3-4 rib portions. Season with salt & pepper. Put on rack in shallow baking pan. Bake 30 minutes. Remove from rack. Drain off fat. Return ribs to baking pan, meaty-side down. Brush with sauce. Reduce heat to 300°F. Bake 30 minutes. Turn ribs & brush with sauce. Top each rib with an onion slice. Bake 1 hour, brushing with remaining sauce until ribs are tender & brown. Add lemon slices to ribs during last ½ hour of baking.

6 servings

4 cups whole kernel corn
1 cup chopped celery
⅓ cup chopped onion
⅓ cup sugar
⅓ cup vinegar
¼ cup chopped dill pickles
2 tablespoons cornstarch
1 teaspoon salt
1 teaspoon caraway seed
¼ teaspoon dry mustard
  pepper
3 tablespoons chopped pimiento

Combine ingredients, except pimiento in saucepan. Stir to dissolve cornstarch. Cook, stirring constantly, until thickened. Remove from heat. Stir in pimiento. Pour into jars. Cover tightly. Refrigerate. Keeps several weeks. Great with grilled meats.

3 pints

2 cups flour
2 cups brown sugar
½ cup butter, softened
1 cup chopped nuts
1½ teaspoons cinnamon
1 teaspoon baking soda
½ teaspoon salt
1 cup sour cream
1 teaspoon vanilla
1 egg
2 cups finely chopped, peeled apples

Preheat oven 350°F.

In large bowl, combine flour, brown sugar & butter. Mix on low speed until crumbly. Stir in nuts. Press 2¾ cups crumb mixture into a 13x9-inch pan.

Add cinnamon, soda, salt, sour cream, vanilla & egg to remaining mixture. Blend well. Stir in apples. Spoon evenly onto crust. Bake 30-35 minutes, until toothpick comes out clean. Cut into squares. Serve warm with whipped cream or ice cream.

12 servings

32

MENU

**Bacon
Artichoke
Dip**

**Grilled Salmon
with
Cucumber Dill Sauce**

**Bibb Lettuce
with Fresh Lemon
Cream Dressing**

Croissants

Frozen
Raspberry
Soufflé

*French White
Burgundy Chablis*

•

*A wonderfully light meal
to serve after going to the
matinée of the
marvelous play that every
one is talking about.
The Artichoke Dip &
Soufflé are made the
day before, making
your afternoon an
unhurried one!!!*
❧

Bacon
Artichoke
Dip

•

1½ cups cooked artichoke hearts,
 chopped
4 slices crisp-cooked bacon,
 crumbled
2 tablespoons chopped onion
2 tablespoons fresh lemon juice
½ cup mayonnaise
 cayenne
1 teaspoon white wine-
 Worcestershire sauce
 additional crisp-cooked bacon,
 crumbled

Combine ingredients. Cover & chill
several hours or overnight. Use
additional bacon pieces on top of
dip as garnish.

1 cup

Grilled Salmon
with
Cucumber Dill Sauce

•

Cucumber Dill Sauce:
½ cucumber, peeled, seeded, diced
 into ¼-inch pieces
1 cup sour cream
1 tablespoon chopped fresh dill
1 tablespoon lemon juice
 salt & pepper

2 pounds salmon fillets, with skin
½ lemon
 dash pepper

Place diced cucumbers in sieve.
Drain 30 minutes. Pat dry on paper
towels. Combine cucumber, sour
cream, dill, lemon juice, salt &
pepper. Cover & chill several hours.
Stir just before serving.

Prepare charcoal fire. Place salmon,
skin side down, directly on grill.
Season with juice of half lemon &
pepper. Cover grill. Cook 15 minutes until salmon flakes with a fork.
Remove from grill with spatula.
Remove skin. Serve with dill sauce.

4 servings

Bibb Lettuce
with Fresh Lemon
Cream Dressing

•

1 tablespoon finely minced onion
1 pint whipping cream
1 teaspoon sugar
 salt & pepper
 juice of 2 lemons
 Bibb lettuce

Combine onion, cream, sugar, salt &
pepper. Just before serving add
lemon juice. Toss with bibb or any
soft-leaf lettuce.

2½ cups

MENU

Bleu Caesar

Baked
Potatoes

**Grilled
Bourbon
Beef**

**Quick
French Bread**

Chocolate
Devil's Food
Cake

*California
Zinfandel*

•

*The neighbors just moved
in last week. Their boxes
are piled high. Invite
them over for a chance to
relax & become
acquainted. This meal
is a delightful, easy way
to break the ice.*

Bleu
Caesar

•

1 clove garlic, finely chopped
½ cup vegetable oil
1 head romaine lettuce
2 heads iceberg lettuce
1 head bibb lettuce
1 tablespoon white wine-
   Worcestershire sauce
¼ teaspoon salt
¼ teaspoon pepper
¼ cup lemon juice
1 egg
¼ cup freshly grated Parmesan
   cheese
¼ cup crumbled bleu cheese
2 cups garlic croutons

Add garlic to oil. Set aside several hours.

In a large bowl, tear lettuce into bite-size pieces. Chill, covered.

Blend seasonings, lemon & egg with garlic oil. Toss with greens. Sprinkle with cheeses & croutons. Toss. Serve immediately.

8 servings

Grilled
Bourbon
Beef

•

1 4-pound English cut or arm bone
   chuck roast, 2-inches thick

Marinade:
1 cup bourbon
½ cup brown sugar
4 tablespoons soy sauce
   juice of one lemon

Combine marinade ingredients. Marinate meat several hours or overnight in refrigerator. Grill 15-20 minutes each side over hot coals. Baste with marinade. Cut into slices.

6 servings

Quick
French Bread

•

1 package rapid-rise yeast
1 cup very warm water
3 cups bread flour
1 teaspoon salt
1 egg, beaten

In a small bowl, dissolve yeast in warm water.

Mix 2½ cups bread flour with salt in large bowl. Make well in center. Add yeast-water mixture. Mix well. When dough forms a ball, continue kneading about 5 minutes. Add more flour if too sticky.

Preheat oven to 375°F.

Place dough in buttered bowl. Cover & let rise in warm place until double in bulk, 30-45 minutes. Punch down. Form into two long loaves. Place on lightly buttered baking sheet. Score with sharp knife in 3 places. Let rise until doubled, about 30 minutes. Brush with beaten egg. Bake 35 minutes.

2 loaves

MENU

Zoo Concert Quiche

Molded Grapefruit Salad

Soft
Bread Sticks

Ravani Greek Almond Cake

*Spanish
White Rioja*

•

On a warm summer's evening, take this to the zoo in a gorgeous basket. Wrap quiche in foil & newspapers to keep warm. Pull out a red-checked table cloth, silver candelabra & fresh flowers. Serve on disposable plates!

Zoo Concert Quiche

•

2 unbaked 9-inch pie crusts
  juice of one lemon
⅛ cup grated lemon peel
¾ pound cooked shrimp
2 cups sliced mushrooms, sautéed
½ pound Swiss cheese, grated
½ cup chopped celery
½ cup chopped scallions
½ cup chopped tops of scallions
1 cup mayonnaise
2 tablespoons flour
1 cup dry white wine
4 large eggs beaten

Squeeze juice of lemon over both crusts. Allow to absorb. Sprinkle each with lemon peel.

Combine shrimp with mushrooms. Add remaining ingredients in order listed. Divide evenly between 2 pie shells.

Bake pies at 350°F. 45 minutes, until middle is set & knife inserted comes out clean.

May be frozen before baking. Thaw at room temperature 45 minutes. Bake at 375°F. 60 minutes.

12-16 servings

Molded Grapefruit Salad

•

3 packages unflavored gelatin
1 cup cold water
1 cup sugar
1 cup boiling water
3 large grapefruit
1 can (8 ounces) crushed
  pineapple, drained
1 cup chopped pecans
1 tablespoon lemon juice

Soak gelatin in cold water. Add sugar & boiling water. Stir until gelatin & sugar dissolve. Halve grapefruit & scoop out pulp, removing seeds. Add grapefruit pulp, juice, pecans & pineapple to gelatin mixture. Mix well. Add lemon juice. Pour into a 6-cup mold. Refrigerate until set, about 4-6 hours.

8 servings

Ravani Greek Almond Cake

•

1 cup sugar
1 cup butter, softened
5 eggs
1 teaspoon almond extract
2 cups self-rising flour
1 cup sugar
1½ cups water
  fresh fruits, sliced berries,
  nectarines, etc.

Preheat oven to 350°F. Butter a 13x9-inch. pan.

Cream butter & sugar. Add eggs, extract & flour. Pour mixture into pan. Bake 20-25 minutes.

Boil sugar & water 5 minutes. Cool. Pour over hot baked cake. Serve with fruit on the side.

8-10 servings

MENU

Heart of Wisconsin Dip

Bratwurst à la Vern

Creamy Vegetable Slaw

Cheesy Bean Bake

Fudgey Brownie Sundaes

Milwaukee's Finest, Ice Cold Beer

•

Typically Wisconsin, this winter meal only needs a crackling fire, 10 inches of snow, a good football game & plenty of Milwaukee's golden brew.

❦

Heart of Wisconsin Dip

•

½ pound cheddar cheese, grated
¼ cup sour cream
 1 clove garlic, chopped
½ tablespoon Worcestershire sauce
½ cup beer, room temperature
   dash cayenne pepper
   round loaf dark rye bread or
   French bread

Combine ingredients except bread. May be served at room temperature, or hot in fondue pot with French bread. Or, hollow out an unsliced round rye bread. Fill with dip. Wrap with foil & bake at 400°F. 15 minutes. Serve with cubed rye bread.

2 cups

Bratwurst à la Vern

•

6 onions, sliced

Sauce:
  1 cup chili sauce
  1 tablespoon Worcestershire sauce
  1 cup ketchup
  2 tablespoons vinegar
½ teaspoon salt
  2 tablespoons brown sugar
½ teaspoon paprika

  6 grilled bratwurst
  1 can (12 ounces) beer

Put onions & sauce ingredients in dutch oven. Add sausage & beer. Simmer, covered, 15-20 minutes, until onions are tender. Serve hot in bratwurst buns.

6 servings

Cheesy Bean Bake

•

 1 cup chopped onions
½ cup chopped green pepper
 2 tablespoons vegetable oil
 3 cups cooked pinto, red or
    kidney beans
 1 cup cooked rice
 1 cup cottage cheese
 3 cups grated cheddar cheese

Preheat oven to 350°F.

Sauté onion & pepper in oil until tender. Fold into beans with rice, cottage cheese & cheddar cheese. Spoon into 2-quart casserole. Bake 30 minutes or until bubbly.

6 servings

MENU

Asparagus
Salad

**Salmon
Bisque**

Wisconsin
Cheese Plate

**Beer
Bread**

**Swedish
Crème**

*Wisconsin
Red Ruby
Gamay*

•

*With the sport of salmon
fishing booming in
Wisconsin, there is
often a prize catch in
the freezer. Serve
Bisque in mugs, with
or without rice, for a
casual dining event.
Bake Beer Bread in an
interesting mold.*

❧

Salmon
Bisque

•

4 slices bacon, cut into 1-inch pieces
½ medium green pepper, chopped
1 large onion, chopped
2 red potatoes, peeled & chopped
3 cups chopped plum tomatoes,
    including juice
1 cup dry vermouth
1 tablespoon Worcestershire sauce
3 bay leaves
2 cloves garlic, minced
2 pounds salmon, cut into ½-inch
    pieces
    salt & pepper
    cayenne
1 cup rice, cook according to
    package instructions
    dill sprigs
    sour cream or crème fraîche

In a 5-quart pan over medium heat,
cook bacon until crisp. Add green
pepper, onion & potatoes. Cook 5
minutes. Add tomatoes & their
juice. Stir in vermouth, Worcestershire, bay leaves & garlic. Cover &
simmer until potatoes are tender, 30
minutes. May be prepared in
advance to this point. Add fish. Cover
& cook until fish flakes easily, 5-6
minutes. Season with salt, pepper &
cayenne. To serve, place cooked rice
in bottom of soup bowl. Ladle hot
bisque over rice. Garnish with dill
& a dollop of sour cream or
crème fraîche.

6-8 servings

Beer
Bread

•

3 cups self-rising flour
3 tablespoons sugar
1 can (12 ounces) light or dark beer
¼ cup butter, melted

Preheat oven to 350°F. Butter a
9x5-inch loaf pan.

Combine flour, sugar & beer. Pour
into prepared loaf pan. Pour melted
butter over top. Bake 50 minutes.
Cool completely in pan. Serve with
onion conserve.

1 loaf

Swedish
Crème

•

2¼ cups heavy cream
1 cup sugar
1 teaspoon unflavored gelatin
2 cups sour cream
1 teaspoon vanilla or other extract
    (lemon, almond, etc.)
2 cups sweetened, chopped
    fresh fruit

Combine cream, sugar & gelatin in
medium-size saucepan. Heat gently,
stirring, over low heat 5 minutes until
gelatin has dissolved. Remove from
heat. Cool until slightly thickened.
Fold in sour cream & vanilla. Pour
into parfait glasses or dessert dishes.
Chill, covered, several hours or
overnight. Before serving, top
with fruit.

8 servings

Sausage & Potato Soup

●

1 pound Italian sausage, sliced
⅓-inch thick
1 tablespoon vegetable oil
½ cup chopped onion
2 pounds tomatoes, peeled,
  chopped
4 potatoes, peeled, chopped
¼ cup finely chopped parsley
1 cup celery, sliced diagonally
2 tablespoons finely chopped
  celery leaves
1½ cups beef stock
1 bay leaf
½ teaspoon thyme
1 tablespoon lemon juice
  salt & pepper

Brown Italian sausage slices in
oil. Add chopped onions. Cook 5
minutes. Add remaining ingredients.
Bring to a boil, reduce heat. Simmer, uncovered, until potatoes are
tender, 40 minutes.

4-6 servings

Mixed Greens with Leona's Sour Cream Dressing

●

1 clove garlic
1 teaspoon salt
3 scallions including greens,
  chopped
½ cup parsley, chopped
1 cup sour cream
1 cup mayonnaise
1 teaspoon Worcestershire sauce
¼ teaspoon hot pepper sauce
1 tablespoon vinegar
1 tablespoon lemon juice
2 quarts mixed greens, field
  lettuces, mâche, arugula, etc.

Mince or mash garlic & place in a
small sauce dish. Cover with salt &
let rest 15-20 minutes. Mix scallions,
parsley, sour cream, mayonnaise,
Worcestershire sauce, hot pepper
sauce, vinegar & lemon juice; add
garlic. Mix well & refrigerate. Will
keep for two weeks.

At serving time toss dressing with
lettuces. Pass pepper mill.

3 cups

Super Lemon Pie

●

3 eggs separated
  grated peel & juice of 1 lemon
4 tablespoons boiling water
1 cup powdered sugar, sifted
1 baked 9-inch pie shell

Beat egg whites until stiff.

Beat yolks until lemon colored. Add
peel & juice of lemon. Gradually
add boiling water. Add sugar. Cook
mixture in a double boiler 3-4 minutes, until thickened. Cool. Fold in
beaten egg whites. Pour mixture
into pie shell. Bake 2-4 minutes at
400°F. until pie turns light golden
brown on top.

6 servings

MENU

**Sausage
&
Potato Soup**

**Mixed Greens
with Leona's
Sour Cream Dressing**

Whole Wheat
Sour Dough
Bread

**Super
Lemon Pie**

*Italian
Red Brunello
di Montalcino*

●

*It's a cool autumn day.
The smell of fall is in the
air & a sweater feels
good. What a day to go
leaf peeping!*
❦

Simple Gatherings
uncomplicated & convenient

*French
White Burgundy
Meursault*

•

*A simple three-course meal
to put you completely at
ease. Use placemats &
everyday dinnerware
to keep it comfortable
for everyone.*

Dairyland
Crab Spread

•

2 packages (3 ounces each) cream
   cheese, softened
¾ cup mayonnaise
½ pound cheddar cheese, grated
1 can (4 ounces) chopped ripe olives
½ pound cooked, flaked crab meat
¼ cup finely chopped onion
2 hard-cooked eggs, chopped
1 teaspoon dry mustard
½ teaspoon paprika
½ teaspoon pepper

Combine cream cheese & mayonnaise. Stir in remaining ingredients. Chill. Serve with a variety of
crackers or vegetable crudités. May
be broiled on wheat crackers or toast
cutouts to serve hot.

2½ cups

Sautéed
Chicken
Tarragon

•

4 chicken breast halves, skinned
   & boned
2 tablespoons butter
   salt & pepper
¾ cup light cream
1 teaspoon cornstarch
¼ teaspoon salt
1½ teaspoons chopped fresh
   tarragon or ½ teaspoon dried
1 teaspoon capers, crushed

Pound chicken breasts between
sheets of plastic to ¼-inch thick.
Melt butter in pan over medium heat
until it sizzles. Sauté chicken 1-2
minutes per side. Remove to heated
platter. Season with salt & pepper.
Combine remaining ingredients. Add
to pan. Bring to boil. Stir & cook
until thickened. Spoon over chicken.

4 servings

Brandied
Peaches

•

Per serving:
1 peach half
1 tablespoon butter
2 teaspoons dark brown sugar
1 tablespoon brandy

Place peaches, pitted side up, in pie
plate or shallow container to fit.
Add butter, sugar & brandy to center of each peach. Broil 3-5 minutes
until bubbly. Serve hot with ice
cream if desired. Use rum, cognac,
hazelnut or another liqueur in place
of brandy.

Grilled Marinated Pork Chops

•

Marinade:
  1 cup fresh orange juice
  2 cloves garlic, minced
  2 tablespoons light soy sauce

  4 pork chops, 1-inch thick

Combine marinade ingredients. Put chops in pan to fit. Pour marinade over chops. Turn to coat. Marinate at least 4 hours, preferably overnight, turning occasionally. Grill over hot coals or broil. Warm remaining marinade. Serve with chops.

4 servings

Sweet-Sour Vegetables Pommery

•

  2 cups broccoli flowerets
  2 cups cauliflowerets
  1 small red pepper, cut into 1-inch pieces
  ¾ cup sliced scallions

Dressing:
  ½ cup vegetable oil
  ½ cup white wine vinegar
  ½ cup sugar
  2 tablespoons Pommery or whole-grain mustard
  salt & pepper

  ¼ cup toasted pine nuts

Combine vegetables in bowl. Mix dressing ingredients. Toss with vegetables. Marinate overnight. Before serving, sprinkle with pine nuts.

4-5 servings

Chocolate Mousse Pie

•

  ½ cup butter
  1 cup flour
  1 tablespoon sugar
  ⅛ teaspoon salt

Filling:
  1 package (6 ounces) semi-sweet chocolate chips
  1 egg
  2 egg yolks
  1 teaspoon rum
  2 egg whites, beaten stiff
  1 cup heavy cream, whipped
    whipped cream for garnish
  1 square baking chocolate, shaved

Preheat oven to 450°F.

Cut butter into flour, sugar & salt. Mix well. Press into 9-inch pie pan. Bake 10 minutes. Cool on wire rack.

Melt chocolate chips. Beat in egg & yolks, one at a time. Blend well. Add rum. Fold in egg whites. Fold in 1 cup of the whipped cream. Spoon into pie shell. Chill several hours or overnight. Garnish with whipped cream & shaved chocolate.

6-8 servings

Quick Baked Haddock

•

*German White
Rheingau Spätlese*

•

*Milwaukee is famous for
its Friday Night Fish Fry.
No need to go out
when the menu is this
easy & delicious.*

⅓ cup bread crumbs
  salt & pepper
1 tablespoon minced herbs
2 pounds haddock fillets, pat dry
  with toweling
1 egg, beaten
½ cup butter, melted
  paprika
  lemon wedges

Preheat oven to 375°F. Butter a
13x9-inch pan.

Combine bread crumbs, salt, pepper
& herbs. Dip fillets in egg, then
crumbs. Place fillets in pan. Drizzle
with melted butter. Bake 30 minutes. Sprinkle paprika on top. Serve
with lemon.

4 servings

Cabbage Slaw for Keeps

•

1 medium head cabbage, finely
  shredded
1 onion, chopped
1 green pepper, chopped
¼ cup sliced pimiento-stuffed olives
½ cup sugar

Dressing:
1 cup white vinegar
½ cup vegetable oil
½ cup sugar
1 teaspoon salt
1 teaspoon celery seed
1 teaspoon prepared mustard
¼ teaspoon pepper

Place vegetables in large bowl.
Combine dressing ingredients in
saucepan. Boil 3 minutes. Add hot
dressing to cabbage. Mix well. Cover.
Chill at least 24 hours. Keeps
until gone!

10 servings

Poires au Gratin

•

4 ripe, but firm, pears, peeled,
  cored & sliced ⅜-inch thick
  cinnamon-sugar
⅓ cup apricot jam
¼ cup dry white vermouth
4-5 dried macaroon or amaretti
  cookies
2 tablespoons butter, cut into pieces
  ice cream or whipped cream

Preheat oven to 325°F. Butter a shallow 1-quart baking dish.

Arrange pear slices in prepared dish.
Sprinkle with cinnamon-sugar.
Blend jam & vermouth. Pour over
pears. Crumble macaroons on top.
Dot with butter pieces. Bake 25-30
minutes until pears are tender.
Serve hot or cold with vanilla ice
cream or whipped cream.

4-6 servings

MENU

**Country
Bean
Soup**

**Cucumber Orange
Spinach Salad with
Caraway Seed
Dressing**

**Refrigerator
Bran
Muffins**

California Burgundy

•

*Just home from work &
dinner is in the
refrigerator! Prepare
Soup, Muffin batter &
Dressing in advance.
30 minutes after
arriving home, enjoy a
warm & satisfying meal.*
❧

Country Bean Soup

•

½ pound northern beans
½ pound red kidney beans
½ pound pinto beans
  water
2 tablespoons butter
1 onion, chopped
1½ pounds smoked pork hocks
1 bay leaf
¾ pound Polska Kielbasa, sliced
  ½-inch thick
1 tablespoon thyme
  salt & pepper

Rinse beans. In stockpot, heat beans & 8 cups water to boiling. Boil 2 minutes. Remove from heat. Cover. Let stand 1 hour. Drain beans in colander & rinse in cold water.

Return pan to heat. Sauté onion in butter 5 minutes. Add hocks, bay leaf & 7 cups water. Heat to boiling. Return beans to pan. Simmer 45 minutes. Add sausage. Cook 15-20 minutes. Remove bay leaf & hocks. Cool slightly. Trim hocks. Add meat to soup. Add thyme, salt & pepper. Best if made 1 day in advance.

8-10 servings

Cucumber Orange Spinach Salad with Caraway Seed Dressing

•

2 bunches spinach, torn into
  bite-size pieces
2 cups mandarin oranges
1 large cucumber, peeled, seeded
  & julienned

Dressing:
¾ cup mayonnaise
1 tablespoon honey
1 teaspoon lemon juice
1 teaspoon caraway seed

⅓ cup toasted almonds

Add spinach, oranges, cucumbers to salad bowl. Cover & chill. Combine dressing ingredients. Cover & chill. Toss salad with dressing & almonds just before serving.

6-8 servings

Refrigerator Bran Muffins

•

3 eggs
3 cups buttermilk
2¼ cups white or brown sugar
¾ cup vegetable oil
3 cups bran cereal
1 cup raisins
2 teaspoons baking soda
¼ cup boiling water
4 cups graham flour
3 teaspoons baking powder
2 teaspoons salt

Combine eggs, buttermilk, sugar, oil, bran, raisins, baking soda & water. Let stand. Mix flour, baking powder & salt. Combine with bran batter. Store in refrigerator. Use as needed. Pour into muffin tins. Bake 20 minutes at 450°F.

3 dozen

MENU

Chicken Marsala

Green Bean Bundles

Shredded Red Cabbage
&
Red Onion Salad

Oven-Browned
Potatoes

Lemon Pepper Loaf

Rich
Chocolate Cake

*Italian
Red Bardolino
or Gattinara*

•

*Large family birthdays
or gatherings can be
hosted with joy utilizing
the oven-cooked menu.*

Chicken Marsala

•

36 pieces chicken
  salt & pepper
  paprika
¾ cup butter, divided
1 pound mushrooms, sliced
¼ cup flour
1½ cups chicken stock
6 tablespoons dry Marsala wine
3 sprigs fresh rosemary or ½
  teaspoon dried

Season chicken with salt, pepper &
paprika. In a large skillet, brown
chicken in ½ cup butter. Remove to
baking pans. Add remaining butter.
Sauté mushrooms 5 minutes. Add
flour. Stir until smooth. Add stock,
Marsala & rosemary. Cook until
thick. Pour over chicken. Bake,
covered, at 350°F. 1 hour.

18 servings

Green Bean Bundles

•

2 pounds whole green beans,
  trimmed
8 scallions including long
  green stems
1 red pepper, cut into ¼-inch
  thick strips
⅓ cup butter
1 clove garlic, finely chopped
½ teaspoon crushed thyme
¼ teaspoon white pepper

Cook beans in salted water 3 minutes.
Plunge into ice water. Drain. Blanch
scallions 15 seconds. Remove &
pat dry. Cut onion off stem.

Gather a serving-size bundle of green
beans. Tie scallion stem around
beans. Knot. Place bundles in buttered 8-inch square pan. Slip several
red pepper strips under knot.

Melt butter in small pan. Sauté
garlic 3 minutes. Add thyme &
pepper. Pour over beans. Cover &
refrigerate. Bring to room temperature. Bake at 375°F. 7-10 minutes until
heated through.

8 servings

Lemon Pepper Loaf

•

1 pound loaf unsliced white bread
½ cup butter, softened
1 tablespoon chopped chives
½ teaspoon grated lemon peel
½ tablespoon lemon juice
¼ teaspoon freshly ground black
  pepper
1 tablespoon Dijon-style or other
  prepared mustard
2 teaspoons poppy seed
8 slices crisp-cooked bacon,
  crumbled
½ pound Swiss cheese, sliced

Cut bread into 9 slices, cutting into,
but not through, bottom crust. In
small bowl, cream butter until light
& fluffy. Add chives, lemon peel,
lemon juice & pepper. Mix
thoroughly. Add mustard, poppy
seed & bacon. Set aside 3 tablespoons butter mixture. Spread
remainder on all cut surfaces of
bread. Place 1 slice cheese in each
cut. Spread reserved butter mixture
on top & sides of loaf. Bake at
350°F. 15-20 minutes.

9 servings

California Napa Chardonnay

•

Elegant May dinner when flowers are from the garden, asparagus is fresh from the market & you want sprightliness on the table.

❧

Fresh Asparagus with Herbed Caper Dip

•

Herbed Caper Dip:
  1 package (8 ounces) cream cheese, softened
  ½ cup sour cream
  3 scallions, minced
  2 tablespoons capers
  2 tablespoons minced parsley
  1 tablespoon Dijon-style mustard
  1 teaspoon Herbs de Provence
    salt & pepper

  2 pounds fresh asparagus, trimmed

For dip, beat cream cheese & sour cream until light & fluffy. Stir in remaining ingredients. Chill. Best made 1 day in advance. Keeps up to 5 days. Serve asparagus spears in pretty basket with dip.

1½ cups

Vermouthy Veal

•

  2 pounds very thin veal slices
3-4 tablespoons flour
  ⅓ cup butter
  1 clove garlic, minced
  1 small onion, chopped
  1 small green pepper, chopped
  1 small red pepper, chopped
  ½ pound mushrooms, chopped
  1 tablespoon lemon juice
  ½ cup dry vermouth

Lightly flour veal. Melt butter in sauté pan. Brown veal pieces. Add garlic, onions, peppers & mushrooms. Sprinkle with lemon juice. Add vermouth. Can be made in advance to this point. Cover & cook on low heat 25 minutes until veal is tender. Substitute turkey slices or chicken breasts for veal.

6 servings

Fruit & Lettuce Salad with Orange Yogurt Dressing

•

  4 cups torn Boston lettuce
  1 can (11 ounces) mandarin oranges, drained
1-2 bananas, sliced
  ½ cup dried black currants
  ½ cup chopped Macadamia nuts, almonds or cashews
  ½ cup mayonnaise
  ½ cup mandarin orange yogurt

Place lettuce in bowl. Top with fruits, currants & nuts.

Combine mayonnaise & yogurt. Chill several hours. Serve dressing with salad.

4 servings

*Italian Red
Brunello di Montalcino*

*The Canapés are in the
freezer, light the grill &
sit back to enjoy the
evening. Pop the Dessert
in the oven while you
assemble the Pasta.
You'll entertain often
when it's this easy.*

Mushroom Canapés

•

¼ cup butter
 1 cup finely chopped onion
 1 pound mushrooms, finely
   chopped
⅓ cup flour
⅓ cup milk
½ teaspoon salt
⅛ teaspoon pepper
 1 pound loaf extra-thin sliced
   bread (white, dill, rye, etc.)
   grated Parmesan cheese
   sliced pimento-stuffed olives,
   optional

Melt butter in skillet. Sauté onions
& mushrooms 10 minutes until liquid is nearly evaporated. Add flour.
Cook 1 minute. Add milk, salt &
pepper. Cook until mixture is very
thick. Set aside to cool. Trim crusts
from bread. Cut bread into triangles
or variety of shapes with canapé
cutters. Spread mixture on bread.
Arrange on baking sheets. Sprinkle
with Parmesan. Freeze until firm.
Place in plastic bags until needed.
To serve, preheat broiler. Arrange
canapés on baking sheets. Broil 5
minutes until browned. Garnish with
olive slice.

30 servings

Basil Spaghetti Carbonara

•

 3 slices bacon, chopped
½ pound prosciutto ham, julienned
 1 small onion, sliced
½ cup sliced mushrooms
 3 tablespoons dry Marsala
 3 tablespoons butter
8-ounces thin spaghetti, cooked
   & drained
 1 egg, beaten
   salt & pepper
 3 tablespoons sliced fresh basil
   leaves
¼ cup freshly grated Parmesan
   cheese

In a large skillet, brown bacon. When
almost crisp, add prosciutto. Cook
3 minutes. Remove to plate. Sauté
onion 3 minutes. Return bacon &
ham to pan. Add Marsala. Simmer 2
minutes. Add butter. Remove from
heat. Add hot spaghetti to pan. Toss.
Add egg, salt & pepper. Toss again.
Pour onto warm serving platter.
Sprinkle with basil & Parmesan.

2-4 servings

French Apple Pie

•

 6 cups peeled, sliced apples
½ teaspoon nutmeg
½ teaspoon cinnamon
1¼ cups sugar, divided
2-3 tablespoons butter
 1 egg, beaten
¾ cup flour
 1 teaspoon baking powder
¼ teaspoon salt
   whipped cream or ice cream

Preheat oven to 375°F. Arrange apple
slices in buttered 10-inch pie pan.

Combine nutmeg, cinnamon &
½ cup of the sugar. Sprinkle over
apples. Dot with butter. Combine egg,
flour, baking powder, salt & remaining sugar. Sprinkle over top of pie.
Bake 50 minutes. Serve warm or
cold with whipped cream or a scoop
of ice cream.

6 servings

Snapper Amande

•

¼ cup coarsely chopped almonds
3 tablespoons butter, softened
1 tablespoon grated lemon peel
½ teaspoon paprika
¼ teaspoon salt
⅛ teaspoon pepper
1 pound snapper fillets

Preheat oven to 350°F. Butter a 1-quart baking dish.

Combine almonds, butter, lemon peel, paprika, salt & pepper. Place fillets, skin side down, in baking dish. Top fillets with butter-nut mixture. Bake 15-20 minutes until fish flakes easily.

2 servings

Broiled Blue Cheese Tomatoes

•

4 medium tomatoes, halved
  salt & pepper
1 clove garlic, minced
1 medium onion, minced
3 tablespoons fresh bread crumbs
4-ounces blue cheese, crumbled

Preheat oven to 350°F.

Season tomatoes with salt & pepper. Arrange in muffin tin. Combine garlic & onions. Divide evenly over tomatoes. Combine bread crumbs & cheese. Sprinkle over tomatoes. Bake 20-25 minutes or broil 5 minutes until cheese is light brown & tomatoes are heated through.

8 servings

Marcie's Grasshoppers

•

½ gallon French vanilla ice cream, softened
½ cup crème de menthe
⅓ cup white crème de cacao
  chocolate twigs garnish

Blend ice cream & liqueurs. Refreeze. To serve, remove from freezer 5-10 minutes before scooping into parfait glasses or ice cream dishes. Garnish with chocolate twigs.

8-10 servings

MENU

Snapper Amande

Garlic-Dill
Extra-Fine
Egg Noodles

Broiled Blue Cheese Tomatoes

Marcie's Grasshoppers

•

*French
White Muscadet*

•

Intimate dinner for two after a hard day's work. Dinner takes very little time to prepare. Spruce up your table & refresh yourselves with an inviting menu to linger over.
❧

•

*After a day of holiday
shopping, munch on the
Pinwheels with a mug
of Soup while the Potatoes
are heating. Toss the
salad with your favorite
dressing. Your evening
will be free to wrap the gifts!*
❦

Celery
Pinwheels

•

5 stalks celery
1 package (8 ounces) cream
   cheese, softened
4-5 tablespoons ground toasted
   almonds

Clean, trim & dry celery. Beat cream
cheese until light & fluffy. Add
almonds. Pack cheese into celery ribs.
Fill liberally. Press stalks together
pinwheel fashion, one inside the
other until a tight circle is formed.
Tie at each end. Wipe away excess
cheese. Chill until firm. To serve,
slice stalks crosswise, ⅜-inch thick.
Use as garnish or an hors d'oeuvre.

12-16 pieces

Old Fashioned
Cream of Tomato
Soup

•

6 tablespoons butter
6 tablespoons flour
¾ teaspoon salt
3 cups milk
3 cups peeled, quartered tomatoes
2 bay leaves
1 small onion, chopped
   pinch baking soda
   salt & pepper
½ cup heavy cream, whipped

Melt butter in saucepan over low
heat. Blend in flour & salt. Cook
2-3 minutes. Add milk. Stir until mixture thickens & bubbles. Set aside.

In another saucepan, cook tomatoes,
bay leaves & onions 10 minutes over
low heat. Add soda just before
removing from heat. Discard bay
leaves.

Combine cream sauce & tomato
mixture. Season with salt & pepper.
Top each serving with 1 tablespoon
whipped cream.

4-6 servings

Salmon
Stuffed
Potatoes

•

4 large baked potatoes
¼ cup milk
2 tablespoons butter
1 egg, beaten
3 tablespoons grated Parmesan
   cheese
2 scallions, finely chopped
   including greens
   salt & pepper
8-ounces cooked, flaked salmon

Cheese Sauce:
2 tablespoons butter
2 tablespoons flour
1 cup milk
   salt & pepper
1 teaspoon dry mustard
8-ounces Bel Paese cheese, cubed

Cut baked potatoes in half. Scoop
out pulp. Mash potatoes with milk,
butter, egg & Parmesan. Stir in scallions, salt & pepper. Fold in salmon.
Mound into potato shells. Bake at
375°F. 20 minutes.

For the sauce, in a small saucepan
over medium heat melt butter. Add
flour, salt, pepper & mustard. Cook
1-2 minutes. Add milk. Stir until
smooth & thickened. Add cheese.
Stir until melted. Serve sauce over
potatoes.

4 servings

MENU

California Mendocino Chardonnay

•

A snappy menu for entertaining casually with panache. Top the table with a bright red cloth & a bowl brimming with yellow daisies. Use yellow bandana 'kerchiefs as napkins. Pzazz!

Tomato-Mustard Chicken

•

1 tablespoon butter
1 tablespoon vegetable oil
4 skinless, boneless chicken breast halves, sliced thin
1 onion, chopped
½ teaspoon thyme
½ teaspoon tarragon
¼ cup dry white wine
1 cup chicken stock
2 cups seeded, chopped tomatoes
1½ tablespoons tomato paste
1 clove garlic, minced
1 tablespoon Dijon-style mustard
3 tablespoons minced parsley

Heat butter & oil in skillet over medium heat. Sauté chicken slices 3-4 minutes. Remove from pan. Add onion & herbs. Cook 5 minutes. Add wine, stock, tomatoes, tomato paste & garlic. Simmer, stirring occasionally, 10 minutes. Increase heat to high. Cook 3 minutes. Stir in mustard & chicken. Cook 2 minutes. Sprinkle with parsley. Serve with pasta or noodles if desired.

4 servings

Parmesan-Eggplant Strata

•

1 large eggplant, peeled & diced
½ loaf white bread, crusts removed, diced
8 slices crisp-cooked bacon, crumbled
6 eggs, beaten
1 cup milk
1 teaspoon Italian herbs
salt & pepper
½ cup grated Parmesan cheese
3 tablespoons butter

Preheat oven to 325°F. Butter a 2-quart baking dish.

Parboil eggplant in salted water 5 minutes. Drain well. Combine eggplant, bread & bacon. Pour into baking dish. Combine eggs, milk, herbs, salt & pepper. Pour over eggplant. Top with cheese. Dot with butter. Bake 45 minutes until golden brown.

8 servings

Strawberry Meringues

•

3 egg whites, room temperature
¼ teaspoon cream of tartar
½ cup superfine sugar
¾ teaspoon vanilla
1 cup heavy cream
2 teaspoons sugar
2 tablespoons orange-flavored liqueur
1 quart strawberries, sliced

Preheat oven to 350°F. Line baking sheets with paper.

Beat egg whites & cream of tartar until soft peaks form. Add sugar, 2 tablespoons at a time. Beat until stiff & glossy. Add vanilla. Spoon meringue onto baking sheets in mounds of desired size. Make "nest" shape with spoon in center of mound. Bake 1 hour until set. Cool 10 minutes. Carefully remove from paper. Store in air-tight container.

Whip cream with the sugar until soft peaks form. Stir in liqueur. Spoon cream into meringues. Top with berries.

4-6 servings

California Fumé Blanc

•

*After the first softball game,
invite the team for an
informal dinner to
discuss strategies. Bermuda
Delights may be served
as an open-face
sandwich or appetizer.*

❧

Mock
Crab

•

1 can (8 ounces) sauerkraut,
   rinsed & drained
1 cup grated sharp cheddar cheese
2 tablespoons chopped green
   pepper
2 tablespoons chopped pimiento
2 tablespoons chopped onion
2 tablespoons bread crumbs
1 tablespoon sugar
   dash hot pepper sauce
¼-½ cup mayonnaise
1 cup cooked tiny shrimp
   lemon slices
   parsley

Finely cut sauerkraut with scissors.
Combine with remaining ingredients. Chill at least 2 hours. Serve garnished with lemon slices & parsley.
Serve with wheat crackers.

2 cups

Sausage
& Lentil
Soup

•

1 pound lentils
9 cups water
½ teaspoon thyme
1 teaspoon salt
1 teaspoon pepper
1 bay leaf
1 pound pork sausage
1 pound hot Italian sausages
1 cup sliced carrots
1 cup sliced celery
1 clove garlic
1 cup chopped onion
1 can (28 ounces) plum tomatoes,
   chopped
2 teaspoons Italian herbs
1 cup dry white wine
½ cup broken spaghetti pieces

Rinse lentils. Combine with water,
thyme, salt, pepper & bay leaf.
Bring to boil. Simmer, covered, 20
minutes.

In a large skillet, brown sausages. Cut
Italian sausages into ½-inch pieces.
Add to soup. Sauté carrots, celery,
garlic & onions in skillet 6 minutes.
Add to soup with tomatoes & herbs.
Simmer 1 hour. 15 minutes before
serving, add wine & spaghetti.

8 servings

Bermuda
Delights

•

Dijon-style mustard
thin-sliced whole grain wheat
   bread
thin slices Bermuda onion
thin slices ripe tomato
thin slices goat's milk cheddar or
   sharp cheddar cheese

Spread Dijon-style mustard on bread
slices. Top with onion & tomato.
Place 2 strips goat cheddar criss-
crossed on tomato. Broil until
cheese melts. Use cocktail rye for
hors d'oeuvres.

Luncheon Gatherings
fresh daytime entertaining

*This versatile brunch,
lunch or light dinner
menu will become
a favorite.*
❧

Fresh
Virgin Marys

•

7½ pounds tomatoes, coarsely
   chopped
1 cup chopped celery
2 cups chopped onion
1 clove garlic, minced
⅛ cup sugar
1 tablespoon salt
½ teaspoon pepper
1 teaspoon horseradish
3 tablespoons fresh lemon juice
1 teaspoon Worcestershire sauce

Combine tomatoes, celery, onion &
garlic in 6-quart pan. Bring to boil
over medium-high heat. Reduce
heat. Simmer 20 minutes. In
blender, whirl mixture until smooth
in batches. Pour into sieve. Discard
pulp & seeds. Stir in sugar, salt, pepper, horseradish, lemon juice &
Worcestershire. Store in freezer containers. Best to make in advance if
using fresh.

3 quarts

Eggs
Sonora

•

1 can (10 ounces) enchilada sauce
2¼ cups chopped tomatoes
¼ cup chopped green chilies
¼ cup chopped celery
¼ cup chopped green pepper
½ cup chopped onion
   salt & pepper
   pinch sugar
2 ripe avocados, mashed
2 teaspoons fresh lemon juice
2 cups refried beans, heated
8 corn tortillas, warmed
1 cup grated cheddar cheese
1 cup grated Monterey Jack cheese
1 pound bacon, crisp-cooked &
   crumbled
12 eggs, scrambled
   sour cream

In a saucepan, combine enchilada
sauce, tomatoes, chilies, celery,
green pepper, onion, salt, pepper &
sugar. Simmer 20-30 minutes.
Combine avocado & lemon juice.
Set aside.

On warmed tortillas, place a layer of
beans, cheeses, bacon, eggs, sauce
& avocado. Top with a dollop of
sour cream.

8 servings

Mexican
Rice

•

1 large onion, chopped
4 tablespoons olive oil
2 cloves garlic, minced
2 cups long grain rice
1½ cups peeled, chopped tomatoes
4 cups beef consommé
1½ teaspoons cumin
   salt

In large saucepan over medium heat,
sauté onion in oil until tender, not
browned, 3-5 minutes. Add garlic &
rice. Cook 3-5 minutes, stirring
often. Add tomatoes, consommé,
cumin & salt. Bring to boil over
high heat. Reduce heat. Simmer, covered, until liquid is absorbed 20
minutes. Fluff with fork before serving.

10-12 servings

ENTREE BREAD BEVERAGE

MENU

Chicken Confetti Salad

Shaved Cucumber & Onion Salad

Walnut Bread

Marbleridge Farm Tea

Pineapple Sorbet with Sugar Cookies

Lemon Flavored Sparkling Water

•

What a delightful patio luncheon for 12. Use brightly colored paper plates, napkins & plenty of flowers.

❧

Chicken Confetti Salad

•

1 head lettuce, torn into bite-size pieces
1 head cauliflower, separated into flowerets
1 Bermuda onion, sliced
1 sweet red pepper, chopped
1 cup broccoli, chopped
¾ pound bacon, crisp-cooked & crumbled
2 cups diced, cooked chicken

Dressing:
3 tablespoons sugar
1½ cups mayonnaise
¾ cup grated Parmesan or romano cheese
1 tablespoon crushed green peppercorns
2 tablespoons milk

Combine lettuce, cauliflower, onion, red pepper, broccoli, bacon & chicken. Chill 1 hour. Mix dressing ingredients, Refrigerate until serving time. Toss salad with dressing just before serving.

12 servings

Walnut Bread

•

2 packages dry yeast
¼ cup warm water
4-5 cups bread flour
½ tablespoon salt
4 teaspoons sugar
½ cup walnuts, finely chopped
1 cup milk
2 tablespoons vegetable oil
2 eggs

Mix yeast with warm water. Set aside 10 minutes until dissolved. In mixing bowl, combine flour, salt, sugar & nuts. Add milk, oil, eggs & yeast mixture.

Beat on low speed with mixer or bread hook. When blended, adjust speed to medium. Mix 15 minutes. If dough hook is not available, mix half of flour with other ingredients until well blended. Stir in remaining flour by hand. Knead 10 minutes. Cover & let stand 15 minutes.

Preheat oven to 375°F. Butter a baking sheet. Turn out dough, cut into 6 pieces. With floured hands, knead into loaf shapes. Place on baking sheet. Cover. Let loaves rise until doubled in bulk. Bake 25-30 minutes, until golden brown.

Dough can be shaped into 2 loaves & baked in two 9x5-inch pans.

6 small or 2 large loaves

Marbleridge Farm Tea

•

6-ounces frozen lemonade concentrate, thawed
1 cup packed, fresh garden mint leaves
4 tea bags
6 cups cold water

Combine ingredients in a 2-quart pitcher. Stir with a wooden spoon to bruise mint leaves. Steep 24 hours in refrigerator. Remove tea bags & mint leaves. Stir & serve over ice.

2 quarts

MENU

*Washington State
Johannisberg Reisling*

•

*A great light dinner after
work or play. Soup &
Cake should be made
the day before. For
last minute guests, put a
cloth on the kitchen
table & add candles.*
❦

Spring Soup

•

2 tablespoons butter
2 leeks, cleaned & chopped,
   including tender greens
1 small onion, chopped
6 cups hot water
2 potatoes, peeled & thinly sliced
2 carrots, peeled & thinly sliced
2 teaspoons salt
¼ cup uncooked rice
8 stalks asparagus, cut into ½-inch
   pieces
½ pound spinach, chopped
1 cup light cream

Melt butter in large pan. Add leeks
& onion. Simmer over low heat
until tender, 5 minutes. Add hot
water, potatoes, carrots & salt. Bring
to a boil. Reduce heat. Simmer 15
minutes. Add rice & asparagus.
Simmer 25 minutes. Add spinach &
simmer 10 minutes. Stir in cream.
Bring to a boil. Note: Flavor improves
if soup is chilled overnight. Heat
through before serving time.

6-8 servings

Toasted Celery Seed Bread

•

¾ cup butter, softened
¼ teaspoon salt
   cayenne pepper
⅜ teaspoon paprika
¾ teaspoon celery seed
1½ pound loaf white bread,
   unsliced, crusts removed

Preheat oven to 450°F.

Blend butter & seasonings. Cut loaf
in half lengthwise, almost through
to bottom. Cut at 2-inch intervals
crosswise, almost to bottom. Spread
butter mixture over all cut surfaces
except bottom. Can be assembled
in advance. Bake on baking sheet
5 minutes.

8 servings

Tipsy Peach Cake with Brown Butter Frosting

•

½ cup shortening
2 cups sugar
2 eggs
2½ cups flour
1½ teaspoons baking soda
¼ teaspoon baking powder
1½ teaspoons salt
¾ teaspoon cinnamon
½ teaspoon ginger
½ teaspoon allspice
3 large peaches, pitted
½ cup bourbon
½ cup water
¼ teaspoon almond extract
½ cup pecans
1 cup raisins

Brown Butter Frosting:
⅓ cup butter
3 cups powdered sugar, sifted
½ teaspoon vanilla
3 tablespoons heavy cream

Preheat oven to 350°F. Butter & flour
a 13x9-inch pan.

Cream shortening & sugar. Add eggs.
Sift dry ingredients. Add to
creamed mixture.

Put peaches, unpeeled, into blender.
Add bourbon, water & extract.
Purée & measure. Add more
peaches, if needed, to make 2½
cups. Mix peaches with batter. Add
raisins & nuts. Blend well. Pour into
pan. Bake 60-65 minutes until cake
tests done. For frosting, brown butter over medium heat until a delicate
brown, not scorched. Blend butter
with sugar. Stir in vanilla & cream.
Mix until smooth. Frost cake.

12-15 servings

*California
Gewürztraminer*

•

*Light the fireplace, sip a
glass of wine while the
Ratatouille bakes.
Spread a cloth in front
of the fire to have a
picnic on a winter's
afternoon.*
❦

Ratatouille en Croûte

•

1 small eggplant, cut into 1-inch
   cubes
1 medium onion, sliced
1 clove garlic, chopped
2 tablespoons olive oil
3 tomatoes, peeled & cut into
   wedges
1 medium zucchini, sliced
½ green pepper, cut into strips
¼ cup snipped parsley
1 teaspoon salt
¼ teaspoon pepper
½ teaspoon basil
1 package (3 ounces) cream cheese
½ pound puff pastry
1 egg, beaten with 1 teaspoon water

Preheat oven to 425°F.

Cook onion & garlic in oil in large
skillet until tender. Add eggplant,
tomatoes, zucchini, green pepper,
parsley, salt, pepper & basil. Simmer
10 minutes. Cool.

Roll pastry into a 16x9-inch rectangle on a floured surface. Spoon
ratatouille lengthwise down center of
pastry. Dot with cream cheese.
Blend egg & water. Brush edges of
pastry. Fold pastry over to enclose
filling. Secure edges with tines of a
fork. Place on a baking sheet. Slash
top in four places with point of a
sharp knife, cutting through pastry.
Brush with egg-water mixture. Bake
20-30 minutes until puffed &
golden. Slice to serve.

6 servings

Bibb Lettuce with Pecans & Oranges

•

4 heads Bibb lettuce
¾ cup pecan halves, toasted
2 oranges, peeled & sliced
⅓ cup vinegar
½ cup sugar
1 cup vegetable oil
1 teaspoon salt
½ small onion, chopped
1 teaspoon dry mustard
2 tablespoons water

Place lettuce, pecans & oranges into
a salad bowl.

Combine vinegar, sugar, oil, salt,
onion, mustard & water in a
blender. Dressing can be made ahead
& refrigerated. Toss with salad just
before serving.

8 servings

Carrot Cake

•

2 cups flour
1 teaspoon baking soda
2 teaspoons cinnamon
1 teaspoon salt
2 cups sugar
1½ cups vegetable oil
3 eggs
2 cups finely grated carrots
1 cup crushed pineapple,
   well drained
1 cup shredded coconut
1 cup chopped walnuts
1 teaspoon vanilla

Frosting:
1 package (8 ounces) cream
   cheese, softened
½ cup butter, softened
2 teaspoons vanilla
4 cups sifted powdered sugar

Preheat oven to 350°F. Butter & flour
a 13x9-inch pan.

Sift flour, soda, cinnamon & salt. Set
aside. Beat sugar, oil & eggs until
well blended. Gradually add flour
mixture. Fold in carrots, pineapple,
coconut, walnuts & vanilla. Pour into
pan. Bake 1 hour. Cool.

For frosting, beat cream cheese, butter & vanilla. Gradually add powdered sugar, beating until smooth.
Frost cake.

12-15 servings

Lemon-Sherry Chicken Suprème

•

¼ cup flour
1 teaspoon salt
1 teaspoon paprika
6 whole chicken breasts, halved, skinned & boned
¼ cup butter
¼ cup water
1 tablespoon cornstarch
2½ cups light cream, divided
¼ cup sherry
½ teaspoon grated lemon peel
1½ tablespoons lemon juice
1½ cups grated Swiss cheese
½ cup chopped parsley

Preheat oven to 350°F.

Combine flour, salt & paprika in flat dish. Coat chicken with flour mixture. Melt butter in a large skillet. Brown chicken on both sides. Arrange chicken in 13x9-inch baking dish.

Mix cornstarch with ½ cup cream. Stir into pan drippings. Cook, stirring, over low heat. Gradually add remaining cream, sherry, lemon peel & juice. Cook & stir until sauce thickens. Pour over chicken. May be refrigerated or frozen at this point.

Bake 30 minutes, covered. Uncover & sprinkle with cheese. Return to oven until cheese melts. Garnish with parsley.

12 servings

Dilled Broccoli Salad

•

3 heads broccoli
¼ cup chopped onion
½ cup sliced stuffed olives
3 hard-cooked eggs, chopped
1½ cups sliced celery
1 tablespoon lemon juice
1 teaspoon dill weed
1 cup mayonnaise
1 head Boston lettuce

Cut broccoli into 3-inch spears. Cook broccoli until crisp-tender about 3 minutes. Drain.

Place broccoli in bowl with onion, olives, eggs & celery. Combine lemon juice, dill weed & mayonnaise. Stir dressing into broccoli mixture. Chill 4 hours. Serve in a Boston lettuce cup.

6 servings

Milwaukee Million Dollar Pie

•

Crust:
2 cups crushed chocolate wafer cookies
½ cup butter, melted

Filling:
1¼ cups butter, softened
1⅓ cups sugar
4-ounces unsweetened chocolate, melted
6 large eggs
3 tablespoons Cognac
2 cups finely chopped pecans
1 pint heavy cream, whipped
semi-sweet chocolate curls

Preheat oven to 350°F.

Mix crumbs & melted butter. Press mixture firmly & evenly onto bottom & sides of two 8-inch pie pans or one 10-inch springform pan. Bake 10 minutes & cool.

Cream butter & sugar. Add melted chocolate. Stir. Add eggs, 1 at a time, beating 3 minutes after each addition. Add Cognac & nuts. Pour into crusts. Top each with whipped cream & curls. Chill 3 hours. Freezes well.

12-16 servings

Photographs

Salade St. Simeon, recipe 145
Beth's Sherried Wild Rice Soup, recipe 12
Martini Sole on the Grill, recipe 29
Mustard Ring, recipe 141
Leg of Lamb with Quince Sauce, recipe 78

*California Blush
Zinfandel*

•

*Entertain the Aunts,
Uncles & Cousins
coming to brunch next
Sunday with ease &
elegance. Present the
Soup in a white tureen
& serve in punch cups
with a dollop of
sour cream &
strawberry on top.*
❦

Cold Strawberry Soup

•

3 cups Burgundy wine
2 pints strawberries, cleaned,
  hulled & sliced
½ cup sugar
1 pint sour cream
  extra berries & sour cream
  for garnish

Simmer Burgundy, strawberries &
sugar for 30 minutes. Chill. Add
sour cream. Purée in blender or
processor. Chill. Pour into serving
bowls. Garnish with sour cream & a
perfect berry.

8 servings

Creamy Egg Brunch Casserole

•

4 slices bacon, chopped
½ pound dried beef, chopped
  coarsely
½ cup butter, divided
½ pound fresh mushrooms, sliced
½ cup flour
1 quart milk
16 eggs
¼ teaspoon salt
  pepper

Preheat oven to 275°F.

Brown bacon in skillet. Remove from
pan. Add beef, ¼ cup butter &
mushrooms. Reserve a few mushrooms for garnish. Sauté lightly.
Sprinkle flour over mixture. Cook 3
minutes. Gradually stir in milk.
Cook until sauce is thickened &
smooth. Stir constantly. Set aside.

Combine eggs, salt & pepper. Scram-
ble eggs in remaining butter until
very soft.

In a 13x9-inch casserole, alternately
add a layer of soft scrambled eggs
& a layer of sauce. Repeat. Garnish
with reserved mushrooms & crumbled bacon. Cover & refrigerate, or
bake immediately 30 minutes.

12 servings

Nana's Banana Bread

•

½ cup shortening
1½ cups sugar
2 eggs
3 large ripe, bananas, mashed
1 teaspoon salt
1 tablespoon vanilla
2 cups flour
1 teaspoon baking soda
½ cup buttermilk or sour cream
¾ cup chopped nuts

Preheat oven to 350°F. Butter & flour
a 9x5-inch loaf pan.

Cream shortening & sugar. Beat in
eggs. Add bananas to creamed mixture with salt & vanilla. Mix until well
blended. Sift flour & baking soda.
Add alternately to batter with buttermilk. Stir in nuts. Pour into loaf
pan. Bake 40-45 minutes.

Recipe makes 22 small cupcakes.
Bake 25-30 minutes.

1 loaf

Pot of Darjeeling Tea

•

*Perfect for entertaining
lightly with style, tea time
has a resurgent
popularity. Add 1 level
teaspoon tea per cup to a
warmed porcelain
teapot. Add freshly boiled
water. Cover & let steep
3-5 minutes. Gently stir
tea. Strain into waiting
teacups. Serve with a bit
of lemon & sugar.*

Poppy Seed
Tea Cake

•

⅓ cup poppy seed
1 cup buttermilk
1 cup butter, softened
1½ cups sugar
4 eggs
2½ cups flour
2 teaspoons baking powder
1 teaspoon baking soda
½ teaspoon salt
2 tablespoons grated orange peel
2 tablespoons sugar
1 teaspoon cinnamon

Combine poppy seed & buttermilk. Refrigerate overnight.

Preheat oven to 350°F. Butter & flour a 10-inch tube or bundt pan. Cream butter & sugar. Add eggs, one at a time, beating well after each addition. Combine flour, baking powder, soda & salt. Add to creamed mixture. Add orange peel. Spoon half the batter into prepared pan. Sprinkle with sugar & cinnamon. Top with remaining batter. Bake 1 hour. Cool 10 minutes. Turn out onto rack.

20 servings

Date
Pudding

•

1 pound pitted dates, chopped
1½ cups chopped English walnuts
1 cup milk
4 eggs
2 cups sugar
1 cup flour
2 teaspoons baking powder
whipped cream

Preheat oven to 350°F.

Soak dates & nuts in milk until dates are soft. Beat eggs & sugar. Add flour, baking powder & date mixture. Pour into 9-inch square pan. Bake 45-50 minutes. Serve warm with whipped cream.

8 servings

Croatian
Kifle

•

2 cups butter, softened
12-ounces cream cheese, softened
4 cups flour
1 can (12 ounces) apricot pastry filling, or thick jam or ¾ cup finely ground almonds
sugar

Combine butter, cream cheese & flour. Use a potato masher to thoroughly mix. Flatten dough. Cover & refrigerate overnight.

Preheat oven to 350°F.

Roll out ⅓ dough onto floured surface to ⅛-inch thick. Cut into 2-inch squares. Place ¼ teaspoon filling in middle of each square. Roll up diagonally. Pinch seam & form into half-moon shape. Place onto baking sheets. Bake 15-20 minutes until lightly browned. Roll immediately in sugar.

12-14 dozen

California Red Gamay

•

A quiche & pie lunch to delight your most discriminating friends. Mound the Truffles onto a small footed serving dish. Decadence!

Connie's Tomato Quiche

•

1 9-inch unbaked pie crust
3 tablespoons flour
  salt & pepper
2 medium tomatoes, cut into wedges
2 teaspoons olive oil
½ cup pitted Sicilian olives, sliced
1 cup minced scallions
3-ounces Bel Paese cheese, cubed
2 eggs, slightly beaten
1 cup heavy cream
1 cup grated provolone cheese

Preheat oven to 400°F. Pierce pie crust all over with fork. Bake 8 minutes. Set aside.

Combine flour, salt & pepper. Dredge tomato wedges in flour. Heat oil in skillet. Sauté tomatoes 5 minutes. Place in pie crust. Reserve 2 tablespoons scallions. Add olives, scallions & Bel Paese to pie crust.

Combine eggs & cream. Stir in cheese. Pour into pie. Bake 45 minutes until filling is set. Top with reserved scallions. Let stand 5 minutes before serving.

6 servings

Welsh Leek Pie

•

1 cup flour
¼ cup finely chopped suet or
  vegetable shortening
  pinch salt
1 teaspoon baking powder
4-5 tablespoons water

1½ pounds lean beef stew meat
¼ cup flour
½ teaspoon salt
  pepper
2 tablespoons vegetable oil
1½ cups beef stock
2 medium potatoes, cubed
1 medium leek, sliced, including
  tender greens

To prepare pastry, combine flour, suet, salt & baking powder in processor or with a pastry blender until uniformly pea-size in consistency. Add water. Mix until smooth ball forms. Chill.

Toss beef cubes with flour, salt & pepper. Brown beef in hot oil 2-3 minutes. Add stock. Cover & simmer 1 hour. Add potatoes & leek. Cook 5 minutes. Spoon into 2-quart casserole.

Preheat oven to 375°F.

Roll pastry out ¼-inch thick. Cover casserole with pastry. Trim edges. Cut out decorative pastry designs. Paint top of pastry with water. Apply pastry cutouts. Cut hole in center of pastry for steam to escape. Bake 1 hour until golden brown.

6-8 servings

Truffles

•

½ cup butter, softened
2 cups powdered sugar
½ cup + 2 tablespoons unsweetened
  Dutch-process cocoa
3 tablespoons Grand Marnier

Coating:
3 tablespoons powdered sugar
3 tablespoons unsweetened Dutch-
  process cocoa

Beat butter in large bowl with wooden spoon. Add powdered sugar, ½ cup at a time, beating well after each addition. Add cocoa. Beat well. Add Grand Marnier. Combine. Cover & refrigerate several hours.

Combine coating sugar & cocoa.

Roll truffles by heaping teaspoonfuls into balls. Roll in coating mix. Refrigerate.

2 dozen

California White Zinfandel

•

*A thank-you luncheon on
the lawn for committee
members. Set up card
tables with breezy, white
paper cloths tied at the
legs with ribbons.*

Cobb
Salad

•

1 large head romaine lettuce, torn
   into bite-size pieces
3 cooked chicken breast halves,
   skinned, boned & shredded
6 scallions, sliced
6 hard cooked eggs, chopped
3 tomatoes, chopped
½ pound bacon, crisp-cooked
   & crumbled
½ pound Swiss cheese, grated
2 avocados, peeled, pitted, cubed
   & tossed in lemon juice
4-ounces blue cheese, crumbled
   oil & vinegar dressing

Place romaine on oval serving platter. Arrange remaining ingredients
in rows, placing chicken in a strip
down the middle. Sprinkle with oil
& vinegar, salt & cracked pepper
before serving.

6 servings

Tabouli

•

1½ cups bulgar wheat
4 cups boiling water
1¼ cups minced parsley
¾ cup minced mint
3 medium tomatoes, chopped
1 cucumber, peeled, seeded &
   chopped
1 clove garlic, minced
¾ cup fresh lemon juice
1 teaspoon salt
⅓ cup olive oil

Pour boiling water over bulgar. Let
stand 2 hours. Drain excess water.
Mix bulgar with remaining ingredients. Chill 4 hours before serving.
Serve in hollowed tomatoes, in pita
bread, in cocktail-size pita bread,
or on bed of lettuce. Serve as a salad,
sandwich or appetizer.

8 servings

Kitchen Sink
Pasta
Salad

•

½ pound linguini, broken into
   pieces
½ pound bow tie pasta
½ pound vegetable rotini
½ pound vegetable wagon wheel
   or shell pasta
¾ cup chopped red onion
2 medium green peppers, chopped
2 medium red peppers, chopped
2 large cucumbers, chopped
2 cups chopped celery
1 cup broccoli flowerets
1 cup cauliflowerets
½ pound hard salami, cubed
½ pound boiled ham, julienned
½ pound mozzarella, cubed
1 cup grated Parmesan cheese
½ cup grated Romano cheese
1 can (7¾ ounces) pitted black
   olives, drained
½ cup sunflower seeds
½ cup soy nuts
1 bunch parsley, chopped
2 teaspoons salt
1½ teaspoons pepper

Garlic Herb Vinaigrette:
¾ cup red wine vinegar
2 cups olive oil
2 tablespoons water
2 cloves garlic, minced
2½ teaspoons Italian herbs
1 teaspoon sugar
   salt & pepper

3 tomatoes, chopped
3 hard-cooked eggs, chopped

Cook pastas al dente. Rinse under
cold water. Drain. Combine pasta
& remaining salad ingredients in a
very large container. Combine dressing ingredients. Toss 1½ cups dressing with salad. Cover & chill 12
hours or overnight. Before serving,
toss with remaining dressing, tomatoes & eggs. Great way to use up bits
of this & that from the refrigerator.

20 servings

MENU

**Italian
Zucchini
Pie**

Whole Wheat
Rolls

**Persian
Peach
Salad**

**Cherry
Date
Cake**

*Italian Chianti Classico
or
Chianti Colli Arentini*

•

*What to do with all that
zucchini? The Pie uses
quantities of zucchini &
freezes well before baking.
Bake 6 Pies for winter
meals. Molto grande!!*
❦

Italian
Zucchini
Pie

•

4-5 cups thinly sliced zucchini
  1 large onion, chopped
  1 clove garlic, minced
  ¼ cup butter
  ½ cup chopped fresh parsley
  ½ teaspoon salt
  ½ teaspoon pepper
  ½ teaspoon oregano
  2 eggs, slightly beaten
  2 cups grated mozzarella cheese
  2 teaspoons Dijon-style mustard
  1 unbaked 9-inch pie crust
    balsamic vinegar

Preheat oven to 375°F.

Sauté zucchini, onion & garlic in butter until tender. Stir in parsley & seasonings. Combine eggs & cheese. Add vegetables.

Spread mustard on bottom of pie crust. Add vegetable mixture. Bake 40-50 minutes until knife inserted in center comes out clean. Serve each slice with a few drops of balsamic vinegar.

5-6 servings

Persian
Peach
Salad

•

4 fresh peaches, peeled, halved
   & pitted
  lettuce leaves

Dressing:
  2 tablespoons Port wine
  1 tablespoon apricot jam
  1 teaspoon ground ginger
½ cup heavy cream, lightly whipped

Arrange peach halves on lettuce leaves.

Heat wine, jam & ginger over low heat until smooth. Strain. Fold into slightly whipped cream. Spoon over peaches.

4 servings

Cherry
Date
Cake

•

1½ cups flour
1½ cups sugar
  1 teaspoon baking powder
  ½ teaspoon salt
  4 eggs
  3 tablespoons butter, softened
  1 cup pitted fresh Bing cherries,
    halved, or maraschino cherries
  2 cups pecan halves
  2 cups walnut halves
  1 pound pitted dates, sliced
    lengthwise

Glaze:
  ½ cup butter
  ¼ cup water
  1 cup sugar
  ½ cup dark rum
    whipped cream

Preheat oven to 300°F.

Sift flour, sugar, baking powder & salt. Add eggs, 1 at a time. Beat well. Add remaining ingredients. Stir in gently. Bake in 10-inch tube or Bundt pan 1 hour 30 minutes. Increase temperature to 325°F. Bake 15 minutes.

For the glaze. Boil butter, water & sugar 5 minutes. Add rum. Set cake in pan on rack. Pierce cake with skewer. Slowly pour glaze onto cake. Allow to soak into the cake while cooling. Remove from pan. Store, refrigerated in tightly covered container several weeks. Add fruit juice or rum to moisten. Serve with whipped cream.

20 servings

MENU

**White
Sangria**

**Shrimp
&
Rice Salad**

**Tina's
Tomatoes**

Pineapple
Cheesecake

*Invite your friends for
lunch. Serve the Shrimp
Salad in red cabbage,
halved & hollowed out
on bright pink plates.
Use plenty of pink
& dark red peonies &
carnations for the
centerpiece.*
❧

White Sangria

•

1 bottle (750ml) dry white wine
½ cup Curaçao
1 lemon, sliced very thin
1 orange, sliced very thin
1 lime, sliced very thin
1 bottle (10 ounces) club soda

Mix wine & Curaçao. Add lemon,
orange & lime slices. Cover & chill
at least one hour. Just before serving,
add ice cubes & club soda.

To make for a crowd, mix 1 bottle
(3 liters) wine, 2 cups Curaçao, with
1 liter plus one 10-ounce bottle club
soda.

6 servings

Shrimp & Rice Salad

•

¾ pound fresh shrimp, cooked,
    peeled & halved
1 cup rice, cook according to
    package directions
1 cup vinaigrette dressing
1 tablespoon teriyaki sauce
1 teaspoon sugar
2 cups thin strips of fresh spinach
½ cup sliced celery
½ cup sliced scallions
⅓ cup crumbled, crisp-cooked
    bacon
1 can (8 ounces) sliced water
    chestnuts, drained

Place shrimp & hot rice in bowl.
Cool slightly. Combine vinaigrette,
teriyaki sauce & sugar. Stir into warm
rice. Cover & chill. Fold spinach,
celery, scallions, bacon & water chestnuts into rice just before serving.

6-8 servings

Tina's Tomatoes

•

1 tomato, halved
2 tablespoons sherry
    salt & pepper
    oregano
2 tablespoons mayonnaise
    freshly grated Parmesan

Pierce holes in cut side of tomato.
Pour in 1 tablespoon sherry per
tomato half. Sprinkle with salt, pepper & oregano. Bake at 350°F. 5-10
minutes. Spread 1 tablespoon mayonnaise on each tomato half. Sprinkle
with Parmesan. Broil 2 minutes until
lightly browned.

2 servings

Strawberry Butter

•

1 cup unsalted butter, softened
2 tablespoons powdered sugar
1 pint fresh strawberries, cleaned
   & hulled

Put ingredients in blender. Blend until smooth. Mixture may look as though it is separating; continue to blend until smooth. One pint blueberries, apricots or kiwi fruit may be substituted as variations.

2 cups

Swedish Pancakes

•

3 eggs
¾ cup sifted flour
   salt
⅛ teaspoon baking powder
¼ teaspoon sugar
1¼ cups milk
1 teaspoon vegetable shortening
   per pancake

Preheat a 10-inch flat griddle or iron pan over medium heat. Beat eggs. Add flour, salt, baking powder & sugar. Slowly beat in milk until batter is thin.

Melt shortening on griddle. Spread ¼ cup batter quickly to fill entire surface of pan. Use back of large spoon with a very light touch. Pancake should be very thin. Turn when browned. Spread with Strawberry Butter. Or top with syrup, powdered sugar, fresh fruit, jam, even sprinkle with granulated sugar. Roll up, serve & enjoy!!

9 pancakes

Buckwheat Yogurt Pancakes

•

⅔ cup buckwheat flour
1⅓ cups flour
2 teaspoons baking powder
1 teaspoon baking soda
1 teaspoon salt
2 teaspoons honey or sugar
2 eggs, beaten
¼ cup butter, melted
2 cups yogurt
1¼ cups milk

Mix flours, baking powder, baking soda, salt & sugar. If using honey add it to liquid ingredients. In another bowl combine eggs, butter, yogurt & milk. Add yogurt mixture to dry ingredients. Stir briefly until batter is moist but not smooth. Cook on a hot, lightly-buttered griddle or electric skillet until the edges look dry. Turn to brown other side. Serve with butter & syrup.

4-6 servings

Bacon & Pasta Omelette

•

2 tablespoons butter
1 small onion, finely chopped
½ pound cooked pasta
½ pound crisp-cooked bacon, crumbled
4 eggs, beaten
   splash white wine
   salt & pepper
   Parmesan cheese

Heat butter in large skillet. Sauté onion 5 minutes. Add pasta & bacon. Toss to coat with butter & onion. Combine eggs, wine, salt & pepper. Pour into hot pan. Shake pan to settle ingredients. Cook until golden brown 5 minutes. Turn with spatulas. Cook other side 2 minutes. Invert onto serving plate. Sprinkle with Parmesan. Cut into wedges to serve.

4 servings

Herbed Croutons

•

¼ cup freshly grated Parmesan cheese
2 tablespoons oregano
2 cloves garlic, minced
1 tablespoon basil
½ teaspoon salt
½ teaspoon freshly ground pepper
4-5 cups dry bread cubes, crusts removed
¼ cup olive or salad oil

Preheat oven to 225°F.

In small bowl, mix cheese, oregano, garlic, basil, salt & pepper. In large bowl, toss bread cubes with oil. Toss with cheese-herb mixture until combined. Spread on baking sheets. Bake 1 hour until crisp & light golden, stirring occasionally so all sides toast. Cool. Croutons will keep one month stored in a tightly sealed container.

4-5 cups

Amaretto Cherry Bread

•

1½ cups flour
2 teaspoons baking powder
½ teaspoon salt
½ cup butter, softened
1 cup sugar
3 eggs
½ cup Amaretto liqueur
1 cup chopped walnuts
1 cup sour cherries, pitted, halved & drained

Glaze:
6 tablespoons sugar
6 tablespoons Amaretto liqueur

Preheat oven to 350°F. Butter a 9x5-inch pan.

Sift flour, baking powder & salt. Cream butter & sugar. Add eggs. Fold in dry ingredients, Amaretto, walnuts & cherries. Pour into loaf pan. Bake 1 hour.

For the glaze, mix sugar & Amaretto. While bread is still warm, pierce top of bread with a skewer. Pour glaze over, allowing it to seep into holes. Cool in pan.

1 loaf

MENU

Bacon & Pasta Omelette

Escarole, Watercress, & Curly Endive Salad with Scallions

Herbed Croutons

Amaretto Cherry Bread

Wisconsin Red Chelois

•

A Packer Backer Brunch! Use leftover pasta for the Omelette & toss the Salad with the Herbed Croutons before the game comes on television. The Spicy Salad will really perk up taste buds.

*French White
Alsatian Gewürztraminer*

•

*The menu couldn't be
simpler for a gathering
of friends or neighbors.
The cold Yogurt Soup
is refreshing &
delightfully different.
Serve in dark-colored bowls.*
🍎

Brother's Punch

•

1-ounce vodka
1-ounce prepared frozen
   concentrated raspberry juice
2-ounces grapefruit juice
   mint sprigs

Pour into tall, ice-filled glasses. Serve
with mint sprig garnish.

1 serving

California Yogurt Soup

•

 4 cups plain yogurt
1¾ cups chilled chicken stock
 4 ice cubes
½ cup golden raisins
 2 hard-cooked eggs, chopped
½ cup sliced scallions
 1 peeled, seeded cucumber,
   finely chopped
 1 teaspoon salt
½ teaspoon white pepper
   finely chopped parsley garnish
   finely snipped dill garnish

Combine all ingredients. Chill several
hours. Serve sprinkled with parsley
& dill.

6-8 servings

Jack's Chicken Salad

•

½ cup mayonnaise
½ cup milk
 2 cups cooked, chopped chicken
   or turkey breast
 1 cup chopped celery
 1 cup coarsely chopped walnuts
 1 large unpeeled Granny Smith
   apple, chopped
 4 scallions, thinly sliced
 1 teaspoon tarragon
 2 teaspoons finely snipped dill
 2 tablespoons poppy seed
 2 tablespoons toasted sesame seed
   salt & freshly ground pepper

Combine mayonnaise & milk. Mix
remaining ingredients in large bowl.
Add mayonnaise mixture. Toss to
coat. Serve on lettuce, in a split
croissant or in melon wedges.
Garnish with a few very thin slices
of apple.

6 servings

Cream of Mushroom Soup

•

½ pound mushrooms, sliced
1 medium onion, chopped
1 cup lightly packed chopped parsley
¼ cup butter
1 tablespoon flour
2 cups beef stock
1 cup sour cream or crème fraîche
   freshly chopped parsley, chives or scallions

In a medium saucepan sauté mushrooms, onion & parsley in butter until mushrooms are limp & liquid has evaporated. Stir in flour. Blend in stock. Bring to boil, stirring. Using blender or processor, whirl broth mixture with cream, a portion at a time, until smooth. Can be made ahead. Cover & chill at this point. Reheat to serve. Garnish with fresh chopped parsley, chives or scallions.

4 servings

Croissant Summer Sandwich

•

Herb Cheese:
1 large clove garlic
1 small onion
1 package (8 ounces) cream cheese, softened
1 cup unsalted butter, softened
¼ cup parsley
¼ cup chives
1 teaspoon salt
½ teaspoon pepper
   dash hot pepper

4 croissants, split
4-ounces sprouts: alfalfa, radish or combination
½ pound rare roast beef, thinly sliced
   salt & pepper to taste

In a food processor with steel blade inserted, chop garlic & onion. Add cream cheese, butter, parsley, chives, salt, pepper & hot pepper sauce. Mix until blended. Chill overnight.

Spread both sides of croissant with herb cheese. Place sprouts & roast beef on one half. Salt & pepper the other half. Cover & refrigerate one hour or up to one day in advance.

4 servings

Raspberry-Walnut "Linzer" Bars

•

1½ cups butter, softened
1 cup powdered sugar
1 egg
   salt
½ teaspoon cinnamon
2¾ cups flour
1½ cups finely chopped walnuts or pecans
2 cups raspberry jam
1 tablespoon lemon juice
   powdered sugar

In a large bowl cream butter, sugar, egg, salt & cinnamon until fluffy. Gradually fold in flour & nuts. Chill dough 1 hour.

Set aside ⅓ dough. Pat remaining ⅔ dough into a 15x10-inch jelly roll pan.

Stir together jam & lemon juice. Spread evenly over pastry. On a floured surface, pat or roll out remaining dough into a rectangle. Cut into strips ¼-inch wide. Place strips on top of jam in a lattice pattern.

Bake at 375°F. 35-40 minutes, until pastry is lightly browned. Cool. Sprinkle with powdered sugar. Cut into bars.

30 bars

MENU

Cream of Mushroom Soup

Croissant Summer Sandwich

Fresh Lemonade

Raspberry-Walnut "Linzer" Bars

French Beaujolais Morgon, slightly chilled

•

The summer air is warm & vibrant. How about a few friends over for a casual lunch?
❧

Celebration Gatherings
special occasions, holidays & gifts

VALENTINE'S DINNER
FOR TWO

**Simple Sole
for Two**

**Pears
with
Tarragon Cream**

Lemon-Broccoli Rice
in
Heart Mold

Croissants
with
Herb Butter

**Cupid's Kiss
Raspberry
Cheesecake**

French Champagne

•

*Victorian is the theme
for a small intimate table
with a red tablecloth
topped by an antique lace
coverlet; streamers
of burgundy & red
ribbons on top; silver
candlesticks & crystal
tulip glasses chilled by
champagne brut; a single
red rose in a crystal vase.*

❦

Simple Sole
for Two

•

1 pound sole fillets
1 tablespoon lemon juice
¼ cup grated Parmesan cheese
2 tablespoons butter, melted
1½ tablespoons mayonnaise
1½ tablespoons chopped onions
    chopped parsley & lemon wedges

Preheat broiler.

Place fillets in a flat baking dish.
Brush with lemon juice. Let stand
20 minutes. Combine cheese, butter
mayonnaise & onion. Broil fillets
6-8 minutes until flaky. Spoon mayonnaise mixture on top of fillets.
Broil 3 minutes. Serve garnished with
finely chopped parsley & lemon
wedges.

2 servings

Pears
with
Tarragon Cream

•

Boston lettuce
4 fresh pears, peeled, cored &
  halved, rubbed with lemon
  pitted Bing cherries
  chopped English walnuts

Tarragon Cream Dressing:
2 eggs
4 tablespoons sugar
6 tablespoons tarragon vinegar
  salt
  white pepper
1 cup heavy cream, whipped

Put pear half, cherries & walnuts on
lettuce-lined chilled plates.

In top of double boiler, beat eggs
with sugar until light & fluffy. Gradually add vinegar, salt & pepper.
Place double boiler over gently
boiling water. Continue beating until
thickened. Remove from heat. Cool.
Fold in cream. Serve on salad.

8 servings

Cupid's Kiss
Raspberry
Cheesecake

•

1 package (8½ ounces) chocolate
  wafer cookies, finely crushed
½ cup butter, melted
½ cup sugar

Filling:
2 packages (8 ounces each) cream
  cheese, softened
¾ cup sugar
3 eggs
¼ cup sour cream
1 tablespoon Grand Marnier
1 teaspoon lemon juice
1 pound red raspberries

Hardening Chocolate Sauce:
2-ounces finest quality milk
  chocolate
2-ounces finest quality dark
  chocolate
1 tablespoon vegetable oil

Preheat oven to 350°F.

Combine cookie crumbs, butter &
sugar. Press onto bottom & sides of
9-inch springform pan. Bake 10 minutes. Set aside to cool.

Reserve 10-12 whole raspberries.
Purée remainder. Measure ⅔ cup
raspberry purée for cheesecake.
Strain remainder in a sieve. Reserve.

For filling, beat cream cheese, sugar,
eggs, sour cream, Grand Marnier
& lemon juice until very smooth &
fluffy. Add the ⅔ cup raspberry
purée. Blend well. Pour into prepared crust. Bake 60 minutes. Cool
to room temperature.

For sauce, melt chocolates & oil. Frost
cheesecake with chocolate sauce.
Place reserved whole raspberries in
decorative pattern on top of sauce.
Refrigerate until sauce hardens. Serve
with strained raspberries, sweetened
with a little Grand Marnier, if desired.

10-12 servings

FRIDAY EVENING SABBATH CELEBRATION

Bourbon Mustard Chicken

Honey-Baked Carrots & Apples

Whipped Potatoes
with
Cabbage

Braided
Egg Bread

Stellar Lemon Meringue Pie

*California White
Sonoma
Johannisberg Riesling*

•

*A menu for any special
occasion, with family &
friends to brighten the
table & the congenial glow
of candlelight.*

Bourbon Mustard Chicken

•

¼ cup Dijon-style mustard
¼ cup bourbon
¼ cup dark brown sugar
 1 teaspoon Worcestershire sauce
 1 teaspoon salt
 2 scallions, thinly sliced
4-6 boneless, skinless chicken breast
     halves, pounded ¼-inch thick
 1 tablespoon margarine
 1 tablespoon oil

Combine mustard, bourbon, brown
sugar, Worcestershire, salt &
scallions in non-metal dish. Place
chicken in mixture, turning to coat.
Cover & marinate one hour. Reserve
marinade. Heat margarine & oil in
heavy skillet over medium-high heat.
Sauté chicken 3-4 minutes each side
until golden. Remove chicken. Pour
off fat. Add marinade. Stir & heat
to boiling. Serve over chicken.

4-6 servings

Honey-Baked Carrots & Apples

•

 8 medium carrots, sliced
 6 medium Granny Smith apples,
     peeled, cored & sliced
 ¼ cup honey
 ⅓ cup brown sugar
 2 tablespoons margarine
     paprika
     watercress, garnish

Preheat oven to 350°F. Butter a 9-inch
square pan. Cook carrots in small
amount of boiling water 10 minutes
until crisp-tender. Drain. Combine
carrots, apples & honey. Pour into
pan. Dot with margarine. Sprinkle
with brown sugar & paprika. Cover
& bake 50 minutes. Garnish with
watercress sprigs.

8 servings

Stellar Lemon Meringue Pie

•

 1 9-inch baked pie crust
1⅓ cups sugar
 ½ cup cornstarch
 ¼ teaspoon salt
1¾ cups water
 4 egg yolks, beaten
 2 tablespoons margarine, melted
 1 tablespoon grated lemon peel
 ½ cup lemon juice

Meringue:
 4 egg whites, room temperature
 ¼ teaspoon cream of tartar
 ½ cup sugar
     lemon slices, garnish

In a saucepan over medium heat,
combine sugar, cornstarch & salt.
Gradually stir in water with a whisk.
Cook, stirring constantly until
mixture boils. Boil one minute.
Remove from heat. Whisk yolks into
saucepan. Return to low heat, stirring constantly. Do not overcook.
Remove from heat. Stir in margarine,
lemon peel & juice. Pour into
pastry shell. Cover with plastic.
Refrigerate 3 hours.

For the meringue, preheat oven to
425°F. Butter & flour a baking sheet.
Beat egg whites & cream of tartar
until soft peaks form. Add sugar by
tablespoonfuls. Beat until sugar dissolves & meringue is stiff & glossy.
Mound meringue in a 9-inch circle
on baking sheet. Bake 5 minutes
until golden. Cool 2 minutes. Using
2 large spatulas, lift meringue on
top of pie. Garnish with lemon slices.

8 servings

Leg of Lamb
with
Garlic-Quince Sauce

•

6-pound semi-boneless leg of lamb
  salt & pepper
3 cloves garlic, slivered
  fresh tarragon sprigs
1 cup quince jelly, melted

Sauce:
  1 whole head garlic
    pan drippings
½ cup water
1 cup quince jelly

Preheat oven to 400°F.

Rub lamb with salt & pepper. With point of sharp knife, make slits in lamb. Insert garlic & tarragon. Place lamb on rack in roasting pan. Place head of garlic for the sauce in pan. Bake 1½ hours or until meat thermometer reads 130°F. for medium-rare, 145°F. medium-well done. Frequently baste with melted jelly. Remove from oven. Tent with foil. Let rest 15 minutes before carving. For sauce, pour off any accumulated fat from roasting pan. Add ½ cup water. Pop each clove garlic from skin. Place in pan juices with jelly over medium heat. Stir up bits of drippings from bottom of pan. Pour into blender. Purée until smooth. Serve with lamb.

8-10 servings

Pictured page 64.

Pasta
Soufflé

•

9 tablespoons butter
1 clove garlic, minced
1½ tablespoons Dijon-style mustard
1⅔ cup milk
  6-ounces Jarlsberg cheese, grated
¼ pound ham, cut into thin strips
1½ cups quartered, cooked
    artichoke hearts
¼ teaspoon cayenne
1 teaspoon pepper
6 eggs, separated
½ pound fresh angel hair or other
    pasta, cooked & drained

Preheat oven to 350°F. Make a wax paper collar to fit a 1½-quart soufflé dish. Butter inside of collar & dish. Dust with Parmesan cheese. Set aside.

In a medium-size saucepan, melt butter. Sauté garlic 1-2 minutes. Stir in mustard. Add milk, cheese, ham, artichokes, cayenne & pepper. Cook, stirring until cheese melts & is hot & bubbly. Remove from heat. Cool. Add egg yolks, 1 at a time, stirring well after each addition. Add pasta. Stir to coat. Beat egg whites until stiff. Stir ⅓ whites into pasta mixture. Blend thoroughly. Gently fold in remaining whites until well blended. Pour into prepared soufflé dish. Bake 40 minutes. Increase heat to 450°F. Bake 10 minutes longer. Remove collar. Serve immediately! Also use as an entrée.

8 servings

Burgundy
Onions

•

6 large yellow onions, sliced
  ¼-inch thick
3 tablespoon butter
1½ cups Burgundy wine
  salt & pepper

Separate onions into rings. Melt butter in large skillet. Sauté onions until tender & golden. Add wine, salt & pepper. Cover & simmer over low heat 15 minutes. Remove cover, increase heat & cook until wine reduces to a glaze.

8 servings

Broccoli Bacon Salad

•

2 large heads broccoli, chopped &
   blanched 1 minute
½ cup raisins
¼ cup chopped scallions or
   red onion
1 cup mayonnaise
¼ cup sugar
2 tablespoons cider vinegar
12 slices crisp-cooked bacon,
   crumbled

Combine broccoli, raisins & scallions.
Mix mayonnaise, sugar & vinegar.
Toss with broccoli. Chill several hours
or overnight. Top with bacon before
serving.

8-10 servings

Orange-Cabbage Salad

•

1 medium head red cabbage, finely
   chopped
1 large onion, finely chopped
1 whole orange, finely chopped
½ cup sugar
½ cup champagne vinegar
½ cup vegetable oil
1 tablespoon celery seed
1 cup rendered pork cracklings,
   optional

Combine cabbage, onion & orange.
Mix sugar, vinegar, oil & celery seed.
Toss with cabbage mixture. Cover &
chill several hours. Toss with cracklings before serving.

12 servings

Pots of Rum Crème

•

1½ envelopes unflavored gelatin
½ cup rum
1½ cups milk
5 eggs, separated
1½ cups sugar
1 teaspoon vanilla
3 cups heavy cream, whipped
   fresh cherries or strawberries

Soften gelatin in rum. Heat milk
in small pan. Add gelatin-rum mixture. Stir until gelatin completely dissolves. Cool. Beat egg yolks until
light & fluffy. Add sugar. Beat until
thick. Add vanilla & cooled milk
mixture. Fold in whipped cream.
Beat egg whites until stiff. Gently
fold into mixture. Spoon into little
crème pots, demitasse cups or ramekins. Chill. Crème will separate into
2 layers. Garnish with fresh cherries
or strawberries.

12 servings

*Delight your family &
guests with flavor
surprises. The Soufflé is
a pasta lover's dream!
Use a low flowering plant
with pastel-colored eggs
interspersed among the
foliage for the
centerpiece. Match
pastel colors for linens.*

Set the table with pastel-colored Easter eggs as accents. Use colored plates & napkins to match the pastel frosting on the Sweet Rolls. Serve Sandwiches & Sweet Rolls in napkin-lined Easter baskets.
❦

Orange Julep

•

1 quart fresh orange juice
½ cup minced fresh mint leaves
½ cup sugar
   juice of 6 limes
2 cups club soda
   mint sprigs, garnish

Mix orange juice, sugar, mint & lime juice. Chill 1-2 hours. Strain to remove mint. Mix with club soda. Pour into tall glasses filled with chipped ice. Garnish with mint. Refreshing!

8 servings

Pear & Poultry Sandwich

•

4 slices cooked chicken or turkey
4 slices buttered toast
½ cup mayonnaise
⅓ cup finely chopped celery
2 tablespoons finely chopped scallions
¼ teaspoon salt
2 very ripe pears, peeled, cored & thinly sliced
½ cup grated cheddar cheese
   paprika

Preheat oven to 350°F.

Arrange chicken or turkey slices on toast on a baking sheet. Combine mayonnaise, celery, scallions & salt. Spread on poultry. Arrange sliced pears on top. Sprinkle with cheese & paprika. Bake 10 minutes. Great for using leftover turkey!

4 servings

Rich Sweet Rolls

•

1 cup butter, softened
1 cup sour cream
2 cups flour
½ cup sugar
½ teaspoon cinnamon
½ cup chopped pecans

Frosting:
1 cup powdered sugar, sifted
2 tablespoons butter, softened
   pinch salt
½ teaspoon vanilla
1-2 tablespoons milk

Combine butter & sour cream. Blend in flour. Form into a ball. Cover & refrigerate 4 hours or overnight. Divide ball into 4 pieces. Keep dough in refrigerator until needed. Roll each piece into 9-inch circle. Cut each circle into 8 triangle-shaped wedges. Mix sugar, cinnamon & pecans. Sprinkle ¼ mixture evenly over wedges. Loosely roll each wedge from wide edge to the point. Place rolls on baking sheet. Repeat for each portion of dough. Preheat oven to 400°F. Bake 15-20 minutes. For frosting, combine powdered sugar, butter & salt. Add vanilla. Add milk gradually until mixture is spreading consistency. Frost rolls while warm. For Easter, tint frosting with pastel colors.

32 servings

ENTREE	POTATOES	DESSERT

Father's Day Pork Tenderloin

•

Green Bean Potato Salad

•

Mousse au Chocolat Sauce Grand Marnier

•

MENU

Father's Day Pork Tenderloin

Green Bean Potato Salad

Corn-on-the-Cob

Mousse au Chocolat Sauce Grand Marnier

French Red Bordeaux Saint-Estèphe

•

A special meal to treat Dads, Grandfathers or Husbands. The Mousse will knock their socks off!
❦

Marinade:
¼ cup water
1 tablespoon Worcestershire sauce
1 tablespoon instant coffee
1 large clove garlic, minced
1 teaspoon salt
½ teaspoon pepper
2 pork tenderloins, 2 pounds
2 tablespoons butter
1 cup sour cream
1 tablespoon flour

Prepare marinade by combining water, Worcestershire, coffee & garlic. Cut tenderloins into 6 medallions, 2-inches thick. Flatten with mallet. Season with salt & pepper. Place in shallow glass dish. Pour marinade over meat. Turn to coat. Chill several hours or overnight.

Heat butter in skillet. Brown meat. Add marinade. Cover & simmer 20 minutes. Place on serving platter. Keep warm. Combine sour cream & flour. Stir into pan drippings. Cook over medium heat, stirring until thickened. Cook 1 minute. Pour sauce over meat.

6 servings

---

3 pounds tiny new potatoes
1 pound fresh green beans, cut into 1-inch pieces

Dressing:
¾ cup vegetable oil
⅛ cup red wine vinegar
1 teaspoon salt
½ teaspoon pepper
1 tablespoon snipped fresh dill
1 tablespoon Dijon-style mustard
red leaf lettuce
alfalfa or radish sprouts

Peel a strip around the center of each potato. Boil in salted water 10-15 minutes until tender. Drain & cool. Steam beans, partially covered, 10-15 minutes. Rinse under cold water & drain. Combine dressing in blender. Pour over potatoes & beans. Chill. Line a serving platter with lettuce. Spoon salad in center & surround with sprouts.

10 servings

6-ounces semi-sweet chocolate
1-ounce unsweetened chocolate
6 eggs, separated
2 tablespoons dark rum
2 teaspoons vanilla
¼ cup sugar

Sauce Grand Marnier:
½ cup sugar
1 tablespoon cornstarch
¾ cup fresh orange juice
¼ cup Grand Marnier
¼ cup toasted almonds, optional

Melt chocolates in double boiler. Beat yolks until light & thick. Add rum & vanilla. Add chocolate slowly. Beat egg whites to soft peaks. Add sugar & beat until stiff & glossy. Stir ⅓ whites into chocolate mixture. Gently fold in remaining whites. Spoon into dessert dishes or stemmed glasses. Cover & chill several hours or overnight.

For the sauce, mix sugar, cornstarch & orange juice in small saucepan. Bring to boil. Remove from heat. Add Grand Marnier & almonds if desired. Cool & serve over mousse.

8 servings

Thanksgiving Apple Stuffing

•

¼ cup butter
3 scallions, sliced
3 large mushrooms, sliced
2 Granny Smith or other tart apples, peeled & sliced
3 cups dry bread cubes
¼ teaspoon each sage, thyme, savory & marjoram
½ cup applesauce
3 tablespoons apple brandy

Preheat oven to 325°F. Butter a 2-quart casserole.

In a medium saucepan, heat butter. Add onions, & mushrooms. Cook until tender. Add apples. Cook 1 minute. Stir in bread cubes, herbs, applesauce & apple brandy. Add more applesauce if mixture seems dry. Bake, covered, 30 minutes. Make an additional batch to stuff the turkey. Also excellent accompaniment to pork or ham.

4 servings

Autumn Salad

•

Nutmeg-Dill Vinaigrette:
1 tablespoon Dijon-style mustard
¼ cup white wine vinegar
⅛ teaspoon Kosher salt
⅛ teaspoon ground pepper
½ teaspoon dill
½ teaspoon ground nutmeg
½ cup extra-virgin olive oil

3 large unpeeled red delicious apples, very thinly sliced
⅓ cup crumbled Roquefort cheese
4 tablespoons walnuts
1 head romaine, trimmed & cut lengthwise into thirds
1 bunch watercress, trimmed
Kosher salt
cracked pepper
freshly grated nutmeg

For the vinaigrette, combine mustard, vinegar, salt, pepper, dill & nutmeg. Add oil very slowly, whisking constantly. Can be made 3 days in advance. Stir vigorously before using.

In a bowl, combine apple slices, Roquefort, walnuts & 3 tablespoons dressing. Refrigerate, covered, up to 4 hours. At serving time, combine romaine, cress & apple mixture on serving platter. Toss with dressing. Season with salt, pepper & nutmeg to taste.

8 servings

Cranberry-Pineapple Cream Salad

•

2 packages (3 ounces each) cream cheese, softened
2 tablespoons mayonnaise
2 tablespoons sugar
1 can (16 ounces) whole berry cranberry sauce
1 can (8 ounces) crushed pineapple, drained
1 cup heavy cream, whipped
Bibb or Boston lettuce
mandarin orange segments
grape clusters

Beat cream cheese, mayonnaise & sugar. Add cranberry sauce & drained pineapple. Blend well. Fold in whipped cream. Pour into a 5-6 cup mold. Freeze overnight. To serve, arrange lettuce on chilled salad plates. Unmold salad. Slice thinly. Garnish with orange segments & grape clusters.

12 servings

Baked Artichokes & Mushrooms

•

½ cup butter
1 clove garlic, minced
1 pound mushrooms, sliced
2 cups quartered artichoke hearts
2 tablespoons lemon juice
½ teaspoon oregano
1 teaspoon basil
1 teaspoon salt
  ground pepper
½ cup grated Parmesan cheese
2 tablespoons dry bread crumbs

Preheat oven to 350°F. Lightly butter a 1½-quart casserole.

Melt butter in a large skillet. Sauté garlic & mushrooms 5 minutes. Add lemon juice. Add artichoke hearts. Cook 5 minutes longer. Add oregano, basil, salt & pepper. Cook 1 minute. Pour into casserole. Sprinkle with cheese & bread crumbs. Bake 25-30 minutes.

4 servings

Sweet Potato Soufflé with Foamy Sauce

•

2 cups cooked sweet potatoes
  or yams
1 cup butter, melted
1½ cups sugar
¼ teaspoon grated nutmeg
1 tablespoon grated lemon or
  orange peel
¼ cup brandy
6 eggs, well beaten

Foamy Sauce:
3 egg yolks
¾ cup sugar
½ teaspoon vanilla
⅛ teaspoon salt
1 cup heavy cream, whipped

Preheat oven to 350°F. Place 13x9-inch pan with 1-inch boiling water in oven.

In a blender or processor, combine sweet potatoes, butter, sugar, nutmeg, citrus peel & brandy. Combine well. Add eggs. Blend until smooth. Pour mixture into 1½-quart soufflé dish. Put soufflé in pan of water in oven. Bake 1 hour until knife inserted in center comes out clean.

For the foamy sauce, beat yolks. Add sugar gradually. Add vanilla & salt. Beat until thick & pale yellow. Fold in whipped cream. Chill. Makes 1½ cups sauce. Soufflé may be served by itself as a vegetable or topped with foamy sauce as dessert. Sprinkle top of soufflé with extra nutmeg & a pinch of cinnamon for additional flavor.

6-8 servings

Cranberry Walnut Pie

•

1 9-inch unbaked pie crust
2 cups whole cranberries
1 cup whole walnut halves
¼ cup brown sugar
1 egg
½ cup sugar
⅓ cup butter, melted & cooled
½ cup flour

Preheat oven to 325°F.

Place cranberries & walnuts in pie shell. Sprinkle with brown sugar. Combine egg, sugar, butter & flour. Beat well. Spread on top of cranberries. Bake 45-50 minutes.

8 servings

For a buffet-style Thanksgiving dinner, give a simple blessing before guests serve themselves. From that moment on it is understood that guests may begin eating as soon as they are seated. When the last guest is seated, offer toasts to the gathering.

Irish
Cream

•

1 can (14 ounces) sweetened
  condensed milk
1½ cups heavy cream
3 eggs
1 cup good Irish whiskey
¼ teaspoon coconut extract
1½ tablespoons chocolate syrup

Add ingredients to blender or processor. Mix on highest speed 30 seconds. Store in covered container in
refrigerator. Keeps several weeks. Stir
before serving. Of course, calories &
cholesterol left out of the recipe!

Peppermint
Brittle

•

2 pounds white chocolate
30 small candy canes

Line a jelly roll pan with heavy
duty foil.

Break up white chocolate. Microwave
at medium power 6 minutes. Stir.
Microwave 1-2 minutes until melted.
Add candy to chocolate. Press into
jelly roll pan. Chill until set about 1
hour. Break into small pieces by
slamming pan onto counter. Kids
can make for teachers!

Cherry-Chip
Banana
Bread

•

½ cup butter, softened
1 cup sugar
2 eggs
2 medium very ripe bananas,
  mashed
2 cups flour, sifted
1 teaspoon baking soda
¼ cup chopped nuts
¼ cup mini chocolate chips
¼ cup chopped maraschino cherries

Preheat oven to 350°F. Butter a
9x5-inch loaf pan.

Cream butter & sugar. Beat until light
& fluffy. Add eggs, one at a time.
Add bananas. Sift soda with flour. Stir
into creamed mixture. Fold in nuts,
chips & cherries. Pour into prepared
pan. Bake 40-45 minutes. Remove
loaf from pan. Cool on wire rack.
Makes 15 muffins if desired. Bake
25-30 minutes.

1 loaf

Raspberry Vinegar

•

2½ cups sweetened raspberries
2¼ cups white vinegar
1½ cups sugar

Place raspberries & vinegar in a glass bowl or crock. Let stand 24 hours at room temperature. Strain into saucepan. Stir in sugar. Bring to boil over medium-high heat. Boil 10 minutes. Pour into clean bottles. Give as a gift with the following recipe attached:

Raspberry Vinegar Salad
2-3 parts walnut oil
  1 part raspberry vinegar
    Boston or bibb lettuce
    julienned cucumbers
    thinly sliced radishes
    salt
    pepper
    oregano

Mix oil & vinegar. Sprinkle lettuce & vegetables with salt, pepper & oregano. Toss with dressing. Also delicious with pears in the salad.

Half-Hour Apple Butter

•

 2 cups unsweetened applesauce
⅓ cup sugar
 1 teaspoon cinnamon
¼ teaspoon allspice
⅛ teaspoon ginger
⅛ teaspoon cloves

In a heavy saucepan, combine ingredients. Bring to a boil. Cook ½ hour, stirring often. Flavor improves as it is stored in refrigerator. Spread on buttered English muffins, pancakes, waffles or toasted bread.

1¼ cups

S.K. Caramel Corn

•

 1 cup popcorn, popped, about
    16 cups
 1 cup brown sugar
¼ cup light corn syrup
½ cup butter
½ teaspoon salt
 1 teaspoon vanilla
½ teaspoon baking soda
 1 cup peanuts

Place popped corn in large doubled brown paper bag. Combine sugar, syrup, butter & salt in bowl. Microwave on high 2 minutes. Stir. Microwave 3 minutes. Stir after each minute. Add vanilla & baking soda. Stir. Pour over popcorn in bag. Shake well. Microwave 1 minute. Repeat. Shake well. Microwave 30 seconds. Add peanuts, if desired. Repeat. Pour on foil or waxed paper to cool. Store in tightly covered containers.

4 quarts

Present these beauties in interesting wrappings, bottles, jars, baskets, packages, a myriad of presentations . . .

Ginger
Shrimp de Jonghe
Miniatures

•

12 cooked shrimp, finely chopped
½ cup butter, softened
 1 clove garlic, minced
 2 tablespoons minced parsley
 1 teaspoon chopped, preserved
    ginger root
20 bread cutouts, toasted 1 side

Beat butter until light & fluffy. Add
garlic, parsley & ginger. Spread
shrimp mixture on untoasted side of
cutouts. Broil until delicately
browned.

20 servings

Mustard
Glazed
Carrots

•

2 pounds carrots, peeled, sliced
   diagonally
3 tablespoons butter
3 tablespoons Dijon-style mustard
¼ cup brown sugar
   salt
¼ cup chopped fresh parsley

Steam carrots 5 minutes. In small
saucepan, melt butter. Add mustard,
brown sugar & salt. Cook 3 minutes.
Add carrots, turning to coat in
sauce. Cook 5 minutes. Sprinkle with
parsley.

6 servings

Cranberry Sauce
Grand Marnier

•

2 cups sugar
2 cups water
1 pound fresh cranberries
1 envelope unflavored gelatin
3 tablespoons Grand Marnier
   grated peel of 1 orange
   juice of ½ lemon

In a large saucepan, combine sugar
& water. Boil 5 minutes. Add cranberries. Boil 5 minutes longer until
skins pop. Soften gelatin in Grand
Marnier. Add to hot cranberries. Stir
until gelatin is thoroughly dissolved.
Cool. Stir in orange peel & lemon
juice. Pour into glass serving bowl.
Chill. May be frozen.

12 servings

Orange
Date Bread

•

½ cup butter, softened
1 cup sugar
2 eggs
⅔ cup buttermilk
2 cups flour
  pinch salt
1 tablespoon grated orange peel
1 cup chopped dates
½ cup chopped pecans

Topping:
1 cup sugar
2 tablespoons grated orange peel
½ cup orange juice

Preheat oven to 350°F. Butter & flour a 9x5-inch loaf pan.

Cream butter & sugar. Add eggs one at a time. Alternately add buttermilk & flour. Stir in salt, orange peel, dates & pecans. Bake 1 hour. Combine topping ingredients. Stir until sugar is completely dissolved. Pour over hot bread. Cool in loaf pan.

1 loaf

Toffee
Rum
Cheesecake

•

½ cup unsalted butter, melted
1 cup ground graham crackers
1 cup ground pecans
2 tablespoons sugar
2 tablespoons brown sugar

Filling:
2 pounds cream cheese, softened
¾ cup sugar
¾ cup brown sugar
3 tablespoons rum
½ cup crushed butter brickle bits
  or English toffee
  pinch salt
4 eggs

Topping:
2 cups sour cream
¼ cup brown sugar
2 tablespoons rum
½ tablespoon maple sugar
  butter brickle bits

Preheat oven to 350°F.

Combine butter, crumbs, nuts & sugars. Blend well. Press mixture on bottom & sides of 10-inch springform pan. Set aside.

For the filling, beat cream cheese & sugars until light & fluffy. Add eggs, one at a time, beating well after each addition. Add rum, butter brickle bits & salt. Blend thoroughly. Pour into crust. Bake 45 minutes. For topping, beat sour cream, brown sugar, rum & maple sugar until sugar dissolves. Spread on top of cheesecake. Sprinkle top with additional butter brickle bits. Continue baking 15 minutes. Remove from oven. Cool on rack. Refrigerate until serving.

10-12 servings

After Dinner
Eggnog

•

1 cup frozen custard ice cream
2 cups rich dairy eggnog
1 cup brandy
⅛ cup rum
  small scoops ice cream
  freshly grated nutmeg

Just before serving, place ice cream, eggnog, brandy & rum in blender. Whirl until frothy. Serve in stemmed glasses. Top with small scoop of ice cream & nutmeg.

12-15 servings

*"A Toast! the glistening
holly bough;
Which crowns the board
of mirth & pleasure;
Sing Noel, Noel!
for 'tis now;
Of joy & peace
we have full measure!"
Frank X. Finnegan*

CHRISTMAS DINNER
À LA DICKENS

**Avocado-Caviar
Salad**

**Christmas Goose
with
Cumberland Sauce**

**Pennsylvania-Style
Stuffing**

Lemon
New Potatoes

**Frosted
Cauliflower**

**Broccoli Timbales
with Ginger-Orange
Carrots**

**Eggnog Mousse
with
Raspberry Sauce**

*French White
Alsace Gewürztraminer*

•

Avocado-Caviar Salad

•

1 head Boston lettuce
2 ripe avocados, peeled, pitted,
   rubbed with lemon
1 cup sour cream
2-ounces American golden caviar
2-ounces best quality black caviar
   lemon slices

On chilled salad plates, arrange
several lettuce leaves. Top with ½
avocado, pitted side up. Fill hollow
with sour cream. Spoon 1 teaspoon
golden caviar on 1 side of the sour
cream, 1 teaspoon black on other.
Garnish with lemon slice twist divid-
ing the two caviars.

4 servings

Christmas Goose with Cumberland Sauce

•

10-pound goose

Cumberland Sauce:
 2 tablespoons red currant jelly
   juice of 2 oranges
⅓ of an orange, including peel,
   finely chopped
½ cup black currants
½ cup light corn syrup
½ cup butter

Stuff goose with Pennsylvania-Style
Stuffing. Roast goose 20 minutes at
450°F. Reduce heat to 325°F. Roast at
25 minutes per pound. Let stand,
covered, 10 minutes. Carve & serve
with Cumberland Sauce.

For the sauce, combine ingredients
in saucepan. Bring to boil. Simmer
15 minutes. Serve hot over goose,
wild game, duck breasts or other
poultry. *(2½ cups)*

8-10 servings

Pennsylvania-Style Stuffing

•

1 pound breakfast sausage links,
   cut into 1-inch pieces
1 pound bacon, diced
1 large onion, chopped
1 cup finely chopped celery
½ pound mushrooms, sliced
2 Granny Smith apples, cored &
   sliced
1 cup chopped fresh parsley
1 teaspoon sage
1 teaspoon thyme
1 pound loaf firm white bread, cut
   into 1-inch cubes
2 cups chicken stock
   salt & pepper

Sauté sausage & bacon until crisp &
brown. Add onion, celery, mushrooms, apples, parsley & herbs. Sauté,
stirring occasionally, 5 minutes. Stir
in bread cubes & chicken broth. Season with salt & pepper. Makes
enough stuffing for 10-12 pound
turkey or goose. Good with other
poultry.

8-10 servings

Frosted Cauliflower

•

1 large whole head cauliflower, trimmed of leaves & cored
2 cups peas
1 medium onion, sliced
½ teaspoon Chinese 5-spice seasoning
1 teaspoon salt
¼ cup light cream
¼ cup toasted pine nuts or sesame seed

Steam cauliflower until tender, 15-20 minutes. Drain. Place on heated serving platter. Keep warm. Cook peas & onions until tender. In blender or processor, add peas, onions, 5-spice & salt. Purée until smooth. Frost cauliflower with purée. Sprinkle with pine nuts, sesame seed, crushed flavored croutons or crisp-cooked, crumbled bacon. Surround with cooked baby carrots for another presentation. To serve, cut cauliflower into wedges.

10 servings

Broccoli Timbales with Ginger-Orange Carrots

•

1½ pounds broccoli, trimmed into flowerets to fit ramekins
7 eggs
1½ cups heavy cream
½ teaspoon salt
⅜ teaspoon white pepper freshly ground nutmeg pinch cayenne

Ginger-Orange Carrots:
36 baby carrots or cut carrots
1¾ cups fresh orange juice
1½ tablespoons peeled, grated, fresh ginger root fresh cilantro, garnish

Preheat oven to 350°F. Place 13x9-inch pan in oven with 1-inch boiling water. Generously butter 8 ramekins or custard cups.

Blanch broccoli flowerets in boiling salted water 2 minutes. Drain. Combine cream, salt, pepper, nutmeg & cayenne. Beat well. Arrange broccoli in ramekins, stem-side up. Pour egg mixture into ramekins. Set molds in hot water in oven. Bake 40 minutes until knife inserted in center of ramekin comes out clean. For carrots, combine carrots, orange juice & ginger in saucepan. Simmer over medium-low heat until tender, 10-12 minutes. Invert molds onto heated serving platter. Intersperse drained carrots between timbales. Garnish with cilantro leaves.

8 servings

Eggnog Mousse with Raspberry Sauce

•

3 envelopes unflavored gelatin
6 tablespoons cold water
5 cups rich dairy eggnog
⅓ cup sugar
½ teaspoon grated nutmeg
2 cups heavy cream, whipped

Raspberry Sauce:
3 cups sweetened raspberries
2 tablespoons cornstarch
2 tablespoons brandy chocolate leaves, garnish

In a small bowl, sprinkle gelatin over cold water to soften. Heat 1 cup eggnog. Add sugar. Stir to dissolve. Add gelatin. Stir until gelatin melts completely. Pour into large bowl. Add remaining eggnog & nutmeg. Chill until slightly thickened, about 1 hour. Fold in whipped cream. Pour into 8 cup mold or individual molds. Chill 8 hours or overnight. For the sauce, drain raspberry juices into small saucepan. Dissolve cornstarch & brandy. Add to saucepan. Cook until thickened. Add raspberries. Chill. To serve, unmold mousse onto platter. Drizzle with sauce. Pass remaining sauce.

8 servings

Gifts & tidings have been exchanged. It is time for serious dining. Place napkins, folded point down, inside the wine glasses. Place a coin or sugared almond in one of the points, bringing the recipient extraordinarily good luck in the year to come. Place thick red grosgrain ribbon down the center & a few across the top of a white cloth for holiday color. ❧

Milwaukee's Bal du Lac Caviar

•

6 hard-cooked, extra large eggs, finely chopped
½ cup finely chopped onion
6 tablespoons butter, melted
½ cup mayonnaise
    pinch salt
¼ teaspoon pepper
1 pint sour cream
1 jar (4.6 ounces) black caviar
    curly endive
    poppy seed or other favorite crackers

Combine eggs & onions. Stir in butter, mayonnaise, salt & pepper. Put into plastic-lined 7-inch mold. Chill at least 4 hours. Unmold onto large serving plate. Remove plastic. Frost with sour cream. Gently cover with caviar using the tip of a small spoon. Surround with small leaves of curly endive. Place crackers around endive.

14 servings

Mushrooms Stuffed with Chèvre Blue Cheese

•

24 large mushrooms, stems removed
2 teaspoons grated onion
⅓ cup butter
1¼ cups fine, fresh bread crumbs
2 tablespoons minced parsley
1 tablespoon lemon juice
½ teaspoon salt
¼ cup crumbled goat's milk blue cheese (chèvre)
    melted butter

Arrange mushroom caps in baking dish. Chop stems very fine. Sauté stems & onions in butter over medium heat. Remove from heat. Add bread crumbs, parsley, lemon juice & salt. Combine well. When mixture cools, add crumbled cheese. Spoon stuffing into caps. Brush mushroom tops with melted butter. May be frozen at this point. Bake 5 minutes at 450°F. (increase baking time if frozen). Broil until delicately browned.

8 servings

Vegetable Gratin

•

1½ cups cauliflowerets
1½ cups baby peas
1½ cups baby or sliced carrots
1½ cups broccoli flowerets
1 can (9 ounces) sliced waterchestnuts
1½ cups heavy cream
1 tablespoon fresh chopped basil
    salt & pepper
1 cup fresh bread crumbs
    butter

Preheat oven to 375°F. Butter an oval 2-quart casserole.

Steam vegetables until crisp-tender. Drain.

In a small saucepan, cook cream over medium heat until reduced by half. Add basil. Toss with vegetables. Season with salt & pepper. Pour vegetable mixture into casserole. Sprinkle with bread crumbs. Dot with butter. Bake 30 minutes until hot & bubbly.

8 servings

Artichoke Almond Salad

•

12 cooked artichoke hearts, halved
⅓ pound fresh snow peas, cut into
  ½-inch pieces
⅓ pound fresh mushrooms, sliced
  lettuce leaves

Dressing:
¼ cup red wine vinegar
¼ cup vegetable oil
2 teaspoons Dijon-style mustard
1 teaspoon each: salt, pepper,
  dill, finely chopped garlic
1 cup light cream

½ cup toasted sliced almonds, or
  crushed honey-roasted almonds

Combine vegetables. Mix dressing ingredients. Toss vegetables with enough dressing to coat. Serve on lettuce lined platter topped with almonds. Add shredded cooked chicken for a hearty luncheon salad.

8 servings

Lemon Cream Ring

•

1 package unflavored gelatin
⅔ cup water
½ cup sugar
⅛ teaspoon salt
  grated peel of 1 lemon
  juice of 1 lemon
1 can (6 ounces) frozen lemonade
  concentrate
1 cup heavy cream, whipped
  fresh fruit

In a saucepan over medium-low heat, dissolve gelatin. Stir in sugar & salt. Stir to dissolve. Remove from heat. Add lemon peel, juice & concentrate. Chill to jelly-like consistency. Fold in cream. Pour into 4-cup mold. Chill until firm. Unmold onto serving platter. Decorate with assorted fresh fruits.

8 servings

Chocolate Whipped Cream Torte

•

3-ounces semi-sweet baking
  chocolate
⅓ cup butter
1¾ cup flour, sifted
1½ cups sugar
1½ teaspoons baking soda
1 teaspoon salt
1½ cups buttermilk or sour cream
1 teaspoon vanilla
2 eggs, slightly beaten
½ cup chopped walnuts, optional

Frosting:
2 pints heavy cream, whipped
1-2 tablespoons unsweetened cocoa
2 tablespoons powdered sugar

Preheat oven to 350°F. Butter & flour 2 9-inch round cake pans lined with waxed paper circles.

Melt chocolate & butter in small saucepan over low heat. Cool slightly. Pour into large bowl. Sift flour, sugar, soda & salt. Combine with chocolate mixture. Add buttermilk, vanilla & eggs. Beat well. Add walnuts. Pour into prepared pans. Bake 30-35 minutes. Cool 10 minutes. Remove cakes from pans. Remove paper. Cool on racks.

For frosting, combine whipped cream, cocoa & powdered sugar. Divide each cake into 2 layers. Spread filling between each layer. Frost top & sides. Decorate with sifted cocoa or pipe additional cream rosettes on top of cake. Decorate with candied violets & candied coffee beans. Prepare 1 day in advance.

10 servings

Hang colorful paper streamers from the chandelier to the tabletop. Keep the lights subdued & put a stack of all-time favorite music on the stereo for a nostalgic New Year's Eve fête. Serve champagne at the appointed hour with the Torte. Roll up the carpet for wee hours dancing.
❧

ENTREE PASTA DESSERT

*California
Red Zinfandel*

•

*When there is an occasion
to celebrate above &
beyond the norm, this
is sure to top the
expectations of your
guests. The Salmon &
Pasta are pictured on
page 4. Conviviality &
sharing the event
are terrific rewards.*
❧

Herbed Salmon Steaks

•

Herb Sauce:
½ cup fresh lemon juice
2 tablespoons butter, melted
1 tablespoon fresh chopped
   tarragon or 1 teaspoon dried
1 tablespoon finely chopped shallots
½ teaspoon freshly ground pepper

4 salmon steaks, 1-inch thick

Preheat broiler or prepare grill.

Combine lemon juice, butter, tarragon, shallots & pepper. Mix well. Set aside. Place salmon on rack in a shallow pan. Pour several tablespoons sauce over steaks. Broil or grill 6 inches from heat 7 minutes. Turn steaks. Top with more sauce. Return to heat 5 minutes until fish flakes easily. Serve with any remaining sauce.

4 servings

Pictured page 4.

Asparagus Romano on Tomato Fettucini

•

¼ cup butter
1 large onion finely chopped
2 cloves garlic, finely chopped
1 tablespoon flour
¼ cup dry white wine
½ teaspoon tarragon leaves
½ teaspoon thyme leaves
2½ cups chicken stock
3 pounds asparagus, cleaned, tips only (reserve tender stems for soups)
2 large egg yolks, slightly beaten
½ cup freshly grated Romano cheese
   salt & freshly ground pepper

1 pound tomato fettucini or pappardelle, cooked & drained
   extra grated Romano cheese

In a large sauce pan melt butter over medium heat. Sauté onions 5 minutes. Add garlic. Cook 2 minutes. Add flour, stir. Add wine. Simmer 3 minutes. Add herbs & stock. Ten minutes before serving add asparagus tips. Cook 3 minutes. Off heat, beat in egg yolks. Return pan to medium-low heat, stirring constantly. Cook 5 minutes. Add Romano, salt & pepper to taste. On a heated platter toss fettucini with asparagus sauce. Sprinkle with additional cheese. Serve immediately.

6 Servings

Pictured page 4.

Irresistible Chocolate Mint Demitasse Cream

•

6-ounces semi-sweet chocolate, melted
   pinch salt
1 egg
1 teaspoon vanilla
2 tablespoons sugar
3 tablespoons peppermint schnapps
¾ cup milk
   whipped cream & strawberries, garnish

Combine chocolate & other ingredients in blender or processor. Whirl until smooth. Pour into demitasse cups. Chill. Serve with a dollop of whipped cream topped with a perfect strawberry. Serve with demitasse spoons.

6 servings

Elegant Gatherings

sophisticated dining experiences

MENU

**Pork Tenderloin
in
Puff Pastry**

Asparagus

**Beets
in
Orange Sauce**

**Blue Cheese Flan
with
Dried Apricots & Figs**

*German White
Rheingau Spätlese*

•

*An elegant meal to serve
to friends or family.
Blanch baby spring
asparagus quickly to
retain crispness & color.
Potted primroses
are the perfect
centerpiece. Coordinate
short candles to match.*

❧

Pork Tenderloin
in
Puff Pastry

•

3 pork tenderloins
¾ cup finely minced scallions
1 cup apple cider or juice
3 tablespoons olive oil
¾ teaspoon salt
½ pound mushrooms, sliced
¾ teaspoon thyme, crushed
2 large stalks celery, chopped
20 peppercorns
10 parsley sprigs
1½ pounds puff pastry sheets
   (3 sheets)
2 egg whites, slightly beaten
1 cup chicken stock
¼ cup butter, softened
¼ cup flour

Place pork in shallow dish. Combine scallions, cider, oil, salt, mushrooms, thyme, celery, peppercorns & parsley sprigs. Pour over pork. Marinate at least 12 hours, turning occasionally.

Preheat oven to 350°F.

Remove tenderloins & mushrooms from marinade & drain well. Reserve marinade. Cut each tenderloin in half. Roll out each pastry ⅛-inch thick. Divide pastry in half. Place mushrooms down center of each piece of pastry. Place pork on top. Bring ends of pastry over pork, then bring sides up & seal well. Place pork, seam side down, on a jelly roll pan. Bake 1 hour & 45 minutes. Remove from oven. Brush crust generously with beaten egg whites. Bake 5 minutes longer, until crust is golden. Remove from oven. Let stand 5-10 minutes.

Pour reserved marinade into blender & process until smooth. Pour into saucepan. Add chicken stock. Cook over medium heat. Combine soft butter & flour. Drop mixture by teaspoonfuls into sauce & cook until thickened. Pour sauce over baked tenderloin & serve.

6 servings

Beets
in
Orange Sauce

•

½ cup sugar
1½ tablespoons cornstarch
⅛ teaspoon salt
   grated peel of 1 orange, slice fruit
   for garnish
1 cup water
¾ cup orange juice
4 cups whole baby beets

Mix sugar, cornstarch, salt & grated orange peel in sauce pan. Add water. Stir & cook until thickened. Add orange juice & heat. Pour over hot beets & serve. Garnish with thin slices of orange which have been glazed in sauce.

8 servings

Blue Cheese Flan
with
Dried Apricots & Figs

•

¾ cup crushed, rich, round crackers
2 tablespoons butter, melted

Filling:
2 packages (8 ounces each) cream
   cheese, softened
8-ounces blue cheese, crumbled
1⅔ cup sour cream, divided
3 eggs
⅛ teaspoon pepper
   dried apricots, figs, etc.

Combine crushed crackers & butter. Press onto bottom of lightly buttered 9-inch springform pan. Bake at 350°F. 10 minutes.

Combine cheeses at medium speed until blended. Add ⅔ cup sour cream, eggs & pepper. Beat until fluffy. Pour into crust, bake at 300°F. 45 minutes. Stir remaining sour cream until smooth. Spread carefully over top. Return to oven for 10 minutes. Cool on rack. Refrigerate several hours. May be prepared 1-2 days before serving. Loosen sides from springform with sharp knife & remove. Garnish with dried fruits.

18 servings

MENU

**Almond
Turkey
Cutlets**

**Ginger-
Orange
Rice**

Sautéed Water Chestnuts
with
Bacon & Spinach

**Upside Down
Lemon Meringue
Pie**

*French Red Burgundy
Côte de Beaune*

•

*If a big turkey on
Thanksgiving doesn't fit
into your lifestyle, try
this recipe. Add a side
dish of stuffing
if desired.*
❦

Almond Turkey Cutlets

•

¾ cup ground, toasted almonds
⅓ cup chopped parsley
¾ cup bread crumbs
2 egg whites, beaten with
   1 teaspoon water until frothy
6 turkey cutlets
4 tablespoons butter, divided
6 tablespoons Parmesan cheese
3 tablespoons slivered almonds
1 clove garlic, lightly crushed
¼ cup white wine
   juice of ½ lemon
½ cup heavy cream

Combine ground almonds, parsley
& bread crumbs. Dip cutlets into
egg white mixture, then into parsley
mixture, coating well on both sides.
Chill several hours to set coating.

Melt 2 tablespoons butter in skillet.
Quickly sauté cutlets until brown &
crisp on each side. Sprinkle each cut-
let with 1 tablespoon cheese.
Remove to warm platter.

In same pan, melt 2 tablespoons
butter. Add slivered almonds, & garlic. Sauté until almonds are light
brown. Add wine & lemon juice.
Cook until reduced by ½. Add
cream. Whisk until slightly thickened. Remove garlic clove. Pour sauce
over cutlets. Serve immediately.

4-6 servings

Ginger-Orange Rice

•

3 tablespoons butter
2 tablespoons finely chopped onion
2 teaspoons grated orange peel
½ teaspoon ground ginger
⅛ teaspoon poultry seasoning
⅛ teaspoon ground pepper
½ cup orange juice
2 cups chicken stock
1 tablespoon chopped parsley
1 cup long grain rice

Melt butter. Cook onion in butter
until soft. Blend in orange peel,
ginger, poultry seasoning & pepper.
Add orange juice & stock. Bring to
boil. Add parsley & rice. Stir with
fork. Cover tightly. Simmer over low
heat 25 minutes until rice is tender
& liquid absorbed. Stir with fork
before serving. Best to prepare close
to serving time as possible.

4-6 servings

Upside Down Lemon Meringue Pie

•

4 eggs, separated
¼ teaspoon cream of tartar
1½ cups plus 2 teaspoons sugar,
   divided
   grated peel & juice of 1 lemon
2 cups heavy cream, divided
¼ teaspoon vanilla

Preheat oven to 275°F. Butter a
10-inch glass pie plate.

Beat egg whites until soft peaks form.
Gradually add cream of tartar & 1
cup sugar. Beat until stiff & glossy.
Spread in pie plate fully over the
edge. Bake 1 hour until golden. Turn
off oven. Open door slightly & let
rest inside oven 1 hour.

Beat egg yolks in top of double boiler
5 minutes until thick & lemon-
colored. Over medium heat, gradually add ½ cup sugar, juice &
grated peel of lemon. Beat & heat
until very thick. Cool, stirring
occasionally.

Whip 1 cup cream. Gently fold into
cooled lemon mixture. Pour into
shell & refrigerate 24 hours, covered.

4 hours before serving, whip remaining cream with vanilla & 2 teaspoons sugar. Pipe or swirl over top
of dessert.

8 servings

Fruited
Sangria

•

2 cups orange juice
2 cups pineapple juice
1 cup sweet-sour soda
½ cup cherry juice
½ cup brandy
½ cup triple sec
½ gallon Burgundy or white wine
    orange slices & lime wedges,
    garnish

Blend ingredients together. Serve in tall, ice-filled glasses. Garnish with orange slices & a lime wedge.

20 servings

Surprise
Dip

•

1 cup packed, grated carrots
1 cup mayonnaise
1 cup Parmesan cheese

Mix ingredients together. Bake at 350°F. 30 minutes. Serve hot with assorted crackers.

2-3 cups

Green Pepper
Dip

•

1 green pepper
    water
1 large onion
2 packages (8 ounces each) cream
    cheese, softened
5 tablespoons sugar
5 tablespoons vinegar

Cut up pepper & onion & place in blender. Cover with cold water & blend. Put pulp in strainer & squeeze out liquid. Return pulp to blender & add remaining ingredients. Blend until smooth. Pour into serving container. Chill. May be frozen. Defrost to serve. Surround with fresh summer squash, zucchini, cauliflower, broccoli, etc. to be used as dippers. May also be used as a salad dressing.

3 cups

Shrimp & Couscous Salad

•

½ cup chicken stock
½ teaspoon salt
1 tablespoon butter
⅓ cup couscous
1 cup small shelled, cooked, shrimp
1 cup raw cauliflower &/or broccoli flowerets
8 black olives, sliced
1 tablespoon snipped fresh chives

Dressing:
2 tablespoons wine vinegar
½ teaspoon Dijon-style mustard
½ teaspoon anchovy paste
    salt to taste
2 tablespoons olive oil
2 tablespoons sour cream

3 hours before serving, combine stock, salt, butter & couscous in a saucepan. Heat to boiling. Cover & remove from heat. Let stand five minutes. Fluff with fork. Turn into a bowl & chill, covered.

In a small bowl combine vinegar, mustard, anchovy paste & salt with a fork. Add olive oil & beat until well blended. Stir in sour cream. Chill.

Shortly before serving, combine couscous, shrimp, cauliflower &/or broccoli, olives & chives. Toss with dressing.

2-3 servings

Taiwan Chicken Salad

•

2 whole chicken breasts, skinned & boned
2 cups chicken stock
¾-inch piece fresh, peeled ginger root
4-ounces Chinese rice sticks (MAIFUN), broken into 3-inch pieces
    oil for deep-frying
4 cups torn lettuce
1 bunch scallions, sliced including green tops
2 tablespoons slivered almonds, toasted

Dressing:
¼ cup sugar
¼ cup vinegar
¼ cup vegetable oil
1½ teaspoons salt
1 teaspoon sesame oil
2 tablespoons toasted sesame seed

Slowly simmer chicken breasts in stock with ginger root until chicken is no longer pink, about 30 minutes. Shred meat & set aside.

In a large saucepan, heat vegetable oil, 2-inches deep, to 350°F. Test one rice stick to make sure oil is hot enough; the rice stick should puff immediately. Cook sticks by small handfuls until very lightly browned. Drain on paper towels.

Combine dressing ingredients. Blend until sugar is dissolved.

Just before serving, combine chicken, rice sticks, lettuce & scallions in large salad bowl. Toss gently with dressing & garnish with almonds. Serve immediately.

6-8 servings

White Chocolate Cake

•

⅓ cup grated white chocolate
½ cup boiling water
1 cup butter, softened
2 cups sugar
4 eggs, separated
1 teaspoon vanilla
2½ cups sifted cake flour
1 teaspoon baking soda
1 cup buttermilk
1 cup coconut
1 cup chopped pecans or walnuts

Frosting:
1 package (8 ounces) cream cheese, softened
½ cup vegetable shortening
2 cups powdered sugar
1 teaspoon vanilla

Preheat oven to 350°F. Butter & flour 3 9-inch paper-lined cake pans.

Melt chocolate in boiling water. Set aside to cool. Cream butter & sugar until fluffy. Mix in egg yolks, one at a time, beating well after each addition. Add melted chocolate & vanilla.

Sift cake flour & soda. Add to creamed mixture with buttermilk. Do not over mix. Beat egg whites until stiff. Fold in gently. Stir in coconut & pecans or walnuts. Divide batter between three layer pans. Bake 25 minutes. Cool 10 minutes. Remove from pans. Remove paper.

For frosting, mix cream cheese, shortening, powdered sugar & vanilla. Spread between layers, top & sides.

12-14 servings

A delicious, different-flavor dinner party. Hang Chinese lanterns filled with little Christmas tree lights. If possible remove legs from your table, place top on floor & sit on pillows!!
❦

MENU

**Mustard-Curry
Spinach
Salad**

**Chicken Wellington
with
Port-Currant Sauce**

**Basil Garden Beans
&
Mushrooms**

Chocolate Ice Cream
with
Walnut Fudge Sauce

*German Mosel Auslese
or
California Port*

•

*Invite friends over for an
evening of cards.
Have dinner, then retire
to the "card" room. Enjoy
dessert while playing.*
❧

Mustard-Curry
Spinach
Salad

•

⅔ cup vegetable oil
¼ cup California wine vinegar
2 tablespoons Chablis
2 teaspoons soy sauce
1 teaspoon sugar
1 teaspoon dry mustard
¼ teaspoon curry powder
½ teaspoon salt
1 clove garlic, minced
1 teaspoon cracked pepper
1 pound bacon, crisp-cooked,
   crumbled
4 hard cooked eggs, finely chopped
3 bunches spinach, cleaned,
   dried, & chilled

Combine oil, vinegar, Chablis, soy
sauce, sugar, dry mustard, curry
powder, salt, garlic & pepper. Mix
well. Combine bacon, eggs & spinach. Toss with dressing when ready
to serve.

6 servings

Chicken Wellington
with
Port-Currant Sauce

•

6 whole chicken breasts, skinned
   & boned, halved
   salt & pepper
6-ounces wild rice
¼ cup grated orange peel
2 eggs, separated
3 sheets (8 ounces each) puff pastry
1 tablespoon water
1 jar (10 ounces) red currant jelly
1 tablespoon prepared mustard
3 tablespoons port wine
¼ cup lemon juice

Preheat oven to 375°F.

Season chicken with salt & pepper.
Cook wild rice according to package directions. Stir in orange peel.
Beat 2 egg whites until stiff. Fold
into rice. Set aside.

Roll out each sheet puff pastry
⅛-inch thick. Divide pastry into ¼'s.
Place chicken breast on each pastry
¼. Spoon ¼ cup rice on top. Roll
up. Place seam side down on jelly
roll pan. Beat 2 egg yolks & water.
Brush on dough. Bake 50 minutes.

Heat currant jelly, mustard, wine &
lemon juice. Serve sauce warm with
chicken.

8-12 servings

Basil Garden Beans
&
Mushrooms

•

1½ pounds fresh green or yellow
   wax beans, trimmed
¼ cup vegetable oil
¾ pound fresh mushrooms, sliced
2 tablespoons chopped onions
1 clove garlic, minced
1 green pepper, chopped
¼ cup boiling water
1 teaspoon salt
1 tablespoon fresh chopped basil
½ cup grated Parmesan cheese

Heat oil in pan. Add mushrooms,
onion, garlic & green pepper. Cook
slowly 5 minutes. Add beans, water,
salt & basil. Cover & cook 10-15
minutes. Stir in several tablespoons
cheese. Sprinkle remaining cheese
on top.

6 servings

*French Red Bordeaux
Saint Estèphe*

•

*This typical German
combination of foods,
pork with apples, is
particularly satisfying
when surrounded by
family on a late Sunday
afternoon. The menu is
elegant for company also!*
❦

Pork Tenderloin
with
Vegetable-Caper Sauce

•

  2 pounds whole pork tenderloins
¼ cup butter, melted
  1 small onion, chopped
  1 small carrot, chopped
½ cup beef stock
1½ tablespoons lemon juice
  1 teaspoon grated lemon peel
¾ teaspoon thyme leaves
½ bay leaf
    salt & pepper to taste
½ cup light cream
  2 tablespoons flour
  2 tablespoons capers

Preheat oven to 400°F.

Place tenderloins in 2-quart casserole with butter, onion & carrot. Roast at 400°F. 10 minutes. Reduce heat to 350°F. Add stock, lemon juice, lemon peel, thyme, bay leaf, salt & pepper. Braise, covered, 30-40 minutes until meat is tender. Remove tenderloins from pan & keep warm. Remove bay leaf. Combine cream & flour until smooth. Stir into pan juices. Cook over medium heat, stirring constantly, until thickened. Add capers. Slice tenderloins & serve with sauce. Good with noodles or späetzle & a fruit garnish, such as spiced apple rings or cranberries.

4-6 servings

Baked Apples
in
Apple Brandy

•

10 large baking apples
  1 cup dried currants
1⅔ cups apple brandy, divided
1⅔ cups ground, toasted hazelnuts
⅔ cup packed brown sugar
⅔ cup heavy cream
½ teaspoon ground cinnamon
¼ teaspoon freshly ground nutmeg
  1 cup apple cider
⅓ cup honey
  1 cup whole cranberries
    watercress

Preheat oven to 350°F.

Combine currants & ⅔ cup brandy in large bowl. Let stand ½ hour. Stir in nuts, sugar, cream, cinnamon & nutmeg. Cut ¼-inch slice from tops of apples. Remove cores to ½-inch from bottom, making a 1-inch wide hollow. Arrange apples ½-inch apart in shallow baking dish. Spoon currant mixture into centers of apples. Pour 1 cup brandy & 1 cup cider around apples. Spoon honey over apples. Bake 30 minutes, basting frequently with pan juices until apples are tender. Arrange on serving platter. Garnish with watercress & cranberries. Serve with pan juices.

10 servings

Mary Newton
Cake

•

2 eggs
1 cup sugar
  salt
1 cup flour
1 teaspoon baking powder
½ cup milk
2 tablespoons butter

Preheat oven to 350°F. Butter & flour a 11x7-inch pan.

Beat eggs until light & fluffy. Gradually add sugar & salt. Sift together flour & baking powder. Gradually add to eggs & sugar. Mixture will be thick. Scald milk with butter. Add to batter slowly beating until smooth & creamy. Pour into cake pan. Bake 20-25 minutes until springy to the touch in center of cake. Cake may be served plain like tea cake, dusted with powdered sugar or ice cream. Another favorite combination is with sugared peaches or strawberries like a shortcake.

6-8 servings

French White Vouvray

•

*Set the table with a bright
yellow cloth & napkins
& plenty of blue
iris. Blue plates would
make the light menu even
more special!*

Fancy Scampi

•

 1 pound fresh mushrooms, sliced
2 small onions, finely chopped
½ green pepper, chopped
2 tablespoons butter
3 medium tomatoes, peeled
  & chopped
2 tablespoons flour
1 cup cream
½ teaspoon white wine-
  Worcestershire sauce
1½ teaspoons sherry-pepper sauce
½ cup dry sherry
3 pounds scampi, cleaned
  & cooked

Preheat oven to 375°F. Butter a
2-quart casserole dish.

Sauté mushrooms, onion & green
pepper in butter. Add tomatoes &
cook gently 8-10 minutes. Stir in flour.
Slowly add cream, stirring until
thickened. Add Worcestershire sauce,
sherry-pepper sauce, sherry &
scampi. Simmer 2 minutes. Transfer
to casserole dish & bake 10 minutes.

6 servings

Raspberry Carrots

•

1½ pounds carrots, peeled &
  sliced thin
⅓ cup raspberry vinegar
½ cup olive oil
¼ cup chopped fresh mint
  salt & pepper

In small amount of boiling water,
cook carrots 3-4 minutes until
nearly tender. Drain. Place carrots in
a bowl. Sprinkle immediately with
vinegar. Add olive oil & toss well.
Sprinkle with chopped fresh mint.
Season to taste. Toss again. Refrigerate at least overnight. Keeps several
days. Bring to room temperature
before serving.

6 servings

Crème Brûlée

•

4 cups heavy cream
¼ cup sugar
8 egg yolks
¼ teaspoon salt
2 teaspoons vanilla
½ cup brown sugar

Preheat oven to 350°F. Put large pan
with 1-inch boiling water in oven.

Heat cream & sugar in top of double boiler until sugar dissolves. Put
egg yolks, salt & vanilla in a bowl.
Beat slightly. Combine cream & egg
mixtures. Pour into glass 12x8-inch
pan. Place inside pan of water in
oven. Bake 45 minutes. Cool. Sprinkle brown sugar evenly over top of
brûlée. Place under broiler to melt
& carmelize sugar. Do not burn!
Chill. If dessert is chilled more than
several hours before serving, the
brown sugar will weep.

8 servings

Grilled Ginger Lamb

•

1 leg of lamb, butterflied
¼ cup soy sauce
½ cup Burgundy
½ cup vegetable oil
⅓ cup peeled, grated ginger root
    juice of one fresh lemon
¼ cup minced onion
1½ tablespoons honey
 2 cloves fresh garlic, minced
1½ teaspoons salt
½ teaspoon fresh ground pepper
⅛ teaspoon cayenne
 1 cup beef stock

Pat lamb dry with toweling. Place in large glass pan. Combine soy sauce, Burgundy, oil, ginger, lemon juice, onion, honey, garlic, salt, pepper & cayenne in blender. Whirl 2 minutes. Pour over lamb. Marinate, covered, overnight or at least 6 hours, turning occasionally. Reserve marinade.

Grill lamb 15-20 minutes each side until medium rare. Baste with marinade while cooking. Can be oven broiled.

Add marinade to beef stock. Heat in small saucepan. Pass sauce with sliced lamb.

10 servings

Creamy Lemon Spinach Noodles

•

2 tablespoons butter
3 tablespoons flour
1 teaspoon salt
    white pepper
2 cups light cream
⅓ cup sliced pimiento-stuffed
    olives
½ pound spinach or herbed
    pasta, cooked & drained
¼-⅓ cup grated Parmesan cheese
 2 teaspoons grated lemon peel

In a saucepan, melt butter. Blend in flour, salt & pepper. Heat until bubbly. Add cream gradually, stirring constantly. Bring to a boil & cook 1-2 minutes. Add olives. Toss noodles with sauce in a warm serving dish. Sprinkle Parmesan cheese & lemon peel evenly over top.

6 servings

Strawberry Cake Roll

•

4 eggs
¾ cup sugar
1 teaspoon vanilla
¾ cup sifted flour
¾ teaspoon baking powder
¼ teaspoon salt
    powdered sugar

Strawberry Butter Cream:
1¼ cups unsalted butter, softened
 2 cups powdered sugar
 4 egg yolks
½ cup puréed fresh strawberries
 3 tablespoons strawberry preserves

Whipped Cream Filling:
 1 pint fresh strawberries, chopped
 1 pint heavy cream
½ cup powdered sugar
 1 teaspoon vanilla

Preheat oven to 400°F. Line a 15x10-inch jelly roll pan with waxed paper. Butter lightly.

Beat eggs until light. Add sugar gradually. Beat until thick & lemon colored. Add vanilla. Sift flour, baking powder & salt. Fold into egg mixture. Pour into pan. Bake 10 minutes. Invert pan onto towel sifted with powdered sugar. Remove pan & paper. Roll cake inside towel starting at 10-inch side. Cool.

For the butter cream, beat butter & sugar until light & fluffy. Beat in yolks. Add berries & preserves. May be made in advance. Cover & chill. Soften to room temperature. For the cream filling, whip cream, vanilla & powdered sugar until stiff. Fold in berries.

To assemble: Unroll cake. Spread with cream filling. Reroll. Place seam-side down on serving plate. Frost with butter cream. Chill several hours.

10-12 servings

*Serve the soup in hollowed
out red cabbage bowls.
Do not hollow out too
much! Top with a sprig
from the fennel bulb.*

Fennel
Soup

•

4 large fennel bulbs, trimmed &
   thinly sliced
2-3 large yellow onions, thinly sliced
5 tablespoons butter
   salt & pepper
6½ cups chicken stock
1 tablespoon lemon juice
1 cup heavy cream
¼ cup dry sherry
½ cup chopped fresh parsley
¼ cup finely chopped red pepper

Sauté fennel & onions in butter until
soft. Add salt & pepper. Transfer to
a blender or food processor. Purée.
Return to large pot. Add stock,
lemon juice, cream, sherry & parsley.
Heat, but do not boil. Serve immediately topped with a sprinkle of
red pepper.

10 servings

Pictured page 113.

Cider-Simmered Pork
with
Hazelnuts

•

1½ pounds boneless pork chops
½ teaspoon salt
½ teaspoon dried thyme
½ tablespoon vegetable oil
1 medium onion, chopped
⅓ cup hazelnuts (filberts)
¾ cup cider
2 tablespoons hazelnut liqueur
   salt & pepper
1 tablespoon butter
1 large unpeeled Delicious apple,
   cut into ¾-inch cubes

Rub pork with salt & thyme. Heat
oil in a 10-inch skillet. Brown pork
chops over medium-high heat until
golden, 3-5 minutes per side.
Remove pork & set aside. Add onion
& hazelnuts. Sauté 2 minutes. Add
cider & loosen brown bits from bottom of pan. Return pork to pan.
Cover & simmer until tender, 30-45
minutes depending on thickness.
Remove pork to serving platter &
keep warm. Purée pan juices, hazelnuts, etc. in processor or blender.
Briefly return to pan to heat. Stir
in liqueur.

In small skillet melt butter until
bubbly over medium heat. Add
apple & cook five minutes, stirring
frequently until crisp-tender. Place
sautéed apples on serving platter with
pork. Pass warmed sauce separately.

4 servings

Persimmon
Cookies

•

1 cup persimmon pulp
½ teaspoon lemon juice
½ teaspoon baking soda
½ cup butter
1 cup sugar
1 egg
½ teaspoon cinnamon
½ teaspoon cloves
½ teaspoon nutmeg
2 cups sifted flour
1 cup white or black raisins
1 cup chopped, mixed walnuts
   & pecans

Preheat oven to 350°F.

Add lemon juice & baking soda to
persimmon pulp in a small bowl.
Stir. Set aside. Cream butter & sugar.
Add egg. Beat until light & fluffy.
Add persimmon pulp. Stir. Add flour,
cinnamon, cloves & nutmeg. Mix
well. Stir in raisins & nuts. Drop by
tablespoonfuls onto baking sheet.
Bake 15 minutes.

3 dozen

*Oregon State
Red Pinot Noir*

•

*Spring & lamb are
definitely simpatico!
Remember to serve lamb
rare to medium-rare.
The menu is easy on
hosting chores & long
on color.*
❦

Shrimp Delight
on
Toast Points

•

1 cup butter, softened
1 cup fresh parsley, chopped
½ teaspoon fresh basil
½ teaspoon fresh thyme
½ teaspoon fresh oregano
2 cloves garlic, crushed
   salt & pepper
1½ pounds medium shrimp, peeled
3 cups artichokes, chopped
1 pound Danish Fontina cheese,
   grated

Preheat oven to 350°F.

Mix butter, parsley, basil, thyme, oregano, garlic, salt & pepper. May be prepared 2-3 days in advance. Sauté shrimp in ½ the butter mix. Discard any liquid. Place cooked shrimp & artichokes in shallow baking pan. Dot with remaining butter mixture. Sprinkle cheese on top of mixture. Bake 10 minutes or until cheese melts. Serve hot over toast points.

6 servings

Herbal
Leg of Lamb

•

½ cup Dijon-style mustard
2 tablespoons soy sauce
1 clove garlic, minced
1 teaspoon ground rosemary
¼ teaspoon ground ginger
2 tablespoons olive oil
6 pound leg of lamb
   watercress & mint garnish

Blend mustard, soy, garlic, rosemary & ginger. Beat in olive oil by drops to make a creamy sauce.

Dry lamb well with toweling. Using a pastry brush, spread sauce over lamb. Place on roasting rack. Let rest several hours before cooking. Roast at 350°F. 1¼ hours for medium. Place lamb on HOT platter. Garnish with watercress & mint leaves.

8 servings

Mushroom-Pistachio
Baked
Barley

•

1 large onion, chopped
1 pound mushrooms, sliced
1 cup pearl barley
7 tablespoons butter, divided
2 cups chicken stock, divided
½ cup coarsely chopped pistachios
   salt & pepper

Preheat oven to 350°F. Butter a 1½-quart casserole.

Sauté onion & ½ the mushrooms in 5 tablespoons butter until soft. Add barley. Sauté until barley browns slightly. Turn into casserole. Pour 1 cup chicken stock over barley mixture. Bake, covered, 25 minutes. Add additional 1 cup stock & cook until liquid is absorbed & barley is tender, about ½ hour.

Sauté remaining mushrooms in 2 tablespoons butter. Cook, over low heat until mushrooms become very dry & almost black in color, but not burned. Mix pistachios with mushrooms. Sprinkle on top of barley before serving.

8-10 servings

•

The best of surf & turf for an occasion of merit, a promotion, engagement, or anniversary. Set the table with your finest wares. Use a flowering plant for the centerpiece with small party balloons tied to wooden skewers stuck in the plant or a copy of an announcement with ribbons tied to the skewers. Congratulations!

Perfect Prime Rib

•

Any size prime rib roast, room
  temperature
garlic clove
sesame oil
salt & pepper

Preheat oven to 375°F. Rub roast all over with cut garlic clove. Rub with sesame oil. Season with salt & pepper. Place roast on rack in middle of oven. Roast 1 hour. Turn oven off. Do not open oven at any time. May be held in oven for several hours. Turn oven on again to 375°F. 30 minutes before serving for rare, 40 minutes for medium rare. Works for any size prime rib roast. Ask butcher for a roast to serve the number of guests.

Linguini Con Tuto Mare

•

 1 cup butter
 2 cloves garlic, minced
⅓ pound mushrooms, chopped
½ cup chopped parsley
 2 cups chicken or clam stock
 2 cups chopped clams
 2 cups crab meat
½ pound shelled shrimp
½ pounds linguini, cooked
  & drained

In a large saucepan, melt butter. Sauté garlic, mushrooms & parsley 5 minutes. Add chicken broth, bring to a boil. Reduce heat. Add clams, crab & shrimp. Cook 5-7 minutes. Toss linguini with sauce on large heated platter. Serve immediately.

6-8 servings

Bourbon-Pecan Mocha Tart

•

½ cup butter, softened
2½ tablespoons sugar
 1 egg, beaten
½ cup ground pecans
1⅓ cups flour

Filling:
 3-ounces unsweetened chocolate
 3 tablespoons butter
⅔ cup sugar
 3 tablespoons bourbon
 1 teaspoon instant coffee
 4 eggs, room temperature
 1 cup light corn syrup
 1 teaspoon vanilla
 2 cups coarsely chopped pecans
16 large pecan halves
  whipped cream or ice cream,
  if desired

Preheat oven to 350°F. Butter an 11-inch tart pan.

Cream butter & sugar. Add egg. Beat well. Add pecans & flour. Mix well. Press onto bottom & sides of tart pan. Refrigerate 30 minutes. Bake 15 minutes. Remove from oven. Set aside.

For the filling, add chocolate, butter & sugar in top of double boiler over low heat. Dissolve coffee in bourbon. Add to chocolate. Stir until smooth. Remove from heat. Cool slightly. In a bowl, beat eggs, corn syrup, & vanilla. Stir in chocolate mixture & chopped pecans. Increase oven temperature to 400°F. Pour chocolate mixture into pastry. Top with pecan halves. Bake 25 minutes. Serve warm with ice cream or whipped cream if desired.

10-12 servings

Shrimp & Kiwi Supreme

•

½ cup white wine vinegar
½ teaspoon Dijon-style mustard
¼ cup sugar
¼ teaspoon salt
 1 cup vegetable oil
 6 kiwi fruit, peeled & wedged
40 cooked, shelled medium shrimp
 2 oranges, peeled & sectioned
    red leaf lettuce

Combine vinegar, mustard, sugar, &
salt in blender or food processor.
Mix well. With machine running,
slowly add oil. Add 2 of the kiwi
fruit. Strain dressing to remove seeds.

Arrange cooked shrimp, remaining
kiwi wedges & orange sections
pinwheel-fashion on a bed of red leaf
lettuce. Carefully pour kiwi dressing
over shrimp & fruit to lightly coat.
Serve chilled as a first course
or salad.

8 servings

Chicken with Juniper Berries

•

6 tablespoons butter, divided
2 tablespoons flour
2 cups chicken stock
1 tablespoon juniper berries
1 medium onion, chopped
1 stalk celery, chopped
8 peppercorns, crushed
1 teaspoon salt
2 cups sour cream
2 teaspoons brandy
2 teaspoons gin
3 whole chicken breasts, skinned,
   boned, & halved
2 tablespoons vegetable oil

Melt 2 tablespoons butter in a
2-quart saucepan. Add flour. Cook
2 minutes. Slowly add chicken stock.
Add juniper berries, onion, celery,
crushed peppercorns & salt. Simmer
mixture 30 minutes until fairly
thick, stirring frequently. Remove
from heat. Blend in sour cream.
Return to low heat. Simmer gently
ten minutes. Strain sauce through
a fine sieve. Add brandy & gin. Stir.
Keep warm.

In large sauté pan, over medium
heat, melt 4 tablespoons butter &
oil. Sauté chicken, 3-5 minutes each
side, until done. Place chicken
breasts on a heated platter. Spoon
some sauce over breasts. Pass
remaining sauce. Garnish with tiny
evergreen sprigs.

6 servings

Chocolate Cinnamon Torte

•

 2 cups sugar
1½ cups butter, softened
 2 eggs
 2 tablespoons ground cinnamon
2⅔ cups flour, divided
3-4 ounce block of semi-sweet
    chocolate
 5 cups heavy cream
 1 cup cocoa

Tear 14 sheets waxed paper, 9½-inches
long. Trace bottom of 9-inch cake
pan on one sheet. Cut out circles.

Preheat oven to 375°F. Beat sugar,
butter, eggs, cinnamon & 2 cups
flour at low speed until combined.
Increase speed to medium. Beat 3
minutes. Stir in remaining flour. Do
not overmix. With damp cloth,
moisten BACK of a baking sheet.
Place 1 or 2 circles on back. Spread
a scant ⅓ cup dough in thin layer
on each circle. Bake 8-10 minutes
until lightly browned. Remove from
oven. Cool 5 minutes. Remove
cookie to wire rack. Repeat. Stack
cooled cookies. Cover with plastic.
Prepare 1-3 days in advance.

For chocolate curls, soften chocolate
bar in hands. With vegetable peeler,
scrape along side of chocolate. Place
curls on plate & chill.

Whip cream & cocoa until soft peaks
form. To assemble, peel off paper.
Place cookie on serving platter.
Spread ½ cup cocoa-cream to
edges. Repeat. Spread remaining
cocoa-cream on top. Garnish with
mound of chocolate curls. Chill at
least 4 hours or overnight.

16 servings

Pictured page 172.

MENU

**Palm
Salad**

**Seafood
Chili**

Wild Pecan
Rice

Cornbread
Sticks

**The Best
Chocolate
Sauce**

Mint
Ice Cream

*French White
Burgundy Chablis*

•

*A rich, special "Chili" to
delight a seafood lover's
palate. Serve the ice
cream in green glass sherbet
dishes & garnish with
mint sprigs & whole
strawberries. Stick a
profiterole cookie or two
on the side.*
❦

Palm
Salad

•

1 can (14 ounces) hearts of palm,
  cut into julienne strips
1 bunch radishes, thinly sliced
2 bunches watercress, well trimmed
2 heads Belgian endive, cut into
  ¼-inch pieces
⅓ cup chopped parsley

Dressing:
¾ cup vegetable oil
¼ cup tarragon vinegar
1 egg yolk
1 tablespoon Dijon-style mustard
1 shallot, minced
1 teaspoon salt
¼ teaspoon ground pepper

Blend dressing ingredients together.
Chill. To serve, toss salad ingredients lightly with dressing.

8 servings

Seafood
Chili

•

3 tablespoons olive oil
1 bunch scallions, sliced
1 cup chopped celery
1 green pepper, chopped
2 large potatoes, chopped
3 cloves garlic, minced
2 cups chopped, peeled tomatoes
1 can (15 ounces) tomato sauce
1 cup white wine or chicken stock
1 teaspoon thyme
  salt & pepper
1 tablespoon pesto sauce
1 tablespoon oyster sauce
1 tablespoon green peppercorns,
  mashed
2 cans (10 ounces each) whole
  baby clams
1½-2 pounds firm white fish,
  Haddock, Pollack, Ocean
  perch, chopped
1 pound shrimp, crab, scallops or
  combination, chopped

Sauté scallions, celery, green pepper,
potatoes & garlic gently in olive oil.
Add tomatoes, tomato sauce, wine,
thyme, basil pesto, oyster sauce &
peppercorns. Simmer 30 minutes.
Five minutes before serving add
clams & selected seafood.

6 servings

The Best
Chocolate
Sauce

•

5-ounces bittersweet chocolate
3 tablespoons butter
1⅓ cups sugar
¼ cup cornstarch
¼ cup light corn syrup
¾ cup evaporated milk

Melt chocolate & butter in double
boiler. Mix remaining ingredients.
Add to chocolate. Cook, stirring constantly until sugar is dissolved &
mixture is smooth, 10 minutes. Store
in refrigerator. Heat to serve. May
be flavored with brandy, schnapps,
mocha, nuts, etc.

2 cups

MENU

**Broiled
Herbed
Shrimp**

**Madagascar
Green Peppercorn
Steak**

Braised
Cherry Tomatoes

Polenta
with
Parmesan

**Poached Pears
with
Sauce Anglaise**

*California Chenin Blanc
with Shrimp*

*California Cabernet
Sauvignon with Entrée*

•

*Green peppercorns are
delightful & add zip to
any recipe. The
impressive menu could be
pared down to suit your
entertaining mood.*
❧

Broiled Herbed Shrimp

•

1½ pounds fresh shrimp, peeled
½ cup butter, melted
2 cloves garlic, pressed
2 tablespoons fresh lemon juice
1 tablespoon chopped fresh parsley
1 teaspoon dried oregano
1 teaspoon dried basil
½ teaspoon salt
½ teaspoon freshly ground pepper
3 cups cooked rice
parsley, garnish

Preheat oven to 450°F.

Place shrimp in single layer in shallow baking dish. Combine butter, garlic, lemon juice, parsley, oregano, basil, salt & pepper. Pour over shrimp. Bake 5 minutes, then broil 4-inches from heat 5 minutes. Serve over rice. Garnish with parsley.

6 servings

Madagascar Green Peppercorn Steak

•

4 slices beef tenderloin, 1-inch thick
4 tablespoons green peppercorns, mashed

Marinade:
⅔ teaspoon green peppercorns, mashed
1 tablespoon soy sauce
1 teaspoon sugar
2 teaspoons vegetable oil
1 tablespoon Worcestershire sauce

1 tablespoon butter
1 tablespoon vegetable oil
½ cup brandy
1 teaspoon cornstarch
2 tablespoons water
½ cup heavy cream

Flatten steaks with rolling pin to ½-inch thick. Spread green peppercorns on each steak. Set aside.

For the marinade, mix peppercorns, soy sauce, sugar, vegetable oil & Worcestershire sauce. Pour over steaks. Marinate one hour.

Scrape peppercorns & marinade off steaks & reserve.

Over high heat in a large skillet, add butter & oil.

Sauté steaks 2 minutes each side for medium rare. Add brandy & flambé 1 minute. Remove steaks to heated platter. Combine cornstarch with water. Add to pan juices. Stir. Add cream & reserved marinade. Stir until bubbly. Serve sauce over steaks.

4 servings

Poached Pears with Sauce Anglaise

•

Sauce Anglaise:
1 cup milk
½ cup heavy cream
6 tablespoons sugar
4 egg yolks
2 teaspoons cornstarch
1 teaspoon vanilla

Pears:
8 pears, slightly underripe, peeled, leave stems on
1 tablespoon lemon juice
4 cups water
2 cups sugar
3 whole cloves
1 cinnamon stick
1 tablespoon grated lemon peel

For Sauce, combine milk & cream. Bring just to a boil. Beat sugar into egg yolks until pale & creamy. Add cornstarch. Stir cream into egg yolks, beating vigorously. Return to low heat & cook 15 minutes, until mixture is creamy. Remove from heat. Add vanilla. Chill, covered, overnight.

For the pears, slice a piece off the bottom of each pear so it will stand upright. Place in cold water & 1 tablespoon juice. Set aside.

Add sugar to 4 cups water & bring to a boil. Add cloves, cinnamon stick & lemon peel. Add pears. Keep at rolling boil until pears are tender & easily pierced with a fork, about 30 minutes. Put pears in individual serving dishes. Pour a little cooking syrup over each to glaze. Chill at least 4 hours. Serve with Sauce Anglaise spooned over top.

8 servings

*California
Napa Chardonnay*

•

*There is understated
elegance when presenting
this menu & wine at
your next dinner party.
Pale blue cloth, napkins
& candles with peach
& blue carnations in the
centerpiece & you will
delight the eye as well
as the palate.*

Sole
Caledonia

•

 1 pound fillets of sole
 ½ cup dry white wine
 1 cup asparagus tips
 ½ cup halved cherry tomatoes
 ½ cup sliced mushrooms
 2 tablespoons butter
 2 tablespoons flour
  salt & white pepper
 1¼ cups hot milk
 1 egg yolk
 ½ cup fresh bread crumbs
 ¼ cup freshly grated Parmesan
  cheese

In a large skillet, poach fillets in wine
2-3 minutes. Remove fillets to buttered baking dish. Reserve poaching
liquid. Top fillets with asparagus,
tomatoes & mushrooms. In small
saucepan, heat butter. Stir in flour,
salt & pepper. Add heated milk. Stir
until thickened. Add a little hot
milk mixture to egg yolk. Return to
pan. Bring to boil. Add poaching
liquid. Stir until blended & smooth.
Pour evenly over fillets & vegetables.
Combine bread crumbs & cheese.
Sprinkle evenly over sauce. Bake at
350°F. 30 minutes until browned
& bubbly.

4 servings

Tipsy
Carrots

•

24 baby carrots or equivalent sliced
 carrots
 2 tablespoons orange-flavored
  liqueur
 ¼ cup brandy
 ¼ cup honey
  juice of 1 lemon
 2 tablespoons chopped Italian
  parsley

Cook carrots until crisp-tender in
small amount of salted water 10
minutes. Arrange in buttered 1-quart
baking dish. Combine liqueur,
brandy, honey & lemon in small
saucepan. Bring to boil. Reduce by
⅓. Pour over carrots & marinate
overnight. Reheat in 350°F. oven 20
minutes or microwave. Sprinkle with
parsley.

6-8 servings

Chocolate
Loaf

•

1½ cups ground walnuts, divided
12-ounces semi-sweet chocolate
 pieces
 ¾ cup unsalted butter
 3 tablespoons unsweetened
  cocoa powder
 ⅓ cup sugar
 4 egg yolks
 5 egg whites
  pinch salt

Vanilla Mousseline:
 1 cup milk
 3 egg yolks
 3 tablespoons sugar
 1 teaspoon vanilla
 1 cup heavy cream
 ¼ cup powdered sugar

Line bottom of 1-quart loaf pan with
waxed paper. Liberally butter inside
of pan. Sprinkle 1 cup walnuts over
inside of pan. Gently press into
place. Set aside.

Combine chocolate, butter & cocoa
in 1-quart saucepan. Cook over low
heat until melted. Remove from heat.
Cool. With mixer, add sugar & beat
3 minutes. Beat in yolks one at a
time. Beat egg whites & salt until
stiff & glossy. Stir ⅓ whites into chocolate mixture. Gently fold in remaining whites. Turn into prepared
pan. Cover with plastic. Refrigerate.
May be frozen 3 weeks. Defrost in
refrigerator.

For mousseline, scald milk. Set aside.
Combine yolks & sugar. Beat until
thick & lemon-colored. Whisk milk
into eggs. Return to saucepan. Cook
over low heat, stirring, until mixture
thickens & coats spoon. Do Not
Boil. Strain custard into bowl. Add
vanilla. Cover & refrigerate. May be
made 3 days in advance. Before serving, whip cream & powdered sugar
until stiff. Fold cream into custard.
Turn out loaf onto serving plate.
Remove paper. Press remaining walnuts onto loaf. Slice & serve with
sauce.

10 servings

Notable Gatherings
presented by Wisconsin Chefs, Cooks & Caterers

Escargots Bon Maman

•

24 large mushrooms, stems removed
 3 tablespoons butter
   pinch salt
½ teaspoon finely chopped shallots
24 escargots
⅓ cup dry red wine
 1 cup brown sauce, recipe follows
½ teaspoon chopped garlic
 1 teaspoon chopped parsley

Brown Sauce:
 1 tablespoon clarified butter
 1 tablespoon flour
½ cup beef stock

Sauté mushroom caps in butter in sauté pan over medium heat. Add salt. Remove caps from pan. Divide caps between six escargot dishes. Keep warm. Sauté shallots in same pan 20 seconds. Add escargots. Increase heat. Add wine. Cook 30 seconds. Add brown sauce. Remove escargots & place in mushroom caps. Keep warm. Reduce sauce over high heat 1 minute. Reduce heat to medium. Add garlic & parsley. Lightly spoon sauce over escargots.

For the sauce, heat butter in sauce-pan. Add flour. Cook over low heat, stirring occasionally, until flour & butter are blended & turn the color of brown wrapping paper. Add stock. Blend with whisk until slightly thickened.

6 servings

Veal Tenderloin Robert

•

1½ pounds (16 1½-ounce slices)
   veal tenderloin
   salt & pepper
 2 thin slices prosciutto ham, finely
   chopped
 8-ounces Brie cheese, peeled
   & softened
¼ cup flour
 1 cup unsalted butter
 4-ounces morels or other
   mushrooms
 3 shallots, finely chopped
 1 cup cream
 1 cup chopped parsley
   fresh lemon juice

Pound veal. Season lightly with salt & pepper. Combine prosciutto & Brie. Spread mixture on veal slices. Roll up. Dust veal with flour. Melt butter over medium-high heat in large skillet. Sauté veal rolls until brown on all sides & cooked through. Remove to a warm covered plate.

In same pan sauté mushrooms & shallots in remaining butter. Add cream. Bring to boil. Reduce sauce to desired consistency. Add parsley. Season to taste with lemon juice & salt. Spoon sauce over veal.

6-8 servings

*Grenadier's
Milwaukee, Wisconsin*

Grenadier's has been open since the mid-'70s. Chef Knut Apitz believes the principle of quickly prepared, lightly sauced, low-fat food can apply to anything. Grenadier's offers continental cooking in the true sense of the word, from French, German, Italian, American to Chinese, Indian, or South American.
❦

*French Chef Edouard
Charles Becker brings
a light & colorful touch in
menu design to the
restaurant that
consistently wins acclaim
for its continental food.
The extensive menu is
complemented by more
than 400 wine offerings
from their cellar. Expert
maître d' Frank Bonfiglio's
attention is famous.*
💝

Pheasant Périgourdine

•

2-2½ pound pheasant
    salt & pepper
1 recipe forcemeat, recipe follows
4-ounces salt pork
    cheesecloth
1 cup butter, melted
½ large onion, diced
1 medium carrot, diced
2 stalks celery, diced
2 shallots, quartered
1 teaspoon thyme
½ bay leaf
½ tablespoon flour
1½ cups water
1½ cups chicken stock
¼ cup Madeira
2 medium mushrooms, finely
    chopped
½-ounce truffles, finely chopped
2 round toasts

Preheat oven to 350°F.

Season pheasant inside & out with salt & pepper. Stuff with forcemeat. Cut salt pork into 4 slices. Lay on the pheasant breast. Place pheasant in roasting pan. Cut a piece of cheesecloth to cover bird completely. Soak in melted butter. Lay on top of bird. Roast 50-65 minutes, basting with melted butter & twice with a sprinkle of water. Transfer to warm platter.

Place roasting pan over medium heat. Add onions, carrots, celery, shallots, thyme & bay leaf to drippings. Cook until brown. Add flour. Cook until flour is browned. Add water & stock. Boil rapidly until mixture is reduced by half. Strain through a sieve into a small pan. Over medium heat, add Madeira, mushrooms & truffles. Stir & simmer a few minutes. Season to taste. Serve pheasant on toast. Coat with sauce. Pass remaining sauce.

2 servings

Forcemeat

•

1 thick slice bacon, ground
¼ pound chicken livers, chopped
⅓ teaspoon finely chopped shallot
1 tablespoon finely chopped
    mushrooms
⅓ teaspoon finely chopped truffles
½ teaspoon parsley
2 tablespoons butter
⅓ cup brown sauce
1 egg yolk
    salt, pepper, nutmeg
    bread crumbs

Sauté bacon, livers, shallot, mushrooms, truffles & parsley in butter. Add brown sauce, yolk, salt, pepper & nutmeg. Stir until liquid is incorporated. Press mixture through a sieve. Add bread crumbs until liquid is completely absorbed.

2 servings

Crêpes Flambées Forêt Noire

•

4 crêpes
½ pint excellent ice cream
⅔ cup sugar
¾ cup red wine
2-inch piece orange peel
2 whole cloves, stuck into
    orange peel
1 stick cinnamon
1 cup lightly crushed raspberries
1-ounce Himbeergeist, or
    eau de vie de framboise
2 tablespoons sliced almonds

Roll each crêpe around ¼ cup ice cream. Freeze. May prepare in advance.

In heavy sauté pan over medium heat, stir sugar until melted & light brown. Add wine, orange peel & spices. Increase heat. Boil, stirring, until mixture is reduced to a bubbly texture. Add raspberries & 3-4 tablespoons of their juice. Cook until mixture is smooth & glazed. Remove spices & orange peel. Heat Himbeergeist & ignite. Add to sauce. Spoon flaming sauce over crêpe. Sprinkle with almonds.

2 servings

*Karen is accredited
by the International
Association of Cooking
Professionals. Currently
teaching for MATC &
the Grand Gourmet
School, she also operates
her own cooking school
& catering business,
Creative Cuisine. Karen's
menus & food are
known for their
simplicity, elegance, ease
of preparation &
beautiful garnishes.*

Chilled Cantaloupe Soup in Melon Baskets

•

4 medium cantaloupes
1½ cups apple juice
⅔ cup sugar
½ cup dry sherry
1 tablespoon fresh lemon juice
¾ teaspoon ground ginger
¾ teaspoon vanilla
mint sprigs

To prepare baskets, draw a light circle around circumference of melon. With a V-cutter or knife, make zig-zag cuts around melon on top of line. Pull melon halves apart. Remove seeds. Scoop out pulp. Reserve shells. Cut a tiny slice off bottom of each melon half to sit flat.

In large bowl, combine pulp, apple juice, sugar, sherry, lemon juice, ginger & vanilla. In blender, whirl 2 cups mixture at a time until smooth. Pour into covered container. Chill overnight. Stir before serving. Pour into melon baskets. Garnish with mint sprigs. Serve with a straw or spoon.

8 servings

Green Salad with Fresh Fruit & Papaya Seed Dressing

•

1 large head romaine lettuce, torn into bite-size pieces
1 head leaf lettuce, torn into bite-size pieces
2 papayas, peeled, cut into 1-inch dice, reserve seeds
2 avocados, peeled, pitted, sliced, sprinkle with lemon juice
1 pint strawberries, halved
2 kiwi fruit, peeled, sliced ¼-inch thick

Papaya Seed Dressing:
½ cup sugar
½ cup white wine vinegar
¼ cup minced onion
½ teaspoon dry mustard
1 teaspoon salt
½ cup vegetable oil
3 tablespoons papaya seeds

Arrange greens on 14-inch platter. Place mound of papaya in center of greens. Arrange avocado slices spoke-fashion around papaya. Alternate kiwi & strawberries around outside of platter.

For dressing, place ingredients except oil & papaya seeds in blender. Blend smooth. With machine running slowly add oil. Add papaya seeds. Blend until they resemble coarsely ground pepper. Chill up to 3 days in advance. Drizzle dressing onto salad just before serving.

10 servings

Dilly Yeast Muffins

•

3½ cups unbleached flour
¼ cup sugar
1 teaspoon salt
1 package quick rise yeast
1½ cups milk
⅓ cup butter
1 jumbo egg
2-3 tablespoons snipped fresh dill or 1-1½ teaspoons dried

Lightly butter 18 muffin cups.

In food processor, combine 1½ cups flour, sugar, salt & yeast. In saucepan, heat milk & butter to 130°F. Pulse processor to blend dry ingredients. With machine running, add milk mixture. Let machine run 30 seconds. Add egg & dill. Run 1 minute. Add enough additional flour to make a stiff, but still sticky dough. Batter is very soft. Cover work bowl with plastic. Put in warm place to rise until double in volume, 30 minutes. Stir down.

Preheat oven to 400°F. Fill muffin cups 2/3-full. Cover & let rise 15 minutes until dough almost fills tin. Bake 12-15 minutes. Do not overbake. Should be served warm. May be frozen.

18 muffins

Photographs

*Fennel Soup, recipe 102
California Ham, recipe 148
Hungarian Nut Torte, recipe 145
Picante Crab Fondue, recipe 142
Monte's Beef Tenderloin, recipe 165*

MENU

**Dilled
Leek
Soup**

Armenian
Lamb Shanks

Brown &
Wild Rice

Seasonal
Vegetables

**Kourabiédes
Greek
Shortbread Cookies**

Yugoslavian Red
•

Dilled
Leek
Soup

•

1 pound zucchini, coarsely
   chopped
1 large leek, washed & chopped
4 tablespoons bacon fat
2 tablespoons snipped fresh dill
5½ cups chicken stock
   salt & pepper
1 cup cream

In a large saucepan, cook zucchini
& leek in fat over medium heat 10
minutes until soft, not brown. Add
dill, stock, salt & pepper. Cover &
simmer 20 minutes. Remove from
heat. Cool slightly. In a blender or
processor, purée in batches. When
ready to serve, reheat. Add cream.
Ladle into heated bowls.

4-6 servings

Kourabiédes
Greek
Shortbread Cookies

•

2 cups flour
1 cup powdered sugar
1 cup butter, softened
   powdered sugar

Preheat oven to 300°F.

Sift flour & sugar. Add to butter.
Thoroughly work with fingers. Form
into balls the size of a walnut. Place
on baking sheet. Flatten with the
bottom of a glass dipped in powdered sugar. Bake 20-30 minutes.
Do not let them get brown! Dust with
powdered sugar.

3 dozen

*The Painted Lady
Newburg, Wisconsin*

*Originally called the
"Max Weinand Saloon,"
the Painted Lady has
served as a tavern since
its construction in 1875.
The varied menu features
homemade hot breads,
soups, dressings, desserts
& entrées in a dining
style described as "haute
cuisine à la Newburg."*
❦

Tomato Herbed Fish Fillets

•

2 pounds any fish fillets, cut into
    serving pieces
½ cup bread crumbs
2 cups peeled, seeded & chopped
    tomatoes
½ cup sliced scallions
2 teaspoons oregano
2 teaspoons basil
1 cup mayonnaise
1 cup grated cheddar cheese

Preheat oven to 400°F.

Dredge fillets in bread crumbs.
Arrange in buttered shallow
casserole or individual ramekins. In
a small bowl, combine tomatoes,
scallions, oregano & basil. Spoon
over fillets. Mix together mayonnaise & cheddar cheese. Spread over
fillets. Bake 20 minutes.

6-8 servings

Lemon Fromage

•

3 eggs
2 egg yolks
½ cup sugar
    grated peel of 1 lemon
1 package unflavored gelatin
    juice of 2 lemons
2 cups heavy cream, whipped
1 pint fresh strawberries

Beat eggs & yolks until light & frothy.
Add sugar gradually. Continue beating until mixture is thick & light
colored. Add lemon peel. Soften
gelatin in lemon juice. Melt over hot
water. When dissolved, add to egg
mixture. Beat well. Fold cream into
mixture. Pour into 1-quart melon
mold or another 1-quart mold. Chill
4 hours. Unmold & garnish with
strawberries.

6-8 servings

*Naomi Arbit
The Gourmet Touch*

*Naomi Arbit is a cooking
teacher, home economist,
food consultant &
co-author of 7 cookbooks
distributed nationally
& internationally.
She is the weekly food
columnist for
Community Newspapers in
Wisconsin & Illinois
under the title,
The Gourmet Touch.*
🍎

MENU

**Mushrooms
in
Sour Cream**

**Cream
of
Artichoke Soup**

Caesar Salad

**Arroz
con
Pollo**

Southern
Butter & Nut
Cake

Oregon State Pinot Noir

•

*Marcia's Gourmet House
Racine, Wisconsin*

*"Food with Taste" is the
motto of this popular
catering & gourmet-to-go
specialty store featuring
daily take-out soups,
stews, quiche, salads,
entrées & bakery
specialties. Marcia's
Gourmet House was
featured on ABC-TV's
20/20 program.*

Mushrooms
in
Sour Cream

•

1 pound mushrooms, sliced
⅔ cup scallions, sliced
2 tablespoons butter
1 tablespoon lemon juice
1 tablespoon flour
1 cup sour cream
2 tablespoons snipped fresh dill
¼ teaspoon salt
   freshly ground pepper
   toasted French bread slices

Sauté mushrooms & scallions in
butter & lemon juice 4 minutes. Stir
in flour. Cook slowly 1 minute. Add
sour cream, dill, salt & pepper.
Cook 1 minute. Serve immediately
over toasts.

4 servings

Cream
of
Artichoke Soup

•

3 tablespoons diced onion
3 tablespoons diced carrot
3 tablespoons diced celery
¼ cup butter
2 cups chopped cabbage
½ cup chopped onion
2 cloves garlic, minced
1 can (14 ounces) artichoke
   bottoms, drained & rinsed
4 cups chicken stock, divided
2 teaspoons chervil
2 tablespoons finely chopped
   parsley
1 teaspoon salt
½ teaspoon paprika
¼ cup dry sherry
⅛ teaspoon hot pepper sauce
   fresh ground pepper
1 tablespoon cornstarch
2 tablespoons cold water
2 cups light cream

In large kettle, sauté onion, carrot &
celery in butter 5 minutes. Remove
from pan. Set aside. In same butter,
sauté cabbage, remaining onion &
garlic 5 minutes. Spoon cabbage mixture into blender or processor. Add
artichokes & 2 cups stock. Purée.
Return to kettle. Add remaining
stock, diced vegetables, chervil,
parsley, salt, paprika, sherry, hot
pepper sauce & pepper. Simmer 10
minutes. Combine cornstarch &
water. Add to soup, stirring until
slightly thickened. Add cream. Heat
gently without boiling.

6-8 servings

Arroz
con
Pollo

•

3½ pound frying chicken, cut into
   serving pieces
¼ cup olive oil
   seasoned salt
   pepper
2 cups chopped onion
2 cloves garlic, minced
1 cup chopped celery
1 cup chopped green pepper
4 cups water, divided
2 teaspoons salt
¼ teaspoon powdered saffron
2 bay leaves
2 cups chopped tomatoes
2 cups long grain rice
1 cup petite peas, cooked
   pimiento strips
   olive oil

In large skillet, brown chicken over
medium high heat in olive oil.
Sprinkle with seasoned salt & pepper.
Remove to dutch oven or roasting
pan. Pour off all but ¼ cup fat. Add
onion, garlic, celery & peppers.
Cook 5 minutes. Add to chicken.
Add 2 cups water to frying pan to
deglaze. Pour over chicken. Add
remaining water, salt, saffron, bay
leaves, tomatoes & rice. Bring to boil.
Stir well. Cover & simmer 30 minutes, or bake at 325°F. 30 minutes.
Garnish with peas, pimiento & a
drizzle of olive oil before serving.

4 servings

MENU

Cured Norwegian Salmon with Mustard Sauce

Herb Stuffed Lamb Leg with Garlic Butter Sauce

Toasted Coconut Flan

French Red Burgundy
Côtes du Nuits

•

Claus on Juneau
Milwaukee, Wisconsin

Norwegian chef Claus Bienek offers gourmet French & Scandinavian food in the style of "Cuisine Nouvelle" in his contemporary dining room.

Cured Norwegian Salmon with Mustard Sauce

•

2 pounds fresh salmon fillet, tail portion
1 cup Kosher salt
1 tablespoon freshly ground white peppercorns
1½ cups sugar
1 bunch fresh dill, chopped, about 1½ cups
½ cup sweet sherry
¼ cup Cognac
poached eggs

Mustard Sauce:
1 cup mayonnaise
2 tablespoons Pommard mustard juice from salmon marinade, about 2 tablespoons
2 tablespoons fresh chopped dill

Place salmon fillet in shallow pan. Combine salt, peppercorns, sugar & dill. Evenly spread over fillets. Pour sherry & Cognac over fillets. Cover. Refrigerate 24 hours.

For the sauce, combine ingredients. Serve the salmon very thinly sliced with mustard sauce ladled over a poached egg.

16-20 servings

Herb Stuffed Lamb Leg with Garlic Butter Sauce

•

4-5 pound Wisconsin boneless leg of lamb, butterflied
salt
freshly ground pepper
½ cup coarse brown mustard
2 tablespoons coarsely chopped garlic
½ cup chopped fresh parsley
1 tablespoon each chopped fresh dill, thyme, tarragon & marjoram, or any fresh aromatic herbs

Garlic Butter Sauce:
2 whole heads garlic, peeled
½ cup water
½ cup butter
1 teaspoon lemon juice

Preheat oven to 350°F.

Rub interior of leg with salt & pepper. Spread mustard evenly over meat. Place garlic & herbs down center of leg. Roll up roast. Secure with butcher's twine. Roast until thermometer reads 130-145°F. depending on preference. Remove from oven. Cover with foil.

For the sauce, in a 1-quart saucepan, bring garlic & water to boil. Reduce liquid to ¼ cup. Add butter. Over low heat, whisk until blended. Add lemon juice. Strain sauce through sieve. Serve lamb sliced on Garlic Butter Sauce.

8-12 servings

Toasted Coconut Flan

•

Caramel Coating:
1 cup sugar
¼ cup water

6 egg yolks
6 eggs
2 cups heavy cream
2 cups milk
1 cup sugar
1 teaspoon vanilla
2 cups toasted flaked coconut

Preheat oven to 275°F. Place a 13x9-inch pan with 1-inch boiling water into oven.

In a small saucepan over medium heat combine 1 cup sugar & water. Cook until sugar is rich caramel color. Pour hot caramel into a 2-3 quart soufflé dish, turning the dish to coat the sides & bottom with caramel. Set aside to cool. In a medium size saucepan, heat cream, milk, sugar & vanilla near the boiling point. In top of double boiler whisk yolks & eggs. Add cream mixture to beaten eggs. Heat in double boiler until hot to touch. Do not boil. Sieve mixture into a bowl. Add toasted coconut. Pour flan mixture into prepared soufflé dish. Place soufflé dish into heated pan of water in oven. Bake 65-75 minutes until completely firm. Chill completely. Invert onto serving tray. Serve with poached peaches or pears if desired.

8-10 servings

*Ellen Jensen offers a Fall
Dinner Menu as well
as a Country Luncheon.
Her theory as a caterer is
to customize each menu
by coordinating theme,
client style & setting.
Creative presentation of
food is the key to her success.*

Roast Loin of Pork with Peanut Sauce

•

5-pound loin of pork

Peanut Sauce:
  3 tablespoons peanut oil
  1 yellow onion, chopped
  ½ teaspoon crushed garlic
  ½ teaspoon crushed red pepper
  6 tablespoons soy sauce
  4 tablespoons sherry
    pinch ground ginger
  ¾ cup creamy-style peanut butter
  1 cup chicken stock
  1 cup heavy cream

Roast the loin of pork at 350°F. until meat thermometer reads 175°F.

For the sauce, sauté onion & garlic in oil with red pepper. Add soy, sherry, ginger, peanut butter & stock. Simmer 30 minutes. Strain mixture. Add cream. Serve sliced loin with sauce.

8 servings

Citrus Chicken Spinach Salad

•

1 chicken breast, sliced into ¼-inch
  strips
1 teaspoon Worcestershire sauce
1 teaspoon honey
1 tablespoon orange juice
2 tablespoons beef stock
½ cup hot bacon dressing
⅛ cup sliced mushrooms
2 tablespoons chopped scallions
2 tablespoons chopped fresh
  parsley
¼ cup cold water
1 tablespoon cornstarch
  fresh spinach leaves
⅛ cup sliced toasted almonds

In medium sauté pan, cook chicken strips with Worcestershire, honey, orange juice, stock, dressing, mushrooms, parsley & scallions. Simmer 5-7 minutes until bubbling. Dissolve cornstarch in water. Add to pan. Cook until thickened. Serve on top of fresh spinach. Top with almonds.

1 serving

Pictured page 169.

Homemade Pecan Walnut Pie

•

1¼ cups dark corn syrup
  1 cup packed light brown sugar
  4 tablespoons butter
  ½ cup chopped pecans
  ½ cup chopped walnuts
  4 eggs
  1 teaspoon vanilla
  1 9-inch unbaked pie crust

Preheat oven to 350°F.

Combine corn syrup & brown sugar in saucepan. Bring to boil. Stir until sugar is dissolved. Add butter, pecans & walnuts. Remove from heat. Beat eggs in bowl. Add vanilla. Pour eggs into syrup. Stir well. Pour into pie crust. Bake 45-50 minutes.

8 servings

Shrimp Denise

•

A fascinating legacy of great restaurants is that they live long after their demise in the hearts & minds of former patrons.

½ cup butter, softened
2 cloves garlic, finely minced
2 teaspoons Worcestershire sauce
2 teaspoons steak sauce
½ teaspoon seasoned salt
12 jumbo shrimp, cooked & peeled
12 5-inch pieces bacon
1½ cups cooked wild rice

Combine butter, garlic, sauces & salt. Shape into a loaf. Wrap in plastic. Chill until very firm.

Split shrimp down the back halfway through. Stuff with seasoned butter. Wrap with bacon, fastened with a toothpick. Broil 2 minutes.

Spoon rice evenly into shallow serving casserole. Arrange shrimp attractively on rice. Dot with remaining butter mixture. Bake 375°F. 10 minutes.

2-3 servings

Hamming It Up

•

Mark Paulus offers the ham recipe deemed, "truly nectar of the gods," from his butcher shop.

1 large sheet heavy-duty foil
6-10 pound boneless ham
ground cloves
brown sugar
2 cups apricot nectar

Preheat oven to 325°F.

Place ham on foil. Rub with ground cloves. Pack ½-inch brown sugar on top of ham. Pour apricot nectar over ham. Seal foil. Place in baking pan. Bake 2 hours. Remove ham, reserve juices. Slice for sandwiches. Return to pan juices. Cover leftovers with juices in glass container. Can be frozen & reheated in microwave for easy meals.

15-18 sandwiches (6-pound ham)

Fresh Tuna with Soy & Ginger

•

3 tablespoons soy sauce
1 tablespoon lemon juice
1 clove garlic, minced
½ teaspoon peeled, grated fresh
    ginger root
    salt & pepper
2 tuna steaks, ½-¾ pound each

In glass dish, mix soy, lemon, garlic, ginger, salt & pepper. Add tuna, turning to coat. Cover & refrigerate at least 2 hours, turning occasionally. Remove steaks from dish. Reserve marinade. Broil tuna 4-inches from heat, 6-8 minutes, turning once. Or, grill tuna 6-inches from coals, 8-10 minutes, turning once. Heat marinade to boiling. Serve tuna with marinade.

2 servings

Aunt Grace's All American Three Layer Fudge Cake

•

2 cups sifted cake flour
2 cups sugar
1 teaspoon salt
1½ teaspoons baking soda
½ cup unsalted butter, softened
3-ounces unsweetened chocolate,
    melted
1¼ cups milk, divided
1 teaspoon vanilla
½ teaspoon baking powder
3 eggs

Mocha Butter Frosting:
⅓ cup unsalted butter, softened
3 cups powdered sugar, divided
    pinch salt
¼ cup milk or light cream
1½-ounces unsweetened
    chocolate, melted
½ teaspoon instant coffee powder
1½ teaspoons vanilla

Preheat oven to 350°F. Butter 3 8-inch round waxed paper-lined cake pans.

In large bowl, sift together flour, sugar, salt & baking soda. Add butter, 1 tablespoon at a time. Beat at medium speed until blended. Gradually add chocolate, ¾ cup milk & vanilla. Beat 2 minutes. Add baking powder, remaining milk & eggs. Beat 2 minutes. Divide batter evenly among pans. Tap pan on counter. Bake 35-40 minutes. Cool pans on racks 10 minutes. Remove layers from pans. Carefully peel off paper. Cool completely.

For frosting, beat butter, salt & 1 cup sugar at medium speed until light & fluffy, 2 minutes. Alternately add remaining sugar & milk beating until smooth. Add chocolate, coffee powder & vanilla. Beat 3 minutes, until spreading consistency. Spread between cake layers. Frost sides & top of cake.

8-10 servings

MENU

Refreshing Grapefruit
&
Cucumber Salad

**Fresh Tuna
with
Soy & Ginger**

Spicy
Mayonnaise Sauce

Boiled New Potatoes
with
Parsley

**Aunt Grace's
All American Three
Layer Fudge Cake**

California Red Zinfandel

•

---

*Myra Dorros
Modern Gourmet of
Milwaukee*

Accredited chef & teacher, Myra is a graduate of Madeleine Kamman's Cooking School in Boston & Annecy, France & is certified by the International Association of Cooking Professionals. She writes a weekly food column for the Milwaukee Journal, The Chef's Hat. As a food consultant, she coordinates a program that educates & trains Milwaukee High School students in food-related jobs.

Bibb, Red Cabbage & Scallion Salad with Duck Cracklings

•

3 cups diced duck skin, from
    neck, etc.
4 heads bibb lettuce
¼ cup peanut oil
2 pounds red cabbage, finely
    shredded
2 bunches scallions, cut on bias
    into 1-inch pieces
1 tablespoon honey
¼ cup balsamic vinegar
1 teaspoon lemon juice
    salt & pepper

Render duck skin until crispy &
browned. Strain. Reserve ¼ cup fat.
Arrange bibb lettuce on 6 plates.
Heat duck fat & oil in large sauté
pan. Add cabbage. Sauté 15 seconds.
Add scallions, honey, vinegar, lemon
juice, salt & pepper. Toss 30 seconds.
Serve on lettuce beds. Garnish with
cracklings.

6 servings

Angel Hair Pasta with Black Truffle Sauce

•

1-ounce black truffles, julienned,
    reserve juice
¾ cup Madeira
1 cup veal stock
½ cup heavy cream
8-10 ounces fresh angel hair pasta,
    cooked & drained
    salt & freshly ground pepper

Add truffle juice, Madeira & stock
to sauté pan. Reduce by ½. Add
cream. Boil until reduced to 1 cup.
Add all but 4 strips truffle. Divide
pasta onto 4 plates. Cover with sauce.
Garnish with remaining truffle strips.

4 servings

Veal with Green Olives, Prosciutto & Spinach

•

3 2-ounce slices veal loin
    salt & pepper
    flour for dusting
2 tablespoons clarified butter
1 teaspoon chopped shallot
    juice of ½ lemon
¾ cup white wine
3 brine-cured, pitted, Sicilian
    green olives
6 spinach leaves, blanched
4 tablespoons cold butter
1 tablespoon finely julienned
    prosciutto ham

Slightly flatten veal. Season with salt
& pepper. Dust with flour. Heat butter in sauté pan. When hot, add veal.
Sauté 15-25 seconds each side.
Remove to plate. Keep warm.

Add shallots. Sauté 5 seconds. Add
lemon, white wine & olives. Remove
olives when hot. Add spinach leaves.
Heat & remove from pan. Arrange
on plate in circle. Reduce sauce by
⅔. Add cold butter using whisk
over medium heat. Do not boil. Add
veal & prosciutto to sauce. Remove
& arrange on plate. Pour sauce over
veal. Garnish with olives.

1 serving

MENU

Bibb, Red Cabbage & Scallion Salad with Duck Cracklings

Angel Hair Pasta with Black Truffle Sauce

Veal with Green Olives, Prosciutto & Spinach

*California White
Napa Valley Chardonnay*

•

*John Byron's
Milwaukee, Wisconsin*

*Since opening in 1978,
John Byron's has a
reputation for serving
creative unique specialties.
All ingredients are the
freshest & highest quality
obtainable depending
on seasonal availability.
Chef Sanford D'Amato
changes menus
completely 3-4 times a year.
The wine list, primarily
with a California bent
from smaller producers,
has twice received the
Wine Spectator's
Top 100 Award.*

MENU

Cream of Autumn Squash Soup

Garden Lettuce Salad with Cranberry Blossom Honey Vinaigrette

Shredded Veal with Zucchini & Mushrooms

Egg Noodles

Hazelnut Torte

French White Burgundy Mâcon Pouilly-Fuissé

•

Nick Spinelli, Jr.

Nick graduated with honors from Culinary Institute of America & has worked in New York, Palm Beach, San Francisco, Quebec & Munich. He currently is Executive Chef for the First Wisconsin National Bank. Nick is a well-known teacher of gourmet cooking & the art of garnishing in Chicago & Milwaukee areas.

Cream of Autumn Squash Soup

•

1 small acorn squash, cleaned & cut into ⅛'s
1 small buttercup squash, cleaned & cut into ⅛'s
1 small pie pumpkin, cleaned & cut into ⅛'s
1 large Bermuda onion, chopped
3 quarts chicken stock
¼ cup butter
¼ cup flour
   salt & white pepper
¾ cup milk
   herbed croutons

Place squashes & onion in large pot with stock. Bring to boil. Simmer until squashes are tender. Remove squashes & onion. Reserve stock. Scoop out pulp from squashes. Purée onion & pulp in blender or processor.

Melt butter in saucepan. Add flour. Cook 2-3 minutes. Gradually add stock. Add purée. Stir to blend. Cook 5-10 minutes. Add milk. Cook 5 minutes. Season to taste. Serve in small carved-out pumpkins. Garnish with herbed croutons.

16 servings

Shredded Veal with Zucchini & Mushrooms

•

5 pounds sliced veal, cut into julienne strips
1½ cups flour seasoned with salt & black pepper
½ cup olive oil
1 cup salad oil
5 pounds small zucchini, halved & sliced
3 pounds mushrooms, sliced
2 cups veal or chicken stock
1 cup dry white wine
2 cups lemon juice
1½ cups finely chopped parsley
2 tablespoons cornstarch
½ cup water

Dredge veal strips in flour. Spread out to rest 5 minutes. Combine the 2 oils. In a large skillet, use oil as needed to sauté veal in batches. Remove to plate. Sauté zucchini & mushrooms until crisp-tender. Remove to plate with veal.

In a 2-quart saucepan combine stock, wine & lemon juice. Bring to boil. Simmer 30 minutes. Combine cornstarch & water. Add to sauce. Stir. Add parsley. Remove from heat. Fold in veal, zucchini & mushrooms. Reheat to boil. Serve with pilaf, noodles or boiled potatoes.

16 servings

Hazelnut Torte

•

1½ cups toasted, skinned hazelnuts, finely ground, divided
4 egg whites
1⅓ cups superfine sugar
3 teaspoons vanilla, divided
1 teaspoon fresh lemon juice
1 cup heavy cream
2 tablespoons sugar
   powdered sugar

Preheat oven to 300°F. Butter & flour 2 9-inch paper-lined cake pans.

Beat egg whites until stiff. Gradually add sugar. Beat 2 minutes. Add 2 teaspoons vanilla & lemon juice. Beat 2 minutes. Carefully fold in 1 cup nuts. Spread mixture evenly into pans. Bake 1 hour until layers are set but not brown. Turn out onto wire racks. Remove paper. Cool thoroughly.

Beat cream with sugar & remaining vanilla until stiff. Add additional powdered sugar for sweeter cream. Fold in remaining hazelnuts. Frost layers, sides & top of torte with cream. Chill several hours.

8 servings

Spinach Linguini with Port Wine & Scallops

•

MENU

Spinach Linguini with Port Wine & Scallops

Chicken Diane

Sugar Snap
Peas

*French White
Alsace Riesling*

•

4 tablespoons butter
2 pounds bay or sea scallops
2 shallots, chopped
2 tablespoons tomato paste
¼ teaspoon seasoned salt
1½ cups heavy cream
¼ cup port wine
1 pound fresh spinach linguine, cooked & drained

In large skillet, melt butter. Sauté scallops & shallots 2-4 minutes. Do not overcook. Remove scallops to warm platter. Add tomato paste, salt, cream & port. Bring to boil. Reduce sauce until slightly thickened. Return scallops to pan. Add linguine. Toss to coat. Serve immediately.

4 servings

Chicken Diane

•

3 tablespoons butter
4 skinless, boneless chicken breast halves
½ pound mushrooms, sliced
2 tablespoons flour
1 cup chicken stock
3 scallions, sliced
1 teaspoon Cajun spice blend
pinch oregano
¼ cup heavy cream

Sauté chicken breasts in butter 5 minutes over medium-high heat. Add mushrooms. Sauté several minutes. Remove chicken to warm plate. Sprinkle flour over mushrooms. Stir to coat. Cook 2 minutes over low heat. Add stock, scallions & spices. Return chicken to pan. Cook 10-15 minutes until sauce is slightly thickened & chicken is tender. Blend cream into sauce. Heat through. Serve with noodles or rice.

4 servings

*The Boulevard Inn
Milwaukee, Wisconsin*

The Boulevard Inn has long been known for their outstanding Continental & American cuisine emphasizing fresh seafood & an impressive California wine list.

Shrimp
à la
Greque

•

¼ pound sun dried tomatoes in oil,
  finely chopped, reserve oil
2 cloves garlic, finely chopped
3 tablespoons capers, drained
½ teaspoon oregano
2 pounds shrimp, peeled & cleaned
2 cups crumbled feta cheese

Preheat oven to 450°F.

Place tomatoes & oil in bowl. Add
garlic, capers, oregano & shrimp.
Toss. Arrange equal portions shrimp
mixture in individual ramekins.
Sprinkle with feta. Bake 10 minutes.

6-8 servings

Pasta with Broccoli
&
Anchovy Sauce

•

2 cups broccoli flowerets
3 tablespoons olive oil
3 tablespoons butter
8 anchovy fillets
1 clove garlic, minced
1 pound pasta, cooked & drained
1 cup freshly grated Parmesan
  cheese

Blanch broccoli in boiling salted
water 2-3 minutes until crisp-tender.
Drain. Rinse with cold water. Drain.

Heat oil & butter in large sauté pan.
Sauté anchovies & garlic, mashing
with wooden spoon. Add broccoli.
Cook & stir 3-5 minutes until broccoli is well coated with sauce. Spoon
mixture into a serving bowl. Add
pasta to bowl. Toss with broccoli mixture until well combined. If sauce
is too thick, add more butter & 2-3
tablespoons hot water. Sprinkle with
Parmesan. Serve immediately.

4-6 servings

Jill Heavenrich

*Well known in
Milwaukee for her
culinary arts, she
operated the Jill
Heavenrich Cooking
School specializing in the
fundamentals of
continental cuisine &
entertaining menus.*

Angel Hair Pasta with Cauliflower & Raw Tomato-Basil Sauces

Chicken Breasts, Artichokes & Oysters with Vernaccia Wine

●

●

MENU

Salmon with Shallot Agresto Sauce & Mixed Peppercorns

Angel Hair Pasta with Cauliflower & Raw Tomato-Basil Sauces

Chicken Breasts, Artichokes & Oysters with Vernaccia Wine

Italian White Vernaccia di San Gimignano

●

Marangelli's Milwaukee, Wisconsin

Italian Chef John Marangelli is a master in presenting "the pinnacle of Italian cuisine." He is considered by some to be a culinary treasure. John's artistic combinations of flavors & textures make the palate & memory sing.

Cauliflower Sauce:
1½ cups chicken stock
½ cup milk
½ cup heavy cream
2 cups cauliflowerets
½ cup peeled, chopped celery
6-8 white celery leaves
2 tablespoons freshly grated Parmesan cheese

Raw Tomato-Basil Sauce:
¼ cup extra virgin olive oil
2 cloves garlic, mashed to paste
1 tablespoon finely chopped Italian parsley
1 pound ripe plum tomatoes, peeled, seeded, drained & finely chopped
3 tablespoons coarsely chopped fresh basil

¼ cup butter, softened
1 tablespoon extra virgin olive oil
1 teaspoon fresh lemon juice
8-ounces fresh angel hair pasta, cooked al dente & drained
2 tablespoons freshly grated Parmesan cheese

For the cauliflower sauce, bring stock & milk to boil in medium saucepan. Add cauliflower, celery & leaves. Cook 10-15 minutes. Strain stock into another saucepan. Purée vegetables in blender or processor. Add cream to stock. Bring to boil. Add puréed vegetables. Simmer a few minutes. Off heat, stir in cheese. Set aside.

For raw tomato basil sauce, add oil to saucepan over medium heat. Sauté garlic. Do not brown. Add parsley. Add tomatoes. Stir. Bring just to the boil. Remove from heat. Add basil. Stir. Set aside.

To serve, in a large flat bowl, whip together butter, oil & lemon juice. Add hot pasta. Toss until evenly coated. Add ½ of the cauliflower sauce & Parmesan. Toss. Divide remaining cauliflower sauce onto 4 plates. Use long-tined fork to make 4 rolls of pasta. Set each roll on top of cauliflower sauce. Enlarge center hole of each roll with 2 forks. Fill each hole with raw tomato-basil sauce.

4 servings

Pictured page 170.

4 skinless, boneless chicken breast halves
4 medium-large artichokes
2 quarts ice water
2 tablespoons lemon juice
12 large fresh oysters, shucked, covered in own juices in bowl
2 tablespoons extra virgin olive oil
¼ cup clarified butter
1 clove garlic, lightly crushed
2 tablespoons finely chopped Italian parsley
1 tablespoon finely chopped mint
¼ cup Vernaccia wine
⅜ cup reserved oyster juice
½ cup heavy cream
flour
1 cup extra virgin olive oil, divided
2 large bunches fresh sage leaves
¼ cup Vernaccia wine
salt & freshly ground pepper

Separate loins from breasts. Remove membrane from loins. Cut each remaining breast into 3 strips the size of the loin. Pat dry. Set aside.

Trim stem from artichokes to 1-inch from bottoms. Remove tough outer leaves. Cut tops off artichokes, leaving 2-inch thick base. Remove inner choke. Evenly trim exterior of woody skin. Place in ice water with lemon juice. Set aside.

Carefully lift oysters from their juice. Gently pat dry. Set aside. Strain juice through cheesecloth. Set aside.

In a medium sauté pan over medium-high heat, allow pan to get hot 5-6 minutes. Add olive oil. Drop in oysters. Cook 1 minute until edges curl. Outside will be crisped, inside slightly warm. Transfer to plate.

Rhubarb
Tart

•

Reduce heat to medium, add butter, garlic, parsley & mint. Add wine. Reduce by ½. Add strained oyster juice. Bring to boil. Add cream. Lower heat. Reduce by half several minutes.

Cut each artichoke into 8 wedges. Pat dry. Set aside.

Lightly dredge chicken strips in flour. In a large sauté pan over medium-low heat, add ¼ cup olive oil. Cook chicken a few strips at a time until light golden & very soft in center. Do not overcook. Remove chicken to plate. Set aside.

Return pan to high heat, add remaining oil. When hot, carefully add artichokes all at once. *Be Careful Of Hot Oil.* Lightly brown artichokes several minutes. Drain off oil. Return pan to high heat. Add sage & wine. Reduce by ½. Add chicken strips. Mix together. Stir in oyster-cream sauce. Bring to boil. Remove from heat. Season with salt & pepper.

On each plate, arrange chicken strips & artichokes in ray pattern. Reheat oysters in very hot oven or broil a few seconds. Place in center of ray. Pour sauce on top.

4 servings

MENU

Zucchini
with
Basil Soup

Quiche

Garden Vegetable Salad
with
Tarragon Vinaigrette

**Rhubarb
Tart**

Beaujolais Nouveau

•

½ cup butter
1 cup flour
½ cup powdered sugar

Filling:
2 eggs, beaten
1 cup sugar
¼ cup flour
1 teaspoon baking powder
¼ teaspoon salt
1 tablespoon grated orange peel
½ teaspoon cinnamon
3 cups diced rhubarb
whipped cream
cinnamon-sugar

Preheat oven to 350°F.

Combine butter, flour & powdered sugar. Pat onto bottom & ½-inch up the sides of a 12x8-inch pan. Bake 15 minutes. Cool.

For the filling, combine all ingredients. Spread over crust. Bake 40 minutes until rhubarb is tender. Top with whipped cream & sprinkle with cinnamon sugar.

12 servings

*Monches Mill House
Hartland, Wisconsin*

Owner Elaine D. Taylor offers this typical luncheon menu. The chilled Soup is sprinkled with chopped radishes & cucumbers. The Garden Salad is a combination of marinated carrots, beans, broccoli, brussels sprouts, button squash & cherry tomatoes.

Shrimp & Artichoke Linguini
with
Casino & Provençale Sauces

•

•

Casino Sauce:
- 2 cups butter, softened
- 4 cloves garlic, chopped
- 1 cup finely chopped parsley
- ⅛ cup finely chopped green pepper
- ⅛ cup chopped pimiento, drained salt
- 1 teaspoon pepper
- ¼ cup dry white wine
- 1-ounce anchovy paste

Provençale Sauce:
- ¼ cup olive oil
- ¼ cup halved garlic cloves, crushed
- 1 large onion, chopped
- ½ teaspoon basil
- ½ teaspoon oregano
- 2 tablespoons finely chopped celery
- 2 tablespoons finely chopped parsley
- 4 cups peeled, chopped plum tomatoes
- ½ cup dry white wine
- 3 tablespoons concentrated clam base

- 12 large peeled, butterflied fresh shrimp tempura flour
- ¼ cup olive oil
- 2-3 tablespoons white wine
- 1 cup Casino Sauce
- 1 recipe Provencale Sauce
- 12 cooked artichoke hearts, halved
- 1 pound linguini, cooked & drained

For Casino Sauce, place ingredients in processor. Whirl until blended & smooth. Chill. Use as topping for fish, vegetables, steaks or whenever a full-flavored butter is required.

For Provençale Sauce, heat oil in small saucepan. Add garlic. Cook until golden but not burned. Strain oil into sauté pan. Discard garlic. Over medium heat, sauté onion in oil until limp. Add herbs. Cook 2 minutes. Add celery. Sauté 5 minutes. Add parsley, tomatoes, wine & clam base. Stir. Bring to boil. Simmer 10 minutes. Use for any recipe requiring a rich tomato sauce.

To serve, dust shrimp with tempura flour. Heat oil in 10-inch sauté pan. Add shrimp & wine to pan. Simmer 1 minute. Add Casino & Provençale Sauces. Cover & bring to boil. Uncover pan, add artichokes. On heated platter, toss linguini with sauce. Serve immediately.

6-8 servings

The Anchorage Restaurant Milwaukee, Wisconsin

Seafood specialties have been perfected at the restaurant situated on the banks of the Milwaukee River. The Sauces are wonderfully versatile.

Buffet Gatherings

brunches, cocktail parties, dinners

MENU

**Molly
Hogans**

**Brandied
Chicken Liver
Pâté**

**Eggs
Fantastic**

Toasted
English Muffins
with Herb Butter

Bars
&
Cookies

Cinnamon
Coffee

*Before or after tobogganing
on a sunny winter day,
have guests help themselves
to Molly Hogans & a
terrific brunch for
hearty souls.*

Molly
Hogans

•

6 eggs
1 cup sugar
1 tablespoon vanilla
1 can (12 ounces) frozen orange juice
1 can (6 ounces) frozen limeade
1 quart gin or vodka
2 bottles (2 liters each)
  lemon-lime soda
2 oranges, sliced
  maraschino cherries

Add eggs to blender. Mix. Slowly
add sugar, vanilla & juices. Blend
well. Pour into large container. Add
gin or vodka. Refrigerate at least
one hour.

Fill tall glasses with ice. Add 2 ounces
juice-gin or vodka mixture. Top
with lemon-lime soda. Garnish with
orange slice & cherry.

25 servings

Brandied
Chicken Liver
Pâté

•

½ cup butter
1 pound chicken livers
½ cup sliced onion
1 small bay leaf
½ teaspoon dry mustard
¼ teaspoon curry powder
1 teaspoon salt
¼ cup excellent brandy

Melt butter in skillet. Add chicken
livers, onion, bay, mustard, curry
& salt. Cover & cook 8 to 10 minutes.
Remove bay leaf & add brandy.
Cool 5 minutes.

Whirl smooth in a food processor or
blender. Pack into a buttered
crock. Cover & chill several hours or
store in freezer.

Serve with assorted breads, crackers
or raw mushrooms.

12 servings

Eggs
Fantastic

•

12 eggs
⅓ cup sour cream
1 pound sausage, any type
1 medium onion, chopped
¼ pound fresh mushrooms, sliced
½ pound cheddar cheese, grated
½ pound mozzarella cheese, grated
½ pound Swiss cheese, grated
  salt & pepper

Beat eggs & sour cream. Pour into
buttered 13x9-inch casserole. Bake
400°F. 10 minutes until eggs are set.

Sauté sausage, onion & mushrooms.
Season with salt & pepper. Drain
fat. Spread meat mixture over
eggs & top with grated cheeses.
Bake 325°F. 30 minutes until
cheese melts.

Can be served with picante or salsa
sauce over eggs.

8-12 servings

*California
Gamay
Beaujolais*

•

*Curtain time is 8 pm,
but there is time for a
pre-theater cocktail party.
Pass trays to keep the party
lively. Don't worry
about leftovers!*
❦

Camembert Puffs

•

½ pound puff pastry or patty shells
½ cup Dijon-style mustard
⅓ cup sesame seed
6-8 ounces Camembert cheese,
    cubed
    hot vegetable oil

Roll puff pastry ⅛-inch thick. Cut into 3-inch squares. With a pastry brush, spread a thin layer of mustard in center, not on edges of pastry. Sprinkle sesame seed over mustard. Place a cube of cheese on sesame seed. Moisten edge of pastry with water. Seal in a triangle shape. Chill in refrigerator 30 minutes or more.

Fry puffs in 375°F. oil about 1 minute until golden brown. Salt if desired. Serve piping hot.

Puffs may be frozen before cooking. Freeze on baking sheet. Place in plastic bag. Fry puffs a few seconds longer if frozen.

18-24 servings

Guacamole Shrimp Tortilla Chips

•

1 pound medium shrimp
    (about 25), cooked, cleaned
    & halved
2 ripe avocados
1 teaspoon salt
2½ tablespoons lemon juice
1 clove garlic, minced
2 tablespoons chopped scallions
    dash chili powder & cayenne
50 round tortilla chips
50 cilantro leaves or flat leaf parsley

Chill shrimp. Mash avocados with fork. Add salt, lemon juice, garlic, scallions, chili powder & cayenne. Mix well. Just before serving spread tortilla chips with guacamole & top with half a shrimp. Garnish with cilantro or parsley.

50 servings

Pictured page 6.

Three Pepper Prize Spread

•

1 package (8 ounces) cream cheese
    or Neufchâtel, softened
½ cup grated parmesan cheese
1 medium sweet red pepper,
    finely diced
1 medium sweet green pepper,
    finely diced
1 medium sweet yellow pepper,
    finely diced
1 small onion, finely chopped
1 tablespoon fresh chopped basil

Beat cream cheese until light & fluffy. Fold in remaining ingredients. Chill until serving. Bake 350°F. 15 minutes. Spread on toast points, muffin halves, crackers, etc.

2 cups

Korean Bulgogi

•

Beef & Ginger Dim Sum

•

Almond Crisps

•

*Light Dry
Sherry
or
Jasmine
Tea*

•

Present these Far Eastern morsels as a tea-time alternative to the cocktail party. Set a table in your garden & let Mother Nature provide the backdrop to your event.

❧

138

Marinade:
½ cup soy sauce
1½ cups water
1 teaspoon sesame seed
1 teaspoon vegetable oil
1 carrot, grated
3 cloves garlic, minced

1½ pounds sirloin tip roast, sliced
into very thin strips
vegetable oil
Silver dollar cocktail buns

Combine soy, water, sesame seed, oil, carrot & garlic. Marinate beef strips overnight. Remove beef from marinade. Heat small amount of vegetable oil in wok over medium-high heat. Stir-fry beef a few seconds. Add marinade. Remove to chafing dish. Serve with tiny cocktail buns.

8-12 servings

Filling:
1 pound lean ground beef or pork
2 slices fresh peeled ginger,
finely chopped
1 cup cooked, chopped spinach
1 tablespoon soy sauce
2 teaspoons rice wine or dry sherry
1 tablespoon cornstarch
½ teaspoon sesame oil

1 package (16 ounces) round
wonton skins, or square skins
with corners cut off
Dipping Sauce:
⅓ cup beef stock
⅓ cup soy sauce
⅓ cup rice vinegar or dry sherry
2-3 slices fresh peeled ginger,
finely chopped
2-3 cloves garlic, finely chopped
2 teaspoons sesame oil
2 teaspoons sugar

Combine filling ingredients. Let stand 20 minutes. Put about 1 teaspoon filling in center of each skin. Bring skin up around filling. Pinch skin together so filling is enclosed. Finished dim sum should look like a miniature draw string purse. The dim sum may be frozen on baking sheets before cooking. Store in plastic bag. Combine sauce ingredients. Let stand 10 minutes to blend flavors.

Steaming dim sum: Place dim sum on a lightly oiled steamer rack in a pot or wok filled with 1-inch water. Cover pot. Steam over boiling water 15 minutes. *Pan frying dim sum:* Put 2 tablespoons peanut oil in bottom of skillet or wok over medium-high heat. Add dim sum in 1 layer. Reduce heat to low. Cook 5 minutes or until browned. Add ⅓ cup beef stock. Cover & cook 5 minutes or until liquid has evaporated.

Serve with dipping sauce.

8-10 servings

---

2 egg whites
½ cup sugar
¼ teaspoon vanilla
⅓ cup flour
4 tablespoons butter, melted
½ cup sliced almonds, toasted

Preheat oven to 375°F. Lightly butter baking sheet.

In a medium bowl combine egg whites with sugar. Beat until stiff. Add vanilla. Fold in flour, butter & almonds. Blend well. Drop batter by teaspoonfuls onto baking sheet several inches apart. Bake 5-6 minutes, until lightly browned. Cool 2 minutes. Remove from pan while still slightly warm.

5 dozen

Onion Mushroom
Olive Salad

•

1 pound whole mushrooms
1½ cups pitted black olives
1½ cups pitted green olives
1 large red onion, sliced &
   separated into rings
1½ cups artichoke bottoms

Dressing:
½ cup olive oil
½ cup red wine vinegar
½ cup white vinegar
1 tablespoon dill
1 clove garlic, minced
1 teaspoon oregano
1 teaspoon salt
½ teaspoon pepper

Place mushrooms, olives, onions &
artichokes in large covered container. Blend dressing ingredients.
Cover mushroom mixture with
dressing. Seal container tightly.
Refrigerate at least 4 hours. Keeps
several weeks. Serve as an appetizer
or as a salad atop spinach leaves.

8 servings

Feta
Mint Tart

•

1 9-inch unbaked tart shell
1 package (8 ounces) cream cheese,
   softened
5-ounces feta cheese,
   room temperature
2 tablespoons butter, softened
¼ cup heavy cream
3 eggs
2 tablespoons chopped fresh mint
   fresh ground pepper
   mint sprigs

   red & green grape clusters

Preheat oven to 375°F.

Beat cream cheese until fluffy. Add
crumbled feta. Beat until blended.
Add butter, cream, eggs, mint & pepper. Pour into prepared, pastry-lined
tart pan. Bake 40-45 minutes, until
tart is puffy & brown. Cool 5 minutes on wire rack. Remove tart from
pan. Garnish with mint sprigs &
grape clusters.

8-12 servings

Pocket Gyros
with
Yogurt Sauce

•

1¼ pounds lean ground beef
1¼ pounds lean ground lamb
¼ cup chopped fresh oregano
1 tablespoon fresh thyme leaves
1 medium onion, finely chopped
2 large cloves garlic, finely chopped
¾ teaspoon salt
¾ tablespoon ground pepper

8-10 pita breads
3 tomatoes, chopped
1 large onion, thinly sliced

Yogurt Sauce:
1 cup plain yogurt
¼ cup finely chopped cucumbers
¼ cup finely chopped onion
1 clove garlic, minced
2 teaspoons olive oil
¼ teaspoon salt
¼ teaspoon pepper

Preheat oven to 325°F.

Combine beef, lamb, oregano, thyme,
onion, garlic, salt & pepper. Pack
into 9x5-inch loaf pan. Bake 1 hour
& 15 minutes. Cool. Slice meat
¼-⅜-inch thick.

Combine sauce ingredients. Chill.
Serve meat in split pita pockets with
tomatoes, onions & yogurt sauce.

8-10 servings

MENU

Onion Mushroom
Olive Salad

Wedges of Round
Greek Bread

Feta
Mint Tart

Pocket Gyros
with
Yogurt Sauce

Butter Cookies

Fresh Fruit

*California
Petite Sirah*

•

*The menu stirs up thoughts
of the Aegean Sea
& balmy evenings dining
al fresco. Place fat glass
shades over the candles
& a colorful cloth
on a table for two or twelve.
Serve gyros in napkin
lined baskets. Yasou!!*

FRUIT

Breakfast
Fruit Kebobs

•

4 cups mixed fruits: seedless grapes,
  papaya, melon, pineapple, guava,
  strawberries, mango, etc.
1 lime, thinly sliced
½ cup vanilla yogurt
1 teaspoon honey
¼ teaspoon freshly grated nutmeg
2 teaspoons lime juice
  watercress sprigs

Toss fruit in bowl with lime slices.
Thread on 6-inch skewers. Arrange
on platter. Combine yogurt, honey,
nutmeg & lime juice. Drizzle over
kebobs. Garnish with lime slices &
watercress sprigs.

4-6 servings

ENTREE

Eggs
Florentine

•

9 eggs
½ cup butter, softened
1 pound cottage cheese
½ pound Swiss cheese, grated
½ pound feta cheese, crumbled
4 cups chopped, cooked spinach
½ teaspoon grated nutmeg

Preheat oven to 350°F. Butter a
13x9-inch casserole.

Beat eggs slightly. Add butter &
cheeses. Mix well. Add spinach &
nutmeg. Pour into prepared casserole. Bake 1 hour until knife
inserted in center comes out clean.

8 servings

ENTREE

English Muffins
with Mushrooms &
Canadian Bacon

•

6 tablespoons butter, divided
1 pound Canadian bacon, sliced
  ¼-inch thick
½ pound mushrooms, sliced
2 medium potatoes, peeled &
  sliced very thin
2 cups light cream
½ teaspoon summer savory
  ground pepper
  Toasted, buttered English muffins

In a large pan, sauté bacon in
2 tablespoons butter over medium
heat, 2-3 minutes. Remove to platter. To same pan, add 2 tablespoons butter. Sauté mushrooms a
few minutes. Remove to platter.
Sauté potatoes in remaining butter,
about 5 minutes. Return bacon &
mushrooms to pan. Add cream,
savory & several grinds of pepper.
Simmer, covered, 10 minutes until
potatoes are tender. Remove cover.
Simmer several minutes to reduce
sauce slightly. Serve over muffins.

4 servings

Mustard Ring

•

4 eggs
¾ cup sugar
1½ envelopes unflavored gelatin
1½ tablespoons dry mustard
½ teaspoon turmeric
¼ teaspoon salt
1 cup water
½ cup flavored white vinegar, tarragon, champagne, dill, etc.
1 cup heavy cream

Beat eggs in top of double boiler over medium-low heat. Mix sugar & gelatin. Add to eggs. Add mustard, turmeric, salt, water & vinegar. Cook until thick. Cool. Stir in unwhipped cream. Pour into 4 cup ring mold. Chill. To serve fill center with fruit, steamed vegetables or cherry tomatoes.

8-10 servings

Pictured page 62.

Blueberry Coffee Cake

•

½ cup butter, softened
1 cup sugar
2 eggs
2 cups flour, sifted
2 teaspoons baking powder
½ teaspoon baking soda
½ teaspoon salt
½ cup buttermilk
½ teaspoon vanilla
1 cup fresh blueberries
1 tablespoon sugar
1 teaspoon cinnamon

Preheat oven to 375°F. Butter 9x5-inch loaf pan.

Cream butter & sugar. Add eggs. Mix well. Add flour, baking powder, baking soda & salt alternately with the buttermilk. Add vanilla. Beat until smooth. Fold in blueberries. Combine sugar & cinnamon. Sprinkle on top of batter. Bake 55 minutes. Let rest 10 minutes. Remove from pan. Cool. Slice & serve with butter if desired.

1 9x5-inch loaf

Glazed Chocolate Chip Cheesecake

•

1¼ cups chocolate wafer cookie crumbs
⅓ cup butter, melted
3 packages (8-ounces each) cream cheese, softened
¾ cup sugar
3 eggs
1 teaspoon vanilla
1 cup semi-sweet chocolate chips, coarsely chopped in blender or processor

Glaze:
½ cup unsweetened cocoa powder
½ cup sugar
½ cup heavy cream
¼ cup unsalted butter, cut into pieces

chocolate leaves or other garnish

Preheat oven to 450°F.

Mix crumbs & butter. Press into bottom of 8 or 9-inch springform pan. Set aside.

Beat cream cheese & sugar at medium speed until blended. Add eggs one at a time, mixing well after each addition. Add chocolate chips & vanilla. Pour into prepared pan. Bake 10 minutes. Reduce heat to 250°F. Continue baking 35 minutes. Loosen cake from edges of pan. Cool before removing sides. Chill.

Combine glaze ingredients in top of double boiler over simmering water. Stir until smooth & shiny, 5 minutes. Cool 5 minutes, stirring occasionally. Pour over cake, tilting to cover evenly. Use spatula to spread over top and sides. Refrigerate several hours. Decorate with chocolate leaves.

10-12 servings

What a great Saturday in May to celebrate with a Derby Party Brunch. Start with Mimosas & end on the eloquent note of a traditional Mint Julep. Spring bouquets of flowers & bright napkins coordinated with jockey-colors set the tempo. Fashion the Mustard Ring into a horse-shoe shape. The do-ahead menu combined with buffet service makes entertaining a breeze.

*Designed to warm up
guests post-ice skating or
cross-country skiing.
Dust off the fondue pot &
gather 'round the fireplace
for an informal, one-table,
help-yourself, food fest.
Don't forget the long-
handled forks to spear
bread cubes.*
❦

Spiced
Cranberry Apple
Glögg

•

   2 quarts cranberry apple juice
6-7 cups Burgundy wine
1½ cups water
   ½ cup sugar
   2 cinnamon sticks
   8 whole cloves
      raisins, almonds, & orange
      slices, garnish

Combine ingredients in large Dutch
oven. Heat gently 1 hour. Do not
boil. Keeps on low heat several hours.
Garnish each mug before serving.

25-30 servings

Picante Crab
Fondue

•

⅓ pound sharp cheddar cheese,
   grated
1 package (8 ounces) cream cheese
1 cup cooked king crab
¼ cup light cream
½ teaspoon white wine
   Worcestershire sauce
1 small clove garlic, finely chopped
⅛ teaspoon cayenne pepper or
   crushed red pepper
   French bread

In double boiler, over medium-low
heat, combine cheeses. Stir constantly until blended & smooth. Add
remaining ingredients. Stir
occasionally. Serve hot from fondue
pot. If fondue thickens, add a little
cream. Serve with French bread cubes.

6 servings

Pictured page 118.

Sausage
Fondue

•

½ pound bulk Italian sausage
1 small onion, chopped
1 clove garlic, minced
1 can (8 ounces) tomato sauce
2 tablespoons cornstarch
¼ cup water
¼ teaspoon salt
⅛ teaspoon pepper
1¾ teaspoons oregano, crushed
¾ pound sharp cheddar cheese,
   grated
½ pound mozzarella cheese, grated
   Italian bread

Brown sausage, onion & garlic. Drain
fat. Mix cornstarch & water. Add to
meat with tomato sauce, oregano, salt
& pepper. Stir. As mixture thickens,
add cheese, ½ cup at a time, stirring
after each addition. Serve from a
fondue pot with cubes of Italian bread.

6 servings

•

*A simple robust menu for
any season. Dress the
occasion up or down to
fit your mood. Adjust
the seafood in the
Manicotti & filling for
the Puff to fit your budget.
The Puff can be an
appetizer, side dish or
main course, depending
on how you slice it.*
❦

Serbian Cheese & Pepper Canapés

•

1 cup butter, softened
4-ounces feta cheese, crumbled
1½-ounces cream cheese, softened
2 large green peppers
1 large red pepper
2 tablespoons vinegar & oil dressing
2 cloves garlic, minced
1 teaspoon salt
½ teaspoon sugar
⅛ teaspoon crushed red pepper
 thinly sliced firm bread,
 cut into canapés

Beat butter & cheeses until light
& fluffy. Cover & refrigerate up to
1 week.

Place whole peppers on oven rack
closest to broiler. Broil 10-15 minutes,
turning every 3-4 minutes. Blisters
will appear on outer skin. Plunge
peppers into cold water. Remove
outer skins, seeds & stems. Chop
peppers finely. Mix dressing, garlic,
salt, sugar & crushed red pepper.
Add peppers. Cover & refrigerate at
least 1 hour, no longer than 24 hours.

To serve, bring cheese to room temperature. Spread cheese on bread
canapés, crusty French bread or rye
crackers. Top with pepper mixture.

12-15 servings

Seafood Manicotti

•

1 tablespoon olive oil
1 pound mixed seafood, shellfish
 & fish fillets

Sauce:
2 cloves garlic
1 can (15 ounces) tomato sauce
1 can (6 ounces) tomato paste
1¼ cups water
2 teaspoons basil
1 teaspoon oregano
1 tablespoon chopped parsley
 salt & pepper

½ pound mozzarella cheese, grated
½ cup cottage cheese
4 tablespoons grated Parmesan
 cheese
2 eggs, slightly beaten
2 tablespoons butter, softened
½ teaspoon salt
½ teaspoon pepper
14 manicotti noodles, uncooked
 extra grated Parmesan cheese

Lightly sauté a selection of seafood
in olive oil. Remove from pan.
Set aside.

Add garlic, tomato sauce, tomato
paste, water, basil, oregano, parsley,
salt & pepper to pan. Simmer 20-30
minutes. Set aside.

Combine cheeses, eggs, butter, salt &
pepper. Add sautéed seafood. Stuff
noodles with mixture. Arrange in
bottom of buttered 13x9-inch pan.
Cover with sauce. Sprinkle with
additional Parmesan cheese. Cover
tightly with foil. Bake at 350°F. 45
minutes.

May be assembled in advance &
frozen. Bake, if frozen, 10 minutes
longer.

6 servings

Double Pizza Puff

•

½ pound puff pastry sheets
1 can (11 ounces) pizza sauce
 sliced ham or prosciutto
 mushrooms
 olives
 capers
 pepperoni
 onions, etc.
 grated provolone cheese
 grated mozzarella cheese
1 egg, beaten

Roll out each pastry sheet to twice
its length & width. Spread one-third
of the sauce on the lower half of the
pastry within ½ inch of the edge.

Be creative, cover sauce with layers
of your favorite pizza ingredients.
Brush edges of pastry with egg. Fold
top over ingredients. Seal. Use fork
to pierce holes in top. Bake 425°F.
15-20 minutes until golden brown.
Cool 5 minutes. Cut into desired
serving portions. Smaller pieces for
hors d'oeuvres, larger wedges for
entrée servings or side dishes.

6 servings per puff

MENU

Assorted Pickled
Peppers, Olives
& Relishes

Cocktail Pita Bread
with
Feta-Cream Cheese

Borscht

**Irish
Soda
Bread**

**Apple
Brownies**

*French Côtes-du-Rhône
Châteauneuf-du-Pape*

•

*Winter picnics are terrific
after a few miles have
slid under your skis.
Port the Borscht in a
1-gallon thermos. Serve
in hot cups. Wrap the
warm Soda Bread in
newspapers & foil.*

Borscht

•

3 pounds chuck steak, cut in large
   pieces
  water
1½ cups cocktail vegetable juice
  2 bay leaves
  ¼ teaspoon basil
  1 large clove garlic, crushed
  1 tablespoon salt
  6 peppercorns
  6 cups water
  4 carrots, chopped
  4 stalks celery, chopped
  1 medium onion, chopped
  1 large leek, chopped
  1 small green pepper, chopped
  1 can (16 ounces) stewed tomatoes
  ½ cup lemon juice
  2 tablespoons sugar
  1 small cabbage, shredded
  2 large potatoes, peeled & chopped
  2 pounds cooked, chopped beets,
    reserve liquid
  ½ cup minced fresh parsley
  3 tablespoons minced fresh dill
  1 pint sour cream

Put meat in a large kettle. Cover with
water. Bring to a boil. Skim surface.
Add vegetable juice, basil, bay leaves,
garlic, salt, peppercorns & remaining water. Bring to boil. Add carrots,
celery, onion & leek. Cover. Simmer
1¼ hours. Add green pepper, tomatoes, lemon juice & sugar. Cook 30
minutes. Add cabbage & potatoes.
Cook 25 minutes. Add beets &
juice, parsley & dill. Simmer 20
minutes. Serve hot with a dollop
of sour cream.

12-15 servings

Irish Soda Bread

•

  4 cups flour
  ¾ cup sugar
  1 tablespoon baking powder
  1 teaspoon salt
  1 teaspoon baking soda
  ⅛ teaspoon cream of tartar
  ½ cup butter, melted
  1 cup raisins
  1 teaspoon caraway seed
1½ cups buttermilk
  2 eggs

Preheat oven to 325°F. Butter a 9-inch
round pan or casserole.

Sift flour, sugar, baking powder, salt,
baking soda & cream of tartar into
a large bowl. Add butter. Blend until
mixture crumbles. Add raisins &
caraway seeds. Mix buttermilk &
eggs. Combine with dry ingredients. Mix
well. Form into a round loaf. Place
in prepared pan. Bake 1 hour & 15
minutes. Remove from pan. Cool on
wire rack.

1 loaf

Apple Brownies

•

  1 cup butter
  ½ teaspoon salt
  2 cups sugar
  2 eggs, beaten
  2 cups flour
  1 teaspoon baking powder
  1 teaspoon baking soda
  1 teaspoon cinnamon
  2 cups peeled, sliced tart apples
  ½ cup chopped walnuts
    ice cream

Preheat oven to 325°F. Butter a
9x9-inch pan.

Cream butter, salt, sugar & eggs. Add
flour, baking powder, baking soda
& cinnamon. Mix in apples & nuts.
Spread in pan. Bake 45 minutes.
Serve warm, à la mode.

12 servings

*California
Sauvignon Blanc
or
French White
Bordeaux Graves*

•

*Entertaining in style,
from salad to torte. Polish
your finery & set
the table with elegance, for
an intimate dinner,
hosting the boss, or
a gathering of favorite
friends. Write the menu
with guests' names on
stiff white stock
to use as place cards.*
❧

Salade
St. Simeon

•

2 small heads bibb lettuce,
    torn into bite-size pieces
1 head radicchio, torn into
    bite-size pieces
1 bunch watercress, stems removed

Dressing:
4 tablespoons extra-virgin olive oil
4 tablespoons balsamic vinegar
    salt & pepper

8-12 slices (¼-inch thick) French
    bread, toasted
8-12 slices goat cheese (chèvre)

Combine greens in bowl. Chill. Mix
dressing ingredients. Just before
serving, melt goat cheese on top of
toasted bread under broiler. Toss
greens with dressing. Serve on
individual salad plates topped
with toasts.

4-6 servings

Pictured page 57.

Shrimp
&
Wild Rice en Cocotte

•

1 cup wild rice
5¼ cups chicken stock, divided
¼ cup butter
1 onion, chopped
1 pound mushrooms, sliced
1 clove garlic, minced
2 tablespoons flour
½ cup dry white wine
½ teaspoon salt
    fresh ground pepper
1 teaspoon tarragon, crushed
1½ pounds cooked, shelled shrimp

Place rice & 4 cups stock in pan.
Bring to boil. Simmer, covered,
45-50 minutes. Uncover. Fluff with
fork. Simmer 5 minutes. Pour off
any excess stock.

Sauté onion, mushrooms & garlic in
butter 5 minutes. Add flour. Stir
over medium heat 3 minutes. Add
remaining stock & wine gradually.
Stir until slightly thickened. Add salt,
pepper & tarragon. Combine rice,
mushroom mixture & shrimp. Pour
into 2-quart casserole. Bake,
covered, 350°F. 20-30 minutes until
heated through. Do not overbake.

6 servings

Hungarian
Nut Torte

•

⅔ cup ground walnuts
⅓ cup ground almonds
⅓ cup toasted, ground hazelnuts
¼ cup sugar
6 tablespoons unsalted butter,
    melted

Filling:
1¼ cups packed brown sugar
2 eggs
1 egg yolk
¾ teaspoon baking powder
1¾ cups ground walnuts
1 cup flaked coconut
½ cup flour
3 tablespoons raspberry, hazelnut,
    or almond liqueur, divided
    whipped cream, optional

Preheat oven to 350°F. Butter a 9-inch
springform pan & dust with ground
almonds.

In a bowl, combine walnuts, almonds,
hazelnuts, sugar & butter. Press into
prepared pan. Set aside.

In same bowl, beat brown sugar, eggs,
the yolk, & baking powder. Stir in
walnuts, coconut & flour. Add 1 tablespoon liqueur of your choice. Pour
filling into crust. Bake torte 30-35
minutes until set & dark golden
brown. Brush top of hot torte with
remaining liqueur. Let cool in pan
on rack. Garnish with whipped
cream, if desired.

10-12 servings

Pictured page 116.

Bermuda Triangles

•

1 package (8 ounces) cream
   cheese, softened
2 teaspoons milk
½ teaspoon prepared horseradish
¼ teaspoon salt
¼ teaspoon pepper
1 cup cooked, flaked crab
1 cup small cooked shrimp
2 scallions, finely chopped
4 tablespoons ground almonds
1 package frozen phyllo pastry,
   thawed
½ cup butter, melted

Combine cream cheese, milk, horse-radish, salt & pepper. Fold in crab, shrimp, scallions & almonds.

Keep phyllo sheets covered with damp towel as you work. Brush 1 sheet with melted butter. Top with another sheet. Brush with butter. Top with a third sheet. Divide into 6 strips & cut in half. Place 1 teaspoon filling at one end of each strip. Fold into triangles as for a flag. Repeat with remaining sheets & filling. Place triangles on baking sheet. Butter the tops. Bake at 400°F. 10-12 minutes until golden. May be frozen before baking. Store triangles in plastic bags until needed.

30 triangles

Green Chili Gougère

•

¾ cup water
6 tablespoons butter
¾ cup flour, sifted
3 eggs
   grated Parmesan cheese

Filling:
1 package (8 ounces) cream
   cheese, softened
2 tablespoons minced onion
1 can (4 ounces) chopped ripe
   olives
1 can (4 ounces) chopped green
   chilies

Preheat oven to 400°F.

In a saucepan heat water & butter to boiling. Add flour all at once. Cook, stirring until mixture forms a ball that leaves the sides of the pan. Remove from heat. Add eggs, one at a time, beating vigorously after each addition. Drop by teaspoonfuls onto baking sheet. Sprinkle each with Parmesan cheese. Bake 35-40 minutes until puffy & dry.

Beat cream cheese until light & fluffy. Stir in onion, olives & chilies. Just before serving, split puffs in half. Fill with 1 teaspoon filling. Puffs can be baked in advance & frozen in airtight bags.

3 dozen

Lime Marinated Shrimp

•

¾ cup mayonnaise
2 tablespoons fresh lime juice
1 small onion, sliced very thinly
   dash white wine Worcestershire
   sauce
1 pound cooked, peeled shrimp
   snipped chives & minced parsley
   lime slices

Combine mayonnaise, lime juice, onion & Worcestershire. Gently stir in shrimp. Chill at least 24 hours. Serve garnished with chives, parsley & lime slices.

4-6 servings

Avocado Stuffed Tomatoes

•

1 pint red or yellow cherry
  tomatoes
1 large ripe avocado
2 scallions, minced including
  greens
1 tablespoon lemon juice
½ teaspoon ground cumin
  hot pepper sauce
4 slices crisp-cooked bacon,
  crumbled

Remove a thin slice from top of
each tomato. Scoop out pulp.
Drain, upside down on paper toweling 30 minutes. Mash avocado
coarsely with fork. Stir in scallions,
lemon juice, cumin & hot pepper
sauce. Add more or less lemon,
cumin & hot pepper sauce to taste.
Fill tomatoes with avocado mixture.
Top with bacon pieces.

24 servings

Sesame Wafers

•

2 cups butter, softened
1½ cups sugar
3 cups flour
1 cup toasted sesame seed
2 cups shredded coconut
½ cup finely chopped almonds

In large bowl, cream butter & sugar
until light & fluffy. Beat in flour.
Stir in sesame seed, coconut &
almonds until well mixed. Dough
will be very stiff. Divide dough into
thirds. Place on long sheet of wax
paper. Shape into roll. Wrap &
refrigerate until firm. Cut into
¼-inch slices. Place on baking
sheets. Bake at 300°F. 30 minutes
until slightly brown. Remove
immediately.

14 dozen

Three-Step Dark Chocolate Truffles

•

1 package (6 ounces) semi-sweet
  chocolate chips
½ cup orange juice
3 tablespoons light rum
1 package (8½ ounces) chocolate
  wafer cookies, crushed
3 cups sifted powdered sugar,
  divided
1 cup finely chopped walnuts
1 container (4 ounces) chocolate
  jimmies
1-1½ tablespoons water
  unsweetened cocoa, optional

Melt chocolate chips in top of
double boiler. Remove from heat.
Add orange juice & rum. Stir. Add
crushed chocolate wafers. Stir in 2
cups powdered sugar & nuts. Blend
well. Cover. Chill 2 hours.

Roll pieces of dough into 1-inch
balls. Roll ball in jimmies, pressing
firmly as you roll. Place on baking
sheet. Chill overnight. Blend
remaining powdered sugar & 1-1½
tablespoons water to make glaze.
Add cocoa to taste, if desired. Dip
chilled chocolate balls halfway into
glaze to coat top.

4 dozen

*This menu is bound to be
a hit With-or-Without-
the-Pool for a summer
cocktail buffet party.
Start early to enjoy the
sunset. Enjoy dreamy
Latin music borrowed
from the library.*

Hot & Spicy Shrimp Dip

•

2 packages (8 ounces each) cream cheese
¼ pound chopped, cooked shrimp
¼ cup chopped onion
1 tomato, peeled, seeded & chopped
3 pickled banana peppers, seeded & chopped
1-2 cloves garlic, finely chopped

Gently heat ingredients in top of double boiler. When hot, pour into chafing dish. Serve with tortilla chips or garlic melba rounds.

3½ cups

Marinated Beef Cocktail Sandwiches

•

Marinade:
1 cup soy sauce
½ cup dry sherry
⅓ cup olive oil
3 cloves garlic, minced
1 tablespoon grated, peeled fresh ginger root, or 2 teaspoons ground ginger

3-4 pounds beef top round or sirloin tip roast

Combine marinade ingredients. Place meat in heavy-duty plastic bag. Pour marinade into bag. Seal bag & place in bowl. Marinate beef, refrigerated, 48 hours. Turn bag several times each day. Remove from refrigerator 1 hour before roasting. Place beef in roasting pan. Bake 325°F. 1-2 hours to desired doneness. Baste with marinade 3-4 times while roasting. Cool. Refrigerate several hours. Slice or shave meat. Serve cold on cocktail buns.

40 servings

California Ham

•

1 whole or boneless ham, any size or variety

Marinade:
2 large oranges, quartered
2 cups dry white wine
6 dried hot chili peppers, crushed
20 peppercorns
1 cup chopped celery leaves
2 carrots, sliced
½ cup chopped parsley

Pierce ham all over with skewer. Place in heavy-duty plastic bag. Squeeze juice from oranges into the bag. Add the squeezed quarters & remaining marinade ingredients to the bag. Seal. Place in bowl. Refrigerate several days, turning occasionally. Score ham & place in roasting pan. Bake at 325°F. until heated through. Baste with marinade several times. Have guests slice their own to put in ham buns or in tiny cornbread muffins. Spicy & delicious. Number of servings varies according to ham size. Ask the butcher.

Pictured page 114.

Lima-Green Bean Bake

•

Sauce:
   6 tablespoons butter
   2 tablespoons flour
   1 teaspoon salt
   ¼ teaspoon pepper
      dash cayenne
   ¼ teaspoon Worcestershire sauce
   1 cup light cream
   ½ cup grated Parmesan cheese

1½ cups french-cut green beans
1½ cups baby lima beans

Preheat oven to 300°F. Butter a 1½-quart casserole.

Melt butter in saucepan. Add flour, salt, pepper, cayenne & Worcestershire. Cook 3 minutes. Add cream. When sauce thickens, add Parmesan. Stir until melted. Alternate layers of vegetables & sauce in casserole. Bake, uncovered, 1 hour. Best thing anyone did to a lima.

4-6 servings

Romaine Salad with Brewers Dressing

•

Dressing:
   ⅔ cup beer
   ⅔ cup vegetable oil
   1 teaspoon paprika
   ¼ teaspoon salt
   1 clove garlic, minced
   1 tablespoon celery seed
   1 tablespoon mustard seed
   1 tablespoon stone-ground mustard
      dash hot pepper sauce
   2 tablespoons brown sugar
   2 tablespoons Dijon-style mustard

   romaine lettuce, grated cheddar cheese, sunflower seeds & finely shredded red onions

Combine dressing ingredients in a jar. Shake vigorously. Use dressing within 3 days. Serve with salad ingredients according to number of guests.

1¾ cups

Mocha Fudge Cake

•

   ½ cup strong coffee or espresso
   8-ounces sweet chocolate
   1 cup sugar
   1 cup unsalted butter
   4 eggs

   ¼ cup red currant jelly, melted

Frosting:
   1 cup heavy cream
   ¼ cup powdered sugar
   ¼ teaspoon vanilla

Preheat oven to 350°F. Line a 1-quart soufflé dish or charlotte mold with well-buttered foil.

In a heavy saucepan heat coffee, chocolate, sugar & butter until chocolate melts. Beat in eggs, one at a time, incorporating well after each addition. Pour into prepared pan. Bake 30 minutes until top is crisp & center does not look set. Cool & refrigerate at least 24 hours. Before serving invert cake onto decorative plate. Remove foil. Brush with currant jelly. Refrigerate 15 minutes. Whip cream with powdered sugar & vanilla. Frost cake. Do not worry about leftovers.

8-10 servings

A New Year's All-Day Football Party couldn't be more delectable. Spread the table with this bountiful array of crowd-pleasing offerings & root for your favorite teams.

MENU

**Broccoli
Stuffed
Game Hens**

**Wild Rice
Pilaf**

**Tomato Onion
Summer
Salad**

Parmesan
Monkey Bread

Chocolate Fudge Cake
&
Strawberries

*California Red
Sonoma Pinot Noir*

•

*Game hens are the perfect
entrée for buffets. Make
extra wild rice for the
stuffing when making the
Pilaf. Seating can be a
problem for large
groups. Set up card tables
anywhere there is space
& cover with
tablecloths, a single
candle & a bud vase.*
❧

Broccoli
Stuffed
Game Hens

•

1 small bunch broccoli, trimmed
  into small flowerets
1 cup cooked wild rice
½ cup grated Swiss cheese
  salt & pepper
4 game hens
2 tablespoons butter, melted

Preheat oven to 375°F.

Steam broccoli 5 minutes until crisp-tender. Drain & cool slightly. Combine broccoli, rice & cheese. Salt & pepper inside of hens. Stuff with broccoli mixture. Brush hens with butter. Bake on a rack in baking pan 1¼-1½ hours. For variation, chop giblets & add to broccoli mixture with ½ teaspoon thyme.

4 servings

Wild Rice
Pilaf

•

½ cup wild rice, cook according to
  package directions
1 cup long grain rice, cook
  according to package directions
1 bunch scallions, thinly sliced
½ pound mushrooms, sliced
2 tablespoons butter
¼ cup light soy sauce

Preheat oven to 350°F. Butter a 1½-quart casserole.

Sauté onions & mushrooms in butter 5-7 minutes. Add soy sauce & rices. Mix well. Place in casserole. Bake 20 minutes.

8 servings

Tomato & Onion
Summer
Salad

•

1 clove garlic
4 ripe tomatoes, thinly sliced
1 Bermuda onion, thinly sliced
1 tablespoon fresh oregano leaves
  salt & pepper
4 tablespoons vegetable oil
1 tablespoon tarragon vinegar
  freshly grated asiago cheese

Rub salad bowl with garlic clove. Mince the garlic & add to tomatoes, onions, oregano, salt & pepper. Toss with oil & vinegar. Chill 2 hours. Sprinkle with cheese before serving. For variation, add fresh salad pepper strips, sliced cucumbers, zucchini &/or summer squash & dress with balsamic vinegar & oil. Refreshing & crunchy.

4 servings

Ethnic Gatherings

heritage themes & American regional

*Serve Fajitas in heated,
little enamelware frying pans
with bright bandana
napkins tied on the handles.*
❧

"Gringo" Chile Relleno Casserole

•

1 pound cheddar cheese, grated
16-ounces chopped green chilies
1 pound Monterey Jack cheese, grated
3 cups light cream
4 eggs, beaten
¼ cup cornmeal
1 teaspoon salt
1 teaspoon Worcestershire sauce
1 cup red picante sauce cooked & thickened with 1 tablespoon cornstarch & 1 tablespoon water

Preheat oven to 350°F. Butter a 13x9-inch pan.

Layer cheddar cheese, green chilies, & Jack cheese, in order, into prepared pan. Blend cream, eggs, cornmeal, salt & Worcestershire sauce. Pour over layers of cheese & chilies. Top with picante sauce. Bake 40 minutes. Cut into squares. Ole!

10-12 Servings

Tex-Mex Fajitas

•

2 pounds flank or skirt steaks

Marinade:
½ cup olive oil
¼ cup red wine vinegar
⅓ cup fresh lime juice
⅓ cup chopped onion
1 teaspoon sugar
1 teaspoon Mexican oregano
salt & pepper
¼ teaspoon ground cumin
3 cloves garlic, minced

6 large flour tortillas

Toppings:
   Onion slices
   Green & red pepper strips
   Chopped tomatoes
   Shredded lettuce
   Guacamole
   Sour cream
   Picante sauce

Tenderize the steak. Combine marinade ingredients. Add steaks, coat evenly. Cover & refrigerate overnight. When ready to serve, grill steak over hot coals, preferably mesquite, 4-5 minutes each side. Remove steaks. In a large skillet, grill fresh onion & pepper slices. Slice steaks into thin strips. Fill warm tortillas with steak, onions, peppers, tomatoes, lettuce, guacamole, sour cream, & picante sauce. Wrap tortilla around filling. Serve in skillets. May also be made with chicken breast. Mamacita—Que Bueno!

6 servings

Texas Sesquicentennial Praline Pound Cake

•

1 cup butter, softened
½ cup vegetable shortening
1 pound dark brown sugar
5 eggs
3 cups flour, divided
½ teaspoon baking powder
¼ teaspoon baking soda
¾ cup milk
2 cups chopped pecans
2 teaspoons pecan-flavored extract or vanilla

Preheat oven to 325°F. Butter & flour a 10-inch tube or Bundt pan.

Cream butter & shortening. Gradually add sugar, beating until light & fluffy. Add eggs one at a time, beating after each addition. Sift 2½ cups flour, baking powder & soda. Add to creamed mixture alternately with milk. Dredge pecans in remaining ½ cup flour. Stir into batter. Add extract. Pour into prepared pan. Bake 1 hour & 15 minutes, until toothpick inserted in center comes out clean. It will be very dark brown. Cool in pan 15 minutes. Remove from pan. Cool. Delicious with ice cream. Cake freezes well.

16-24 servings

MENU

**Linguini
with
Lemon Clam Sauce**

Mozzarella
Garlic Bread

**Cauliflower Salad
with
Black Olives**

**Waffle
Cookies**

Espresso
with
Orange Peel

*Italian
White Frascati*

•

*Family or friends can
enjoy the pleasures of the
Italian table where food
"satisfies the stomach
and respects the mind."
Savory but simple,
rich but not too heavy, the
spirit is light & casual.
Use fresh fruit as the
centerpiece to accompany
the Waffle Cookies.*

❦

Linguini with Lemon Clam Sauce

•

½ cup butter, divided
3 tablespoons olive oil
2 cloves garlic, minced
1 shallot, minced
2 cans (8 ounces each) minced
  clams, drained, reserve liquid
3 tablespoons fresh lemon juice
1 tablespoon chopped parsley
2 teaspoons grated lemon peel
¼ teaspoon ground pepper
1 bay leaf
1 pound linguini, cooked
  & drained
  grated Parmesan cheese

Heat 3 tablespoons of the butter &
the oil in a heavy pan. Sauté garlic
& shallot until tender. Add the liquid from clams, lemon juice, parsley, lemon peel, pepper & bay leaf.
Simmer until liquid is reduced to
1 cup. Remove bay leaf. Stir in clams.
Heat thoroughly. Add remaining
butter. Stir. Serve sauce over linguini.
Sprinkle with Parmesan.

4-6 servings

Cauliflower Salad with Black Olives

•

1 head cauliflower, broken into
  large flowerets
6 tablespoons olive oil
3 tablespoons white wine vinegar
1 teaspoon dry mustard
½ teaspoon fresh ground pepper
1 tablespoon capers
1 tablespoon minced parsley
1 jar (2 ounces) chopped pimientos
3 scallions, sliced
½ teaspoon salt
½ cup sliced, pitted black olives

Drop cauliflowerets into boiling
salted water. Cook 5 minutes. Drain
& rinse under cold water. In the bottom of a round bowl, reassemble
flowerets into a head, stems up. Combine oil, vinegar, mustard, pepper,
capers, parsley, pimientos, scallions
& salt. Pour over cauliflower. Cover
& chill at least 2 hours or overnight.
To serve, drain off marinade into a
small bowl. Place serving dish on top
of cauliflower & invert. Add olives
to marinade. Spoon over cauliflower.

6 servings

Waffle Cookies

•

1½ cups butter, softened
1¾ cups sugar
5 eggs, separated
1 teaspoon vanilla, anise, lemon,
  orange, or other extract
2 teaspoons baking powder
5½ cups flour

  waffle iron

Cream butter & sugar in large bowl
until fluffy. Add egg yolks one at a
time. Beat well. Add vanilla or
extract. Combine flour & baking
powder. Add flour to egg mixture.
Beat egg whites until stiff. Fold into
batter until smooth. Form into
walnut-size balls. Bake in a waffle
iron until brown.

2½ dozen

*German
Rheinhessen
Spätlese*

•

*Nothing says "Milwaukee"
better than German food.
Embroidered tablecloth,
hock wine glasses, pretty
china, a loaf of rye bread
& plenty of butter set
the perfect tone. A
stein of beer & soft, hot
pretzels are faultless
preludes to gemütlichkeit—
an atmosphere of
warmth & fellowship.*

Rouladen of Beef

•

2 pounds thin round steak,
    pounded into 6-8 square pieces
    salt & pepper
    Dijon-style mustard
6-8 slices bacon
  1 medium onion, chopped
  ½ pound carrots, chopped
6-8 dill pickle spears
  2 tablespoons vegetable oil

Sprinkle meat with salt & pepper.
Spread each piece with 1 tablespoon
mustard. Lay 1 slice bacon across
each piece of meat. Top with
chopped onion, carrots & 1 spear
pickle. Roll up & secure with toothpick. Sauté rolls in oil until brown.
Add 1-inch water to pan. Simmer,
covered, 1½ hours until tender.
Thicken pan juices with cornstarch
if desired.

6 servings

Pictured page 176.

Rött Kraut

•

1 3-pound head red cabbage,
    finely shredded
2 large cooking apples,
    peeled & chopped
1 large onion, chopped
¼ cup sugar
¼ cup vinegar
6 slices crisp-cooked bacon,
    crumbled
2 tablespoons bacon drippings
1 teaspoon salt
    ground pepper
½ cup boiling water

In a large saucepan, combine all
ingredients. Add water. Bring mixture to a boil. Reduce heat. Let
simmer 1 hour.

8 servings

Püher Schnitten

•

¼ pound butter, softened
½ cup sugar
6 eggs, separated
¾ cup flour
1 teaspoon baking powder
    grated peel of ½ lemon

Topping:
1¼ cups sugar
3½ cups ground, toasted hazelnuts
    (filberts)
1 teaspoon vanilla

Preheat oven to 350°F.

Beat butter & sugar until light &
fluffy. Add egg yolks one at a time.
Add lemon peel, flour & baking
powder. Mix until smooth. Spread
into 13x9-inch pan.

Beat the egg whites until soft peaks
form. Gradually add sugar. Beat
until stiff. Fold in hazelnuts & vanilla.
Spread onto dough mixture. Bake
30 minutes. Cool. Cut into diamond
shapes.

3 dozen

*Yugoslavian
Red Prokupac*

•

*From Czechoslovakia to
the Adriatic coast,
Eastern Europe is well
represented in Milwaukee.
Church festivals are
celebrated with
customary gusto & with
foods like these. Serve
tiny glasses of clear
plum brandy to whet
the appetite!*

Ghivetch

•

1 cup thinly sliced carrots
1 cup sliced green beans
1 cup diced potatoes
½ cup diced celery
2 medium tomatoes, cut into wedges
1 small yellow squash, sliced
1 small zucchini, sliced
1 small Bermuda onion, chopped
½ head cauliflower,
   broken into flowerets
¼ cup green pepper strips
¼ cup red pepper strips
½ cup green peas

Sauce:
1 cup beef stock
⅓ cup olive oil
3 cloves garlic, minced
½ bay leaf, crumbled
½ teaspoon tarragon
2 teaspoons salt
1 teaspoon ground pepper

Preheat oven to 350°F. Combine vegetables in 13x9-inch pan.

In a saucepan, boil sauce ingredients. Pour over vegetables. Cover with aluminum foil. Bake 1 hour.

8-10 servings

Pictured page 2.

Patica

•

4 cups flour
1 teaspoon salt
½ pound pure lard,
   room temperature
1 cup warm milk
2 tablespoons sugar
1 package yeast
2 eggs, beaten

Filling:
3 pounds chopped pecans or
   walnuts
1 heaping cup crushed vanilla
   wafers
1 tablespoon cinnamon
2 cups butter, melted
8-ounces honey
1 cup packed brown sugar
9 eggs, beaten

In a large bowl, mix flour & salt. Cut in lard until uniformly crumbly. In a small bowl, combine milk, sugar & yeast. Add eggs. Mix flour & milk mixtures together to form dough. Cover tightly & chill overnight.

Preheat oven to 350°F. Butter 2 10-inch tube pans.

Combine pecans, wafer crumbs & cinnamon. Mix melted butter, honey & brown sugar. Add to pecan mixture. Add eggs. Mix well.

Remove dough from refrigerator. On a very large surface, roll dough ¼-inch thick, 4 feet wide. On one long side, spread filling mixture evenly up to the edges of dough. Working left to right, gently pull dough around filling with hands & begin rolling it up into a 3-inch diameter x 4-foot long roll. Divide into two sections. Place in prepared pans, patting edges of dough together where they meet. Cover & let rise in warm place 1 hour. Bake 1 hour. Let cool in pans. When completely cooled, remove from pans. Slice very thin to serve. Double wrap to freeze for up to 6 months.

25-30 servings per pan

Moravian Sugar Cake

•

2 packages quick-rise yeast
1 cup warm water
1 cup sugar
½ teaspoon salt
2 eggs, beaten
1½ cups butter, melted
1 cup hot mashed potatoes
5-6 cups sifted flour
1½ cups packed light brown sugar
1 tablespoon cinnamon

Butter 3 9-inch square or round cake pans.

Combine yeast & water. Let stand a few minutes. Mix together sugar, salt, eggs & 1 cup of the butter. Gradually beat in mashed potatoes. Add 1 cup of flour. Beat until smooth. Stir in yeast. Beat in enough remaining flour to form a light, soft dough. Cover & let rise until doubled, about 1½ hours.

Divide dough into 3 portions. Press evenly into prepared pans. Cover & let rise until doubled.

Preheat oven to 350°F.

Blend together brown sugar & cinnamon. Make indentations 1-inch apart on each cake. Sprinkle sugar mixture into each depression. Drizzle remaining ½ cup butter over top of cakes. Bake 20 minutes. Cakes freeze very well. Serve with plum sauce, or another fruit sauce if desired.

6-8 servings each cake

MENU

Hungarian Steak with Caper-Sour Cream Sauce

Potato Dumplings with Caraway Seed

Herbed Kohlrabi

Pickled Baby Beets

Traudl's Plum Küchen

Viennese Coffee

Hungarian Red Egri Bikavér "Bull's Blood"

The fare of this menu suggests a hearty family gathering on a Sunday night to celebrate a homecoming or a birthday. Italian plums come into season late summer. Plan ahead & have the Küchen in the freezer. The wine is ancient in Hungarian history & has symbolic masculine overtones. Offer a schnapps (brandy) as an apéritif.

Hungarian Steak with Caper-Sour Cream Sauce

•

2 pounds beef round steak, ¾-inch thick
  salt & pepper
2 tablespoons vegetable oil
3 medium carrots, bias-cut 2-inches thick
2 medium parsnips, cut into strips
½ cup sliced celery
1 cup boiling water
1 cup beef stock
½ teaspoon salt
  dash pepper
3 tablespoons flour
1 cup sour cream
2 tablespoons capers, drained
  paprika

Preheat oven to 350°F.

Cut steak into serving-size pieces. Season with salt & pepper. Heat oil in a skillet. Brown meat. Remove to shallow casserole or Dutch oven. Top with carrots, parsnips, & celery. Combine water, stock, salt & pepper. Pour mixture over steak & vegetables. Bake, covered, 1-1¼ hours. Remove meat & vegetables to platter. Keep warm. To the pan juices, add water if necessary to make 1 cup liquid. Combine flour & sour cream. Stir into pan juices. Add capers. Cook 2 minutes & stir until bubbly. Serve on top of steak & vegetables. Sprinkle with paprika.

6 servings

Herbed Kohlrabi

•

2 tablespoons butter
1½ pounds kohlrabi, cut into julienne strips
⅔ cup chicken stock
1½ tablespoons sugar
½ teaspoon salt
¼ teaspoon pepper
1 tablespoon chopped parsley
1 teaspoon dried chervil

In a skillet, heat butter. Add kohlrabi, stock, sugar, salt & pepper. Bring mixture to boil. Reduce heat & simmer, covered, until tender but still crisp, 7 minutes. Increase heat to high. Cook, uncovered, stirring constantly until liquid evaporates & vegetable is glazed, 5 minutes. Add herbs. Serve at once. Carrots, turnips, or other root vegetables may be substituted.

4 servings

Traudl's Plum Küchen

•

20 Italian purple plums, pitted & quartered

Pastry:
2 cups flour
1 cup sugar
¾ cup unsalted butter, softened
1 egg
1 teaspoon vanilla
2 tablespoons milk

Custard:
2 egg yolks, beaten
1 tablespoon milk
4 tablespoons sugar

Streusel:
1¼ cups flour
¾ cup sugar
½ cup unsalted butter, softened
1 teaspoon grated lemon peel

  powdered sugar
  whipped cream, optional

Preheat oven to 400°F. Butter & flour 2 8-inch cake or springform pans.

Combine flour & sugar. Cut butter into flour mixture. Add egg, vanilla & milk. Add extra flour if necessary to make dough very smooth. Divide dough in half. Pat onto bottom & 1½-inches up sides of each pan. Place plums in pans.

Combine custard ingredients. Mix well. Pour onto plums. Combine streusel ingredients until crumbly. Top custard with streusel. Bake 10 minutes. Reduce heat to 375°F. Bake 35-40 minutes until golden brown. Cool on rack. Remove from cake pan. Dust with powdered sugar. Serve on cake plate with whipped cream if desired. Fresh peaches, cherries or blueberries may be substituted for plums.

10-12 servings

MENU

Miniature
Spring Rolls

Japanese
Beer

**Cress-Kiwi Salad
with
Pineapple Dressing**

Batayaki

Steamed Rice

Stir-Fried
Oriental
Vegetables

**Mandarin
Orange Cake**

*French Red
Côtes-du-Rhône*

*Sharpen your chopsticks.
Set the table with simple
elegance for this dinner
with an oriental flavor.
Use three flowers
representing earth, man
& sky with airy greens
for the centerpiece.
Plain white dinnerware
& pastel linens will
lighten the table.*

Cress-Kiwi Salad
with
Pineapple Dressing

•

2 large heads Boston lettuce,
  torn into bite-size pieces,
  reserve large outer leaves
2 bunches watercress, stems
  trimmed
1 large avocado, cut into
  1-inch cubes
2 tablespoons lemon juice
2 cups diagonally-sliced celery
4 kiwi fruit, sliced
¼ cup toasted sesame seed

Pineapple Dressing:
¾ cup vegetable oil
¼ cup unsweetened pineapple juice
1 teaspoon grated lemon peel
2 tablespoons lemon juice
1 tablespoon chopped fresh mint
¾ teaspoon salt
½ teaspoon dry mustard
  freshly ground pepper

Line a platter with the large outer
leaves of lettuce. Add torn lettuce
& cress. Toss avocado cubes with
lemon juice. Arrange avocado,
celery & kiwi on top of greens. Sprinkle with sesame seed. Cover & chill
until serving.

Combine dressing ingredients. Chill.
Before serving, gently toss salad
with dressing.

12 servings

Batayaki

•

½ cup butter
4 medium onions, thinly sliced
1 pound mushrooms, thinly
  sliced
2-2½ pounds top sirloin, trimmed
  & thinly sliced

Dipping Sauce:
  juice of 1 lemon
½ cup soy sauce, or amount equal
  to lemon juice

Melt butter in wok or deep skillet over
medium-high heat. Add onions.
Cook 10-15 minutes. Add mushrooms. Sauté briefly. Add meat. Cook
1-2 minutes, until meat is lightly
browned. Place on serving platter.

Combine lemon juice & soy for
dipping sauce. Serve with rice &
dipping sauce in small individual
bowls.

5-6 servings

Mandarin
Orange Cake

•

2 cups flour
2 cups sugar
2 teaspoons baking soda
½ teaspoon salt
2 eggs, beaten
2 cans (11 ounces each) mandarin
  oranges, drained
1 cup packed brown sugar
4 tablespoons milk
3 tablespoons butter

Preheat oven to 350°F. Butter &
flour 2 8-inch cake pans or 1
13x9-inch pan.

Sift flour, sugar, baking soda, & salt.
Add to beaten eggs. Add oranges.
Beat with mixer four minutes. Pour
batter into prepared pans. Bake 40
minutes. Mix brown sugar, milk &
butter in small saucepan. Bring to
a boil. Pour over hot cake right from
the oven. Delicious served with
whipped cream.

12-15 servings

*French
White
Entre-Deux-Mers*

•

The fish boil & Door County are Wisconsin's answer to Cape Cod & the clam bake. Working outdoors, usually behind a restaurant, the chef, a multi-talented person, plays accordion or fiddle when the fish basket goes into a pot over a roaring fire. Dramatically, the music stops, signaling the grand finale. Fuel is thrown onto the fire, allowing the water to boil over, removing the fish oils. The basket is lifted out of the water & whisked into the restaurant where the food is served buffet-style.

Door County Fish Boil

•

18 small new potatoes, scrubbed, unpeeled
18 small onions, peeled
12 whitefish steaks, 1-inch thick
cheesecloth
6-8 quarts water
1 cup salt
melted butter
lemon wedges
parsley

Large kettle with a lift-out basket

Tie potatoes & onions into a cheese-cloth bag. Tie fish in another cheesecloth bag. Fill kettle with water. Bring to rolling boil. Add ½ cup salt. Place potatoes-onions in basket. Place basket in kettle. Cook 10 minutes. Add remaining salt. Add fish to basket.

Cook 10 minutes. Skim surface. Lift basket from water. Drain well. Remove cheesecloth. Serve with butter & lemon. Sprinkle with parsley.

6 servings

Door County Cherry Crisp

•

3 tablespoons cornstarch
½ cup sugar
2½ cups pitted Door County tart cherries, including juice
1 cup brown sugar
1 cup flour
½ cup butter, melted
ice cream or sweetened whipped cream

Preheat oven to 350°F. Lightly butter an 8-inch square pan.

In a medium saucepan combine cornstarch, sugar & cherries. Simmer 7-10 minutes until thickened. Pour into prepared pan. Mix brown sugar, flour & butter until uniformly crumbly. Sprinkle evenly over cherries. Bake 25 minutes. Serve warm topped with ice cream or whipped cream.

6 servings

Lemon Tea Bread

•

1 cup butter, softened
1 cup sugar
5 large eggs
2 teaspoons grated lemon peel
2 cups flour
½ teaspoon baking powder
½ cup dried currants
2 tablespoons sugar

Preheat oven to 350°F. Butter & flour a 9x5-inch loaf pan.

In a bowl, cream butter & sugar until light & fluffy. Beat in eggs one at a time. Add lemon peel. Beat until smooth. Sift together flour & baking powder. Gradually add to butter mixture. Stir in currants. Pour batter into prepared pan. Bake 30 minutes. Sprinkle sugar evenly over top of loaf. Continue baking 30 minutes. Remove from oven. Cool on rack 5 minutes.

Remove from pan. Cool. Serve thinly sliced.

1 loaf

•

*The influence of immigrant
German families on
Milwaukee & Wisconsin
is apparent on our
tables. Distinctly winter
fare, the menu is
lightened with vegetables
to satisfy today's lighter
palate. The elegant
Auslese lends sophistication
for everyone's enjoyment.*
❦

Sauerbraten

•

Marinade:
2 cups vinegar
2 cups water
½ cup chopped onion
4 bay leaves
2 tablespoons paprika
4 cloves

3-5 pounds beef top or bottom round

1 cup flour, divided
4 tablespoons butter
½ cup sliced carrots
½ cup sliced onions
½ cup sliced celery
1 teaspoon thyme
  reserved marinade
1 cup water
½ cup Mosel wine
⅓ cup finely crushed ginger snaps
¼ cup brown sugar
1 teaspoon salt
  ground pepper

In a saucepan, heat marinade ingredients just to the boil. Place meat in non-metal dish. Pour on hot marinade. Marinate several days, turning meat once a day.

Remove meat. Pat dry with paper toweling. Strain marinade into bowl. Set aside.

Dredge beef in ½ cup flour. In a large pot, melt butter & brown meat on all sides. Add carrots, onions & celery. Cook 5 minutes, stirring vegetables. Add thyme & reserved marinade. Cover. Bake at 325°F. 3 hours.

Remove meat to platter. Keep warm. Strain cooking liquid into saucepan. Combine remaining flour with water. Stir into pan with wine & gingersnaps. Bring to boil. Add brown sugar, salt & pepper. Stir, until thickened & smooth. Slice meat accompanied with the sauce.

6-8 servings

Noodle
Kugel

•

½ cup butter, melted
3 eggs, beaten
1 cup sour cream
1 cup cottage cheese
1 can (8 ounces) crushed pineapple
8-ounces medium-wide egg
  noodles, parboiled 3 minutes,
  drained

Topping:
2 tablespoons butter, melted
2 tablespoons brown sugar
  dash cinnamon
4 tablespoons cornflake crumbs

Preheat oven to 350°F. Butter a 9-inch square pan.

Combine butter, eggs, sour cream, cottage cheese & pineapple. Add noodles. Pour into prepared pan.

Combine topping ingredients. Spread on top of noodle mixture. Bake 1 hour. Let rest 5 minutes. Cut into squares. May be assembled one day in advance. Bake just before serving. Or, use an 8-cup ring mold with topping added before the noodles. After baking, invert onto platter. Fill center with vegetables if desired.

6-8 servings

Cranberry
Ice

•

1 quart cranberries
2 cups water
3 cups sugar
2 tablespoons lemon juice
2 cups milk

Place cranberries in saucepan with water. Simmer 20 minutes. Cool a few minutes. In small batches, add to processor or blender. Purée. Pour into a sieve over a bowl. Strain & discard skins.

Add sugar to cranberry juice. Stir until dissolved. Add lemon juice & milk. Stir. Pour into a shallow glass or metal pan. Cover. Freeze until firm. Remove from freezer 30 minutes before serving. Scoop into parfait glasses.

10-12 servings

*Mix & match your most
colorful dinnerware
& napkins to create a
casual ambiance
for a festive South of
the Border menu.
Strata is great hot or
room temperature.*

South of the Border Strata

•

4 cups crushed nacho-flavored
    tortilla chips
2 cups grated Monterey Jack cheese
6 eggs beaten
2½ cups milk
1 can (4 ounces) chopped green
    chilies
¼ cup finely chopped onion
3 tablespoons chili salsa
½ teaspoon salt
¼ teaspoon hot pepper sauce
    cherry tomato halves, garnish

Butter a 1½-quart shallow baking dish.

Sprinkle tortilla chips & cheese
evenly over bottom of baking dish.
In a medium-size bowl, combine
eggs, milk, green chilies, onion,
salsa, salt & hot pepper sauce. Beat
well. Pour over cheese mixture.
Cover & refrigerate several hours or
overnight. Bake, uncovered, in a
preheated 325°F. oven 50-55 minutes,
until set & lightly browned. Let rest
10 minutes. Cut into squares. Top
each square with cherry tomato half
if desired.

6 servings

Lilian's Picadillo Cubano

•

3 tablespoons olive oil
1 large onion, chopped
2 cloves garlic, chopped
1½ pounds ground chuck or round
1 large green pepper, chopped
½ teaspoon basil
½ teaspoon oregano
½ teaspoon paprika
¾ teaspoon cayenne
1 can (8 ounces) tomato sauce
1 pound tomatoes, peeled, seeded,
    & chopped
½ cup raisins
½ cup sliced pimiento-stuffed olives
    salt & pepper

Heat olive oil in large skillet. Sauté
onion & garlic 5 minutes. Add meat
& brown 7 minutes. Add green pepper & spices. Simmer 15 minutes.
Add tomato sauce, tomatoes, raisins
& olives. Cook over low heat 1-1½
hours, until mixture is nearly dry.
Serve in flour tortillas.

6 servings

Frijoles Molidos Costa Rican Black Beans

•

1 pound black beans, washed &
    soaked overnight in 2 quarts water
2 tablespoons butter
1 large onion, finely chopped
1 large green pepper, finely
    chopped
2 cloves garlic, minced
2 quarts water
1½ tablespoons salt
6 slices bacon
1 can (4 ounces) chopped green
    chilies
½ teaspoon paprika
    fresh ground pepper
    grated farmers cheese or any
    fresh cheese

Drain beans. In a 4-quart pan, sauté
onion, green pepper, & garlic in
butter. Add beans, water, & salt. Simmer 2½-3 hours until beans are
soft. Mash or purée beans. In a large
pan, cook bacon until crisp.
Remove from pan. Crumble & set
aside. Add mashed bean mixture
to pan. Add chilies, paprika & pepper. Stir in reserved bacon. Just
before serving, sprinkle with grated
cheese. May be used as a side dish
or as an appetizer with nacho chips.
Reheats easily.

6-8 servings

*California
Petite Syrah*

•

*Bowls of olives & almonds
are perfect appetizers.
Serve the colorful salad
in large terra cotta
saucers. Use the bread
& fresh fruit as
the centerpiece.
The baked dinner makes
entertaining easy.*
❦

Feta
Mint
Salata

•

1 large head romaine lettuce,
　torn into bite-size pieces
2 medium tomatoes, cut into
　½-inch wedges
1 large cucumber, sliced
6 large radishes, sliced
1 small bunch scallions, sliced
6-ounces feta cheese, crumbled
4-ounces Kalamata olives
1 tablespoon chopped fresh mint

Dressing:
½ cup olive oil
3 tablespoons fresh lemon juice
2 tablespoons red wine vinegar
1 clove garlic, finely minced
1 teaspoon finely chopped fresh
　oregano

Place lettuce in large salad bowl. Add tomatoes, cucumbers, radishes, scallions, cheese & olives. Sprinkle with mint. Combine dressing ingredients. Mix well. Toss with salad. Salt & pepper to taste.

8 servings

Plaki
Baked Fish

•

1 onion, thinly sliced
1 clove garlic, minced
2 tablespoons olive oil
3 cups peeled, chopped plum
　tomatoes, with juice
1 tablespoon snipped fresh dill
1 tablespoon chopped fresh
　oregano
1 teaspoon chopped fresh basil
1 teaspoon ground pepper
2 pounds red snapper fillets

Preheat oven to 350°F. Butter a shallow 2-quart baking dish.

In a medium saucepan, sauté onion & garlic in olive oil until soft but not brown, 5 minutes. Add tomatoes, dill, oregano, basil & pepper. Stir. Cook 5 minutes. Place fillets, skin side down, in prepared baking dish. Pour tomato mixture over fish. Bake, uncovered, 20-25 minutes.

6 servings

Sliced Potatoes
with
Olive Oil & Herbs

•

8 medium potatoes, thinly sliced
⅓ cup olive oil
1 tablespoon fresh thyme leaves
1 tablespoon chopped fresh savory
1½-2 teaspoons salt
　freshly ground black pepper

Preheat oven to 425°F.

Dry potato slices on toweling. Place in large bowl. Mix olive oil, thyme, savory, salt & pepper. Toss with potato slices until each slice is well coated. Spread slices evenly on a baking sheet. Bake 35-40 minutes. Increase heat to 475°F. Cook 5 minutes longer until crisp & golden.

6 servings

MENU

**Italian
Veal Chops**

**Garden Pasta
with
Pesto Sauce**

Foccacia
Bread

**Ricotta
Coffee
Velvet**

Italian Red Pinot Grigio

•

*Basil can be purchased at
a farmer's market during
the summer to make
Pesto Sauce for year-long
enjoyment. The menu is
a snap to put together
for family or friends.*

Italian
Veal Chops

•

6 veal loin or rib chops
1 tablespoon olive oil
   salt & pepper
6 fresh sage leaves
1 cup beef stock

In a heavy skillet, brown veal chops
on both sides in oil. Season with
salt & pepper. Pour off any fat. Add
sage & stock. Simmer 20-25 minutes. Add several sliced potatoes,
onions & peppers for a one-pot meal.

6 servings

Garden Pasta
with
Pesto Sauce

•

Pesto Sauce:
  2 cups fresh basil leaves
½ cup olive oil
  2 tablespoons pine nuts or walnuts
  2 cloves garlic
  1 teaspoon salt
½ cup freshly grated Parmesan
    cheeese
  2 tablespoons freshly grated
    Romano
  2 tablespoons butter, softened

  1 pound pasta, cooked & drained
  1 cup tiny peas
  1 cup broccoli flowerets
  1 cup chopped tomatoes

In a blender or processor, combine
basil, olive oil, pine nuts, garlic &
salt. Whirl until smooth. Pour into
bowl. Beat in cheeses. When incorporated, add butter. Beat until well
blended. To freeze, do not add
cheeses or butter. Defrost & add
before serving.

To assemble, combine pasta with vegetables. Add Pesto. Toss well. Serve
with additional cheese.

6 servings

Ricotta
Coffee
Velvet

•

  1 pound ricotta cheese
  4-ounces plain or vanilla yogurt
1½ tablespoons instant coffee
  1 cup sugar
⅓ cup bourbon
    whipped cream garnish
    chocolate sauce garnish

Beat or blend ingredients until very
smooth & sugar has dissolved. Chill
several hours or overnight. Pour into
sherbet glasses or tiny pots de
crème. Garnish with whipped cream
& a drizzle of chocolate sauce if
desired. A light dessert that knows
no season.

6 servings

Favorite Gatherings
selections from past JLM cookbooks

MENU

Pear Halves
with
Blue Cheese

**Chicken
Crab
Divan**

Wild Rice

**Carrots & Onions
"Sauter"**

**Mocha
Torte**

*California
Fumé Blanc*

•

*With this versatile menu
you can have an elegant
dinner or add wild rice
to the Divan, & serve the
Pears & Mocha torte for
an impressive three
course luncheon.* ❧

Be Milwaukee's Guest
(BMG) 1959

Be Wisconsin's Guest
(BWG) 1964

Be Our Guest
(BOG) 1976

164

Chicken Crab Divan

•

2 packages (10 ounces each) frozen
     artichoke hearts, thawed
     & drained
4 whole skinless chicken breasts,
     split & boned
¼ cup butter
1 can (6½ ounces) crabmeat,
     drained
¼ cup dry sherry
     salt & pepper
3 tablespoons butter
½ cup small whole mushrooms
¼ cup finely chopped onions
3 tablespoons flour
1⅓ cups heavy cream
1 cup milk
½ cup chopped parsley
     dash cayenne
¼ cup grated Parmesan cheese
     paprika

Arrange artichokes on bottom of
buttered 12x8-inch baking dish. In
large skillet, sauté chicken in butter
15 minutes. Add crab. Cook 5 minutes. Add sherry. Allow to evaporate.
Season with salt & pepper. Remove
chicken & crab. Keep warm.

Add remaining butter to pan drippings. Sauté mushrooms & onions.
Sprinkle with flour. Stir until smooth.
Add cream & milk. Stir until thickened. Add parsley & cayenne.
Remove from heat. Blend in Parmesan. Cover artichokes with half the
sauce. Arrange chicken & crab over
sauce. Pour remaining sauce over
top. Sprinkle with paprika. Prepare
up to 3 days in advance. Bring to
room temperature before baking.
Bake 375°F. 20 minutes. (BOG)

8 servings

Carrots & Onions "Sauter"

•

1 pound carrots, peeled & cut into
     1-inch pieces
½ pound small onions, peeled
     water to cover
     salt
2 bay leaves
½ teaspoon thyme
½ tablespoon sugar
2 tablespoons butter

Put carrots & onions in saucepan.
Cover with water. Add salt, bay
leaves, thyme & sugar. Simmer until
crisp-tender. Drain. Melt butter in
pan. Add carrots & onions. Sauté
until golden. (BWG)

4-6 servings

Mocha Torte

•

1 cup flour
1 teaspoon baking powder
6 eggs, separated
1 cup sugar
1 teaspoon vanilla
3 tablespoons cold water

Filling:
1 cup unsalted butter, softened
1½ cups powdered sugar
2 eggs
2 tablespoons strong coffee
1 cup heavy cream, whipped
2-ounces semi-sweet chocolate
½ cup ground nuts, optional

Preheat oven to 350°F. Butter & flour
3 9-inch cake pans.

Sift flour & baking powder. Set aside.
Beat egg whites to soft peaks. Add
sugar gradually. Beat until glossy &
stiff. In another bowl beat egg yolks
until thick. Add vanilla & cold water.
Fold carefully into egg white mixture. Carefully fold in flour. Pour batter into prepared pans. Bake 20
minutes. Remove from pans immediately. Cool.

For the filling, cream butter & sugar.
Add eggs one at a time, beating
well. Add coffee. Remove ⅓ mixture
to a small bowl. Fold ⅓ whipped
cream into small bowl. Spread
butter-coffee-cream between the
3 cake layers.

Add chocolate to remaining butter
mixture. Add remaining whipped
cream to butter-chocolate mixture.

Spread chocolate-butter mixture on
top & sides of cake. Top with a
generous sprinkling of ground nuts
if desired. Refrigerate for at least
1 hour. (BMG)

10-12 servings

Monte's Beef Tenderloin

•

5-pound beef tenderloin,
 room temperature
 larding or bacon to cover meat
1 clove garlic
6 tablespoons butter
3 tablespoons prepared or
 Dijon-style mustard
½ teaspoon salt
½ teaspoon pepper

Mince or process larding with garlic, butter, mustard, salt & pepper. Mix well to make a paste. Pat over beef. Broil 12 minutes. Bake at 350°F. 15 minutes. Let rest 5 minutes before slicing. Adjust broiling & baking times to size of tenderloin. For 3 pounds, broil 10 minutes, bake 10 minutes. For 6 pounds, broil 15 minutes, bake 15 minutes. (BOG)

10-12 servings

Pictured page 120.

•

Ease in entertaining is the advantage of this menu. Enjoy your guests up to the last minute. Bake squashes in the oven the last 15 minutes while the Mushroom Pie & Tenderloin finish baking. Add a salad course if you like.

Mushroom Pie

•

6 tablespoons butter, divided
2 pounds mushrooms, cleaned
 & dried
 juice of ½ lemon
6 tablespoons flour
1 cup chicken stock
½ cup Madeira sherry
½ cup heavy cream
 salt & pepper
1 pie crust to cover baking dish
1 egg, beaten

Preheat oven to 450°F. Butter a shallow 1½-quart baking dish.

In a large skillet, heat 4 tablespoons butter. Add mushrooms & lemon juice. Cover. Cook 10 minutes, shaking pan often. Remove mushrooms to prepared baking dish. Return skillet to heat. Add remaining butter & flour. Stir in stock. Cook, stirring constantly until sauce is thick & smooth. Add Madeira, cream, salt & pepper. Pour sauce over mushrooms. Top with pie crust. Brush crust with beaten egg. Make 4 slits in top of crust. Bake 15 minutes. Reduce heat to 350°F. Bake 10-15 minutes longer. (BMG)

6-8 servings

Lorraine's Philly Velvet

•

1½ cups crushed chocolate wafers
⅓ cup butter, melted
1 package (8 ounces) cream
 cheese, softened
½ cup sugar, divided
1 teaspoon vanilla
2 eggs, separated
1 package (6 ounces) semi-sweet
 chocolate chips, melted
1 cup heavy cream, whipped
¾ cup chopped pecans, optional
 whipped cream for garnish

Preheat oven to 325°F.

Combine wafer crumbs & butter. Mix well. Press on bottom of 9-inch springform pan. Bake 10 minutes. Cool.

In a large bowl, combine cream cheese, ¼ cup sugar & vanilla. Add egg yolks. Beat until well blended. Add chocolate. In another bowl, beat egg whites until soft peaks form. Gradually beat in sugar. Fold whites into cream cheese mixture. Fold in whipped cream. Fold in pecans if desired. Pour into prepared pan. Freeze. May be made days or weeks ahead of time. Remove from freezer 30 minutes before serving. Garnish with additional whipped cream or chocolate leaves. (BOG)

10-12 servings

MENU

Chicken à la Corral

Sliced Potatoes
& Lima Beans
Vinaigrette

Broccoli Casserole with Almonds

Raspberry Torte

*California
Red Merlot*

•

*Completely portable feast
for tailgating. Have
thermal coolers for hot
& cold foods. Place
oven-heated brick in
bottom of thermal chest
to keep casserole hot.
Chicken can be grilled
on site or prepared
at home. Set the table with
finery or disposable
dinnerware.*

Chicken à la Corral

•

4 pound broiler chicken, quartered
   salt & pepper

Sauce:
 2 teaspoons oregano
 1 tablespoon chopped parsley
 2 cloves garlic, minced
 ¼ cup lemon juice
 ½ cup olive oil

Place chicken in broiler pan or
prepare grill. Season with salt &
pepper. Combine sauce ingredients.
Broil or grill chicken 20 minutes
each side. Baste frequently with
sauce. Serve chicken with remaining sauce. (BWG)

4 servings

Broccoli Casserole with Almonds

•

2 packages (10 ounces each) frozen
  chopped broccoli
2 tablespoons butter
2 tablespoons flour
2 cups milk
¾ cup grated Parmesan/
  Romano cheese
1 teaspoon salt
¼ teaspoon ground pepper
¼ pound sliced, sautéed mushrooms
½ cup chopped almonds
4 slices crisp-cooked bacon,
  crumbled
½ cup buttered bread crumbs
  dash paprika

Preheat oven to 350°F. Butter a
1½-quart casserole.

Cook broccoli in small amount of
boiling water or steam until crisp-
tender. Drain. Place in prepared casserole. In a saucepan, melt butter.
Blend in flour. Add milk. Cook, stirring until thick. Add cheese. Stir
until melted. Season with salt & pepper. Add mushrooms. Remove from
heat. Put almonds & bacon on top
of broccoli. Pour cheese sauce over
casserole. Sprinkle with bread
crumbs & paprika. Bake 20 minutes
until browned & bubbly. (BMG)

6 servings

Raspberry Torte

•

1 package (10 ounces) butter or
  shortbread cookies, crushed
6 tablespoons butter, softened
2 cups powdered sugar
1 egg, beaten
1 teaspoon vanilla
1 quart fresh raspberries or
  2 packages (10 ounces each)
  frozen raspberries, thawed,
  drained, reserve ½ of juice
1 cup heavy cream, whipped

Put ½ crumbs in buttered 9x9-inch
pan. Cream butter & sugar. Add egg
& vanilla. Beat until smooth. Spread
over crumbs. Top with raspberries
& reserved juice. Spread whipped
cream over raspberries. Sprinkle
with remaining crumbs. Refrigerate
overnight. (BWG)

6-8 servings

Wisconsin Cheddar Cheese Soup

•

¼ cup butter
½ cup diced carrots
½ cup diced green pepper
½ cup minced onions
⅓ cup flour
4 cups rich chicken stock
6-ounces Wisconsin medium
   cheddar cheese, grated
6-ounces Wisconsin aged cheddar
   cheese, grated
   salt & pepper
   milk to thin soup, optional

Melt butter in 3-quart saucepan.
Add vegetables. Sauté until tender
but not brown. Add flour. Stir. Add
stock. Stir until thickened. Add
cheeses, stirring constantly. Season to
taste. Simmer 15 minutes. Thin with
a small amount of milk if desired.
(BWG)

4-6 servings

Broiled Mushroom Sandwiches

•

1 package (3 ounces) cream cheese,
   softened
1 tablespoon butter
1 egg yolk
1 teaspoon white wine-
   Worcestershire sauce
½ cup finely ground mushrooms
6 slices bread, toasted on 1 side

Beat cheese & butter. Add egg yolk
& Worcestershire. Stir in mushrooms. Spread mushroom mixture
on untoasted side of bread. Broil 5
minutes. Can be served as appetizer.
(BMG)

6 servings

Spicy Oatmeal Cake

•

1 cup quick rolled oats
1⅓ cups boiling water
1¾ cups flour
1¼ teaspoons baking soda
1 teaspoon salt
1 teaspoon cinnamon
½ teaspoon nutmeg
⅔ cup butter
1 cup sugar
1 cup packed dark brown sugar
2 eggs
½ cup chopped nuts

Broiled Caramel Topping:
¼ cup butter
1 cup packed dark brown sugar
1 cup flaked coconut
2 tablespoons light cream

Preheat oven to 350°F. Butter a
13x9-inch pan.

Combine oats & boiling water. Set
aside. Sift together flour, baking
soda, salt, cinnamon & nutmeg. Set
aside. Cream butter & sugars. Add
eggs. Beat well. Stir in oatmeal &
flour mixtures. Add nuts. Stir. Pour
into prepared pan. Bake 35-40 minutes. For topping combine butter,
brown sugar, coconut & cream. Mix
well. Spread on warm cake. Broil
on lowest rack until bubbly & golden
brown. May also make into cupcakes or muffins, baking 20-25
minutes. (BOG)

12 servings

MENU

Grilled Beef Tenderloin

Horseradish-Cream Sauce

Heavenly Spinach

Stornaway Herb Spaghetti

Fresh Berries
&
Triple Crème Cheese

French Red Bordeaux - Margaux

•

You can be in complete control entertaining your favorite person, enjoy conversation & relax. Grill meat while heating the Spinach & Herb Spaghetti 20 minutes before serving. Voilà!

❧

Grilled Beef Tenderloin

•

Seasoning Mixture:
- ¾ cup soy sauce
- ½ cup sugar
- ½ cup toasted sesame seed, crushed
- ¼ cup vegetable oil
- ¼ cup flour
- 2 scallions, sliced
- 1-2 cloves garlic, minced
- ¼ teaspoon ground pepper

3-4 pounds beef tenderloin, cut into filets

Combine seasoning ingredients. 15 minutes before grilling, spread mixture on filets. Grill to desired doneness. (BOG)

6 servings

Heavenly Spinach

•

- 6 tablespoons butter, divided
- ½ pound mushrooms, sliced
- ½ cup mayonnaise
- ½ cup sour cream
- ½ cup grated Parmesan cheese
- 1 package (10 ounces) frozen artichoke hearts, thawed
- 4 packages (10 ounces each) frozen chopped spinach, cooked & drained
  salt & pepper
- 3 large tomatoes, sliced ½-inch thick
- ½ cup dry bread crumbs

Preheat oven to 325°F. Butter a 13x9-inch baking dish.

Sauté mushrooms in 2 tablespoons butter. Combine mayonnaise, sour cream & cheese. Stir in artichokes, spinach & mushrooms. Season with salt & pepper. Pour into prepared dish. Place tomatoes on top of vegetables. Brown bread crumbs in remaining butter. Sprinkle over vegetables. Bake 20 minutes. (BOG)

10 servings

Stornaway Herb Spaghetti

•

- ¾ cup olive oil
- 1 tablespoon butter
- 1 bunch scallions, finely chopped
- 1 bunch parsley, finely chopped
- 1 clove garlic, finely chopped
- 1½ teaspoons fresh chopped rosemary
- 1½ teaspoons fresh chopped basil
  salt
- ¼ teaspoon pepper
- 1 small package (12 ounces) spaghetti, broken into small pieces, cooked & drained
- ½ cup grated Parmesan cheese

Heat oil & butter in skillet. Add scallions, parsley, garlic, herbs, salt & pepper. Heat through. Pour over hot cooked pasta. Toss with Parmesan. May be reheated in oven at low temperature. (BMG)

6 servings

Photographs

Citrus Chicken Salad, recipe 125

Angel Hair Pasta with Cauliflower & Raw Basil-Tomato Sauces, recipe 132

Chocolate Cinnamon Torte, recipe 105

Cabbage & Grapes, recipe 20

Rouladen of Beef, recipe 154

MENU

Mushroom Soup
with
Homemade Croutons

**Hot
Crabmeat
Sandwich**

**Crispy
Potatoes**

**Spinach
Salad**

Warm
Fruit Compote

*New York State
Seyval Blanc*

•

*Line up a dart tournament
in the basement! At
half-time, serve this
satisfying Soup-Sandwich-
Salad dinner to please
all participants,
particularly the host
or hostess.*

❦

Hot Crabmeat Sandwich

•

6-ounces crabmeat
2 packages (3 ounces each) cream
  cheese, softened
3 tablespoons mayonnaise
1 tablespoon chopped onion
½ teaspoon Worcestershire sauce
4 drops hot pepper sauce
  juice of ½ lemon
4 rusks or toasted English muffins
4 slices tomato
  salt & pepper
4 slices sharp cheddar cheese

Combine crab, cream cheese, mayonnaise, onion, Worcestershire, hot
pepper & lemon juice. Cover & chill
overnight. When ready to serve
divide crab mixture evenly on top of
rusks. Top each with a tomato slice.
Season with salt & pepper. Top with
cheese. Bake at 300°F. 30-40 minutes. (BWG)

4 servings

Crispy Potatoes

•

4 large unpeeled Idaho potatoes,
  cut ⅛-inch thick
  salt & pepper
½ cup butter, melted
1 cup grated Parmesan cheese

Preheat oven to 350°F.

Arrange potato slices in single layer
on baking sheets. Season to taste
with salt & pepper. Pour butter over
potato slices. Sprinkle with Parmesan. Bake 45 minutes until crisp.
Drain on paper toweling. (BOG)

6 servings

Spinach Salad

•

Dressing:
2 hard cooked eggs
1 large apple, chopped
1 small onion, chopped
¼ pound blue cheese, crumbled
½ cup mayonnaise
½ cup sour cream
  salt & pepper

1 pound fresh spinach, cleaned
  & chilled

Combine dressing ingredients. Toss
with spinach just before serving.
(BMG)

6-8 servings

Open House
Punch

•

6 bananas
1 can (12 ounces) frozen
  orange juice
1 can (6 ounces) frozen lemonade
1 can (46 ounces) pineapple juice
3 cups water
2 cups sugar
4 quarts chilled ginger ale

Mash bananas in blender with small
amount of orange juice. Combine
with remaining orange juice, lemonade, pineapple juice, water & sugar.
Mix well. Pour into containers that
fit into punch bowl. Freeze until
firm. Two hours before serving, place
frozen mixture in punch bowl. Add
ginger ale. Add vodka, white wine,
or champagne, if desired. (BOG)

50 servings

Dairyland
Casserole

•

3 tablespoons butter, divided
1½ pounds ground chuck or round
⅓ cup sliced scallions
2 cans (8 ounces each) tomato sauce
  dash Worcestershire sauce
1 package (8 ounces) cream
  cheese, softened
½ cup sour cream
1 cup cottage cheese
8-ounces noodles, cooked
  & drained

Preheat oven to 350°F. Butter a
2-quart casserole.

In a large skillet, melt 1 tablespoon
butter. Brown beef. Add scallions.
Add tomato sauce & Worcestershire.
Combine cream cheese, sour cream
& cottage cheese. Place ½ noodles
in bottom of casserole. Cover with
cheese mixture. Put remaining noodles on top of cheeses. Top with
beef mixture. Bake 20 minutes.

May be prepared in advance before
baking. Cover & refrigerate. Bake
45 minutes. (BMG)

8 servings

Brunch
Egg Casserole

•

¼ cup butter
¼ cup flour
1 cup light cream
1 cup milk
¼ teaspoon thyme
¼ teaspoon marjoram
¼ teaspoon basil
1 pound extra sharp cheddar
  cheese, grated
18 hard cooked eggs, sliced thin
1 pound crisp-cooked bacon,
  crumbled
¼ cup finely chopped fresh parsley
  buttered bread crumbs

Preheat oven to 350°F. Butter a
2-2½-quart casserole.

In a medium saucepan, melt butter.
Blend in flour. Add cream & milk.
Cook, stirring until thick. Add herbs
& cheese. Stir until melted. Place
⅓ of sliced eggs in bottom of casse-
role. Sprinkle ⅓ bacon over eggs.
Sprinkle ⅓ parsley. Add ⅓ cheese
sauce over all. Repeat 2 more layers.
Sprinkle top with bread crumbs.
Bake 30 minutes. (BMG)

8-10 servings

Fruit Salad Dressing

•

1 egg, slightly beaten
1 cup sugar
  grated peel & juice of 1 lemon
  grated peel & juice of 1 orange
2 cups heavy cream, whipped

Combine sugar & egg in top of double boiler. Cook until sugar is thoroughly dissolved. Add grated peels & juices. Cool & store in covered jar in refrigerator. Keeps about 1 week. To use, add 2 tablespoons of this concentrated dressing to each cup of whipped cream. Serve as topping for gelatin or fruit salads. Concentrated dressing also good over ice cream. (BMG)

2 cups concentrate

French Breakfast Puffs

•

1½ cups flour
1½ teaspoons baking powder
½ teaspoon salt
½ teaspoon nutmeg
⅓ cup butter, softened
½ cup sugar
1 egg
½ cup milk

Topping:
½ cup butter, melted
½ cup sugar
1 teaspoon cinnamon

Preheat oven to 350°F. Butter 24 2-inch muffin tins.

Sift flour, baking powder, salt, & nutmeg together 3 times. Set aside. Cream butter & sugar until light & fluffy. Beat in egg. Add flour mixture alternately with milk to egg mixture. Blend well. Fill muffin cups ¾-full. Bake 20 minutes. Remove from tins. Roll each puff in melted butter, then in cinnamon-sugar. Variation: For Apple Muffins, reduce milk to ¼ cup. Add ½ cup grated, peeled apple to batter. (BOG)

2 dozen

Frosted Pumpkin Bars

•

2 cups sugar
4 eggs
1 cup vegetable oil
1 can (16 ounces) pumpkin
2 cups flour
2 teaspoons baking powder
1 teaspoon baking soda
1 teaspoon cinnamon
½ teaspoon salt

Creamy Icing:
1 package (8 ounces) cream cheese, softened
6 tablespoons butter, softened
4 cups powdered sugar
1 teaspoon vanilla

Preheat oven to 350°F.

Combine all ingredients except icing. Blend well. Pour into unbuttered 15x10-inch jelly roll pan. Bake 25-35 minutes until toothpick inserted in center comes out clean. Cool. For icing, cream the cheese & butter. Gradually add sugar. Beat until well blended. Stir in vanilla. Frost cooled pumpkin bars with icing. (BOG)

4 dozen

Super Bowl Sunday & the crowds have gathered to enjoy a one o'clock buffet brunch. Serve the Fruit Compote as an appetizer with toothpicks to dip in the fluffy Dressing. Make miniature Puffs & Muffins to ease calorie consciences. Cut Pumpkin Bars into diamond shapes & arrange on a platter.

*Magnums of
Iced California
Brut Champagne*

•

*For a reception of exciting
dimensions, a retirement,
graduation or
wedding, guests can help
themselves or pass
appetizers on silvery
trays. Arrange moiré
ribbons in soft colors on
the serving table to
match the flowers.
Shimmering champagne
flutes, white plates & a
tiered ivory cake greet
guests to the delights
awaiting them.*

Cheese
&
Bacon Puffs

•

1 pound crisp-cooked bacon,
  crumbled
1 cup mayonnaise
1 cup grated sharp cheddar cheese
4 scallions, sliced
1 tablespoon sherry
1 teaspoon white wine-
  Worcestershire sauce
  few drops hot pepper sauce
  melba rounds

Combine bacon, mayonnaise, cheese,
onions, sherry & seasonings. Chill
3 hours or overnight. Keeps up to 3
days. Spread on melba rounds.
Broil until bubbly, 3 minutes. (BOG)

50 servings

Liverwurst
Paté

•

1 teaspoon unflavored gelatin
5 teaspoons Cognac
1 pound fresh, unsmoked liverwurst
¼ cup sour cream
1 teaspoon dry mustard
¼ cup minced onion
2 truffles, finely chopped, optional

Soften gelatin in Cognac. Heat over
low temperature until gelatin completely dissolves. Mash or process
liverwurst with gelatin mixture &
remaining ingredients. Pour into a
plastic-lined 1-pint mold. Chill, covered, several hours or overnight.
Unmold. Serve with toast points or
crackers. (BWG)

6-8 servings

Siberal
Sauce

•

1 cup mayonnaise
2-3 tablespoons spicy tomato relish
1 tablespoon lemon juice
  few drops white wine-
  Worcestershire sauce
3 tablespoons thick, rich cream
  generous splash of gin

Combine ingredients. Cover & chill.
Serve with a selection of iced,
cooked shellfish, "to make a treat
for royalty." (BMG)

1½ cups

Hungarian Veal Goulash

•

1 clove garlic
1 tablespoon bacon fat or
  shortening
3 medium onions, finely chopped
1 tablespoon Hungarian sweet
  paprika
  salt & pepper
2 pounds veal stew meat, cut
  into 1-inch cubes
1½ tablespoons tomato paste
1½ cups tomato juice
2 tablespoons sour cream

Rub heavy skillet with garlic. Discard garlic. Heat bacon fat. Add onions & paprika. Cook until onions become transparent. Season meat with salt & pepper. Add meat to onions. Stir until meat is coated. Add tomato paste & juice. Bring to boil. Reduce heat. Simmer 1½ hours until meat is tender. Stir in sour cream. Continue cooking at a very low heat 30 minutes. Do not boil. To prepare in advance, stir in sour cream. Pour meat into 3-quart casserole. Refrigerate. Bake 50 minutes at 300°F. (BWG)

6 servings

Sprouts Emerald Isle

•

4-ounces cream cheese
¾ cup milk
1 tablespoon sherry
1 tablespoon chopped fresh parsley
1 tablespoon minced onion
½ teaspoon salt
¾ pound fresh brussels sprouts
  or 1 package (10 ounces) frozen,
  cooked crisp-tender
¼ cup bread crumbs

Melt cream cheese in milk over low heat. Add sherry, parsley & onion. Stir until smooth. Pour ½ sauce into bottom of small baking dish. Arrange sprouts over sauce. Add remaining sauce. Top with bread crumbs. Bake 325°F. 30 minutes. (BMG)

4 servings

Pecan Roll

•

6 eggs, separated
¾ cup sugar
1 teaspoon baking powder
1⅔ cups finely ground pecans
2 tablespoons powdered sugar
1 pint French vanilla ice cream,
  softened

Caramel Sauce:
2 tablespoons butter
1 cup heavy cream
¾ cup sugar
1½ cups light brown sugar
  pinch salt

Preheat oven to 375°F. Line bottom of 15x10-inch jelly roll pan with well-buttered wax paper.

In a bowl, beat yolks until light & lemon-colored. Gradually add sugar. Beat until mixture is very thick. Add baking powder. Add pecans. Combine well. In another bowl, beat egg whites until stiff but not dry. Fold egg whites into yolk mixture until smooth & evenly distributed. Pour mixture into prepared pan. Spread smooth. Bake 20 minutes. Sift powdered sugar onto kitchen towel. Turn cake out immediately onto towel. Cool 5 minutes. Remove paper. Roll cake inside towel. Cool. Unroll. Spread with softened ice cream. Re-roll cake. Freeze until serving. For the sauce, melt butter. Add cream. Stir in sugars & salt. Cook, stirring, until sugar is thoroughly dissolved. Slice cake & serve with Caramel Sauce. (BMG)

10-12 servings

Artichokes Adored

•

1 cup mayonnaise
1 cup Parmesan cheese
   bread rounds, toasted on one side
1 package (10 ounces) frozen
   artichokes, cooked, drained
   & quartered

Combine mayonnaise & cheese. Spread small amount on untoasted side of bread rounds. Top with artichoke quarter. Top with additional cheese mixture. Broil until lightly browned. As a dip for assorted crackers, combine cheese mixture & artichokes. Put in small ovenproof dish. Bake until bubbly. (BOG)

8 servings

Spaghetti à la Crab

•

¾ cup butter, divided
2 tablespoons olive oil
5 large shallots, minced
2 packages (6 ounces each) frozen
   Alaskan king crab, thawed,
   not drained
½ cup chopped fresh parsley
1 jar (2 ounces) chopped
   pimientos, drained
2 tablespoons lemon juice
½ teaspoon Italian herbs
1 pound vermicelli, cooked
   & drained
   croutons
   grated Parmesan cheese

Heat ½ cup butter & oil in medium saucepan. Sauté shallots. Add crabmeat. Stir in parsley, pimientos, lemon juice & herbs. Heat 8-10 minutes. Toss hot pasta with remaining butter. Ladle sauce over pasta. Top with croutons & Parmesan. (BOG)

4-6 servings

Sherry Cream Puffs

•

½ cup butter
1 cup boiling water
1¼ cups flour, sifted
¼ teaspoon salt
4 eggs, room temperature

Filling:
½ cup butter
½ cup flour
1½ cups milk
   dash salt
⅔ cup sugar
2 eggs, beaten
½ cup sweet sherry
1 cup heavy cream, whipped
   chocolate sauce

Preheat oven to 450°F. Lightly butter a baking sheet.

Combine butter & water in saucepan over medium heat. Stir until butter melts. Add flour & salt. Stir vigorously over low heat until mixture forms a ball & leaves sides of pan. Remove from heat. Cool slightly. Add eggs, one at a time, beating well after each addition. Drop by tablespoonfuls 2-inches apart on prepared pan. Bake 15 minutes. Reduce heat to 350°F. Bake 25-30 minutes longer. Cool.

For filling, heat butter in medium saucepan. Stir in flour. Add milk. Remove from heat when thickened. Add salt, sugar & eggs, beating well. Add sherry. Cool. Fold in whipped cream.

Split & fill puffs. Serve with a chocolate sauce. (BWG)

12-18 puffs

MENU

Artichokes Adored

Spaghetti à la Crab

Sautéed
Veal Rib Chops

Marinated Hearts of Palm
on
Boston Lettuce

Sherry Cream Puffs

*Italian White
Pinot Bianco
or Pinot Grigio*

•

*Sumptuous dining by candlelight. Impressive to guests yet easy on the hosting duties.
Tie ribbon around the middle of folded square napkins, folded point to the bottom. Pull open points away from ribbon to form a 4-point fan or flower.* ❧

Acknowledgements

Editor
F. Lynn Nelson

Assistant Editor
Carol Manegold

Chapter Chairmen
Quiet Gatherings
Janet Emmerson
Casual Gatherings
Susan Slocum
Simple Gatherings
Suzi Levendusky
Luncheon Gatherings
Diane Armstrong
Celebration Gatherings
Colleen Mortonson & Julie Meier
Elegant Gatherings
Jane Segerdahl & Jaymie Upton
Notable Gatherings
Minnie Chambers & Missie Hawley
Buffet Gatherings
Anne Gallagher & Chris Mitchell
Ethnic Gatherings
Mary Ornst & Mardi Kemp
Favorite Gatherings
Nancy Szatkowski

Production Panel
Diane Armstrong
Valerie Clarke
Rita Larsen
Susan LeFeber
Janet Roethle
Leslie Schumacher

Proofreaders-Indexers
Diane Armstrong
Catherine F. Bauer
Susan Hopwood

Wine Consultant
Daniel H. Nelson

Chairman
Christine S. Krieg

•

Marketing Chairman
Katherine S. Reising

•

Operations Chairman
Allison M. Dittmann

Retail Marketing
Manager
Nancy M. Schmidt

•

Suzi W. Levendusky
Colleen S. Mortonson
Mary M. Ornst

Wholesale Marketing
Manager
Nancee B. Gorenstein

•

Jennifer F. Hillis
Kaye S. Kovacs
Elizabeth R. Loder
Carol A. Mayer
Jaymie I. Upton

Public Relations
Manager
Debra K. Sosey

•

Nancy N. Stall

Operations
Susan H. Covi
Susan D. Jones
Susan L. LeFeber
Marilynn J. Wilke

Fundraising
Jeanne L. Grist
Jane L. Rice

Special Advisors
Vice President Supportive Services
Louise G. Dill

•

Director of Ways & Means
Judy A. Hansen

•

Treasurer
Mary Anne K. Wawrzyn

The GATHERINGS committee would like to commend on behalf of the Junior League of Milwaukee the following people for use of their recipes & invaluable assistance in testing & typing recipes:

Stephanie Ackerman
Suzanne Aiken
Patricia S. Algiers
Linda Allen
Helen Baur Allis
Louise Q. Anderson
Susan Anderson
Kathleen Arenz
Diane Armstrong
Patsy Aster
Amy Balge
Beth Bauer
Cathy Bauer
Leslie Barkow
Linda Barlow
Donna Baumgartner
Helen B. Bechthold
Charlotte Becker
Diane Bedran
Nancy Bell
Cathy Bellovary
Jodi Bender
Terry Beneske
Louise Berg
Mary Bero
Lucy Bibby
Kathe Biersach
Fran Birchhill
Holly Blake
Blue Mound Country Club
Janet Bode
Boder's on the River Restaurant
Kathleen Bonady
Patricia Bond
Carolyn Borelli
Barbara Borges
Georgia Bouda
Bee Boyd
Kathleen Callan Brady
Holly Braun
Claudine Eldred Breidster
Allison Briber
Denise Brondino-Carini
Cathy Brown

Joanne Brown
Eleanor Hamilton Browne
Bobbie Buening
Janet Burdick
Barbara Busch
Paula Calhoun
Denise Cassidy
Minnie Chambers
Annemarie Gabor Christiansen
Jeanne Christiansen
Nancy Nichols Christy
Pam Chumbley
Nancy Collopy
Mary Lou Borders Cook
The Corral Restaurant
Anne Courtney
Debbie Crane
Patty Curtes
Judy Dalecky
Kathy Daly
Alberta Statkus Darling
Mary Darling
Linda Davis
Maureen Day
Agatha Dehmel
Nancy DeMarsh
Mary Russel Dengel
Linda DeRosa
Louise Dill
Melody B. Dill
Deloris Donnelly
Louise Doornek
Kathy Drum
Patti Dwyer
Pam Elliott
Janet Emmerson
Diane R. Emory
Mary Emory
Joy Duquette Engroff
Gala Eppstein
Lynn Epstein
Stephanie Eron
Laura Fabick
Marjorie S. Feerick

Christine Ferber
Jane Fitzgibbons
Teena Flanner
Diane Foley
Tory Folliard
Patricia Ivins Foster
Jocelyn Kilham Fothergill
Marjorie Fowler
Liz Frank
Linda Lease Franklin
Debbie Freeman
Barb Fuldner
Connie Merker Fullwood
Kate Gaertner
Ann Gallagher
Janet Garmer
Marilyn Gary
Micky Gerschke
Rose Glaisner
Beth Gochnauer
Anne Godsey
Susan Goetzinger
Ann Gorenstein
Nancee Gorenstein
Georgiana Gormley
Beth Gottsacker
Mary Montgomery Goulet
Betsy Gritzmacher
Joan Krejci Grzesiak
Ellen Gutierrez
Lindi Haag
Charlene Haas
Keri Hadler
Judy Hansen
Sue Harrington
Judy Haugsland
Missie Hawley
Virginia Wild Hayssen
Jill Sherry Heavenrich
Holly Helf
Peggy Helz
Jill Herbst
Janet Herr
Susan Wilson Hertzberg

Jenny Hillis
Dolores Hodnet
Jane Hodnik
Beth Hoffman
Susanne Holsen
Barbara Holtz
Patricia Holzmann
Susan Hopwood
Kathy Howell
Penny Isermann
Francie Ishmael
Valerie Jablonka
Dee Jamison
Jane Jansen
Barbara Janssen
Jody John
Cindy Johnson
Julie Johnson
Peggy Johnson
Vicki Johnson
Sue Jones
Margaret Joppe
Sue Jordan
Laura Jorgensen
Holly Jurss
Karen Juzenas
Kitti Kadlec
Phoebe Kaminsky
Ginny Kannenberg
Susan Kaufman
Karen Keating
Mardi Kemp
Sandra Ketter
Maryglen Kieckhefer
Shelley Bundy King
Lucinda Kitzke
Linda Klimowicz
Aimee Klundt
Genevieve G. Koenig
Kaye Ellen Kovacs
Lora Watts Krauthoefer
Marina Krejci
Chris Krieg
Barb Krueger

Gerri Krysiak
Anne LaBudde
Edith Courteen Landis
Vida Langenkamp
Mary Lardner
Rita Larsen
Mary B. Laudon
Marge Laughlin
Raquel Garcia Lauritzen
Susan LeFeber
Suzanne LeFeber
Lucile C. Leland
Ann Levendusky
Doray Levendusky
Susan Levendusky
Elizabeth R. Loder
Lola Loepfe
Patricia Longabaugh
Sharon K. Lundgen
Chris Lydon
Patricia Lyons
Vita MacArthur
Janey Minahan MacNeil
Madeleine's Restaurant
Carol Manegold
Sally S. Manegold
Andrea Topetzes Mann
Mary Marshall
Jane Martin
Marcia Matchette
Tracy Mayfield
Diane McCormick
Karen McCormick
Paulie McCown
Patricia G. McCulloch
Marilyn McGriff
Joan Meehan
Julie Meier
Astrid Schlicke Mellencamp
Ann Miller
Mary Keith Miller
Patricia Minks
Anita Mitchell

Gloria Mitchelson
Holly Moebius
Chris Mitchell
Judy Moon
Marjorie Moon
Betty Moore
Lyndon Moore
Deborah Mortensen
Colleen Mortonson
Jill Muehlmeier
Laurie Mueller
Mary Ellen Mueller
Mary Mulcahy
Nadine Mundt
Mary Myers
Liz Neff
Beverly Nelson
F. Lynn Nelson
Kay Nordeen
Phoebe Norton
Katharine Elwell Noyes
Pam Olsen
Linda Olson
Bonnie Ornst
Mary Ornst
Mildred Ornst
Eugenie Bournique Pabst
Joyce Pabst
Kathy Palmer
Marti Palmer
Katie Parent
Jane Wykle Parker
Lynne Pearcy
Nancy Peters
Salli Watts Peterson
Julie Petri
Jane Phillips
Nancy Phillips
Jaquelin Pillsbury
Ildy Poliner
Barbara Quilling
Deborah Quirk

Mary Raitt
Patricia Ranger
Karin Raymond
Laura Rees
Deanna Crary Reeser
Katherine S. Reising
Anne Rice
Mary Rickmeier
Laurie Roberts
Janet Roethle
Cathy Rowe
Susan Ryan
Kathy Sammons
Linda Sapp
Marlene Schilffarth
Mary Marcato Schley
Jan Schmidt
Mary Kay Schmidt
Nancy Schmidt
Maureen Schroeder
Leslie Schumacher
Patty Schuyler
Meredith Scrivner
Jane Seaman
Jane Segerdahl
Andrea Sellinger
Virginia Rahel Shackleton
Judy Sherman
Maureen Sievers
Vicki Sileno
Jane Simpson
Susan Slocum
Beth Smith
Mary Smith
Sue Smith
Linda Solveson
Elizabeth Van Antwerp Sorgi
Joan Spector
Janet Spero
Barbara C. Steinmetz
Susan Steldt
Judith Stephens

Trisha Stephenson
Kim Stobbs
Lynn Stuhr
Dolly Sullivan
Karen Sullivan
Nancy Szatkowski
Kekee Szorcsik
Gale Tanger
Val Teague
Barbara Terschan
Barb Timmerman
Derse Todd
Roseann Tolan
Elaine Toledo
Angela Topetzes
Patricia Treiber
Terry Trott
Shari Truitt
Pam Uihlein
Polly Strauss Uihlein
Jaymie Upton
Nancy Vetter
Kathleen Greene Vogel
Cindy Wachs
Laurel Walker
Carole Walthers
Mary Anne Wawrzyn
Jean Weissmueller
Barbara Moquin Whealon
Grace Smith White
Lesley White
Marilynn Wilke
Connie Willems
Katie Withers
Gail Miller Wray
Christie Wrenn
Mary Wuesthoff
Mary York
Letitia S. Young
Jan Zakrajsheck
Eileen Ziegler
Penny Ziegler
Sharon Zurawski

**The Junior League of Milwaukee would like to thank the following people
for submitting recipes & providing suggestions to GATHERINGS:**

Molly Abrohams
Debbie Antonio
Sharon Armas
Blythe Bathrick
Priscilla Beadell
Lynne Belcher
Linda P. Bell
Mary Borges
Betsy Boswell
Patricia Brash
Mary Brobson
Gordon F. Burgess, M.D.
Patricia M. Burgess
Marguerite L. Burghardt
Julie Carpenter
Ardis Cerny
Linda Christensen
Judy Christl
Martha Conrad Clark
Sandy Dawson
Laurie Digate
Mary Dolaharty
Myra Dorros
Madeline Ells

Sue Erlacher
Barbara Faude
Christine Ferber
Connie Frank
Susan Freedy
Trudy Frentz
Sandy Garmer
Helen Genskow
Judy Gilg
Karen Glanert
Constance Godfrey
Mary Beth Goodspeed
Judy Gorsuch
Suzanne Greene
Eileen Gruesser
Candice Haight
Tina Hartwig
Gretchen Henry
Marlene Hirschberg
I'Nell Hogue
Mary Hopkins
Jayne Jordan
Laura LaVanway

Kathy Lee
Betsy Lierk
Eilene Lust-Stevens
Jeanne Machata
Lois Marincic
Cindy Martin
Mary Mayer
Ruth McCoy
Kathy Mesick
Ada Moegenburg
Jean Neal
Kathy Nelson
Katherine Peppler
Judy Perry
Carol Petersen
Karen Petersen
Elly Pick-Jacobs
Pam Pierce
Julie Polakowski
Mary S. Pollock
Jeanne Reed
Judith Ross
Holly Ryan

Patricia Sara
Mary Lee Schweiger
Barbara Shearer
Deborah Singer Silvestri
Lyn Skeen
Lyn Slater
Judith Stark
Marion Stewart
Nancy Sturm
Sue Swindells
Nicole Teweles
Kathleen Timberman
Joann Villavicencio
Sherida Wank
Jean Wenkler
Tracy Wickwire
Ellen Wiese
Laurel Wilkens
Peg Willson
Ann Winchell
Geraldine Woody
Cheryl Worthington
Eileen Ziegler

The cover has been donated by the Brooks family in memory of:

Genevieve H. Brooks

We would like to thank the following sponsors for their generous contributions to GATHERINGS:

Anheuser-Busch, Inc.
Somebody Still Cares About Quality
Milwaukee, Wisconsin

First Wisconsin Foundation
Milwaukee, Wisconsin

The Grenadier's Restaurant, Inc.
Milwaukee, Wisconsin

HM Graphics, Inc.
Milwaukee's Custom Printer
Milwaukee, Wisconsin

Marshall Field's
Milwaukee, Wisconsin

Usinger's Famous Sausage
America's Finest Since 1880
Milwaukee, Wisconsin

Recipes Sponsored in Honor of:

Mrs. Robert Auspach	*Gladys Grist*	*Janet Loosen*	*Peggy Schuster*
Mrs. Douglas A. Baske	*Mrs. Leonard Gorenstein*	*Emily Luczak*	*Mrs. Douglas Seaman*
Wilma K. Bauer	*Lillian Stroschein Gutknecht*	*Mary Ann Krembs McDevitt*	*Margery Sengbusch*
Nan Blackburn	*Mrs. Robert L. Hillis*	*Bernice L. Meehan*	*Carolyn Skuara*
Barbara Blutstein	*Amelia Hodnik*	*Kathy Mesick*	*Alma Slatten*
Happy Levis Booth	*Jo Hyman*	*Mrs. Keith Miller*	*Walter J. Smith*
Mrs. Marie Botsch	*Emma S. Kaszubowski*	*Lyndon Moore*	*Edward Larscheid Styles*
Josephine Wigdale Brennan	*Mrs. William Keith*	*Mary Mortonson*	*Julia Larscheid Styles*
Mrs. Felix Brown	*Marquirite Killian*	*Pat Norris*	*Dolly Sullivan*
Mary Lou Cardio	*Lauren Krieg*	*Mrs. Daniel P.J. O'Connor*	*Theresa Thiele*
Bobbie T. Cosper	*Raymond Krieg*	*Allison Ornst*	*Mrs. Joseph E. Tierney, Sr.*
Mrs. Owen Crenshaw	*Simone Koch*	*Bob Ornst, Jr.*	*Fay Kalafat Topetzes*
Anne Crowley	*Billie Ann Kubly*	*Isabelle Polacheck*	*Maurine Harvey Truitt*
Margadette M. Demet	*Florence Lahman*	*Karole Read*	*University of Illinois-*
Betty Dill	*Kathleen Brennan Lee*	*Ruth Rice*	*College of Communications*
Matsy Ells	*Helene Lesynski*	*Terrence K. Rice*	*Mrs. Cora Walker*
Elizabeth Ann Fortmann	*John Levendusky*	*Leona K. Roussy*	*Connie Welch*
Louise Fortmann	*Tess Lewis*	*Bob Schmidt*	*Grace S. White*
Mrs. Robert G. Friedman	*Sandra Liebkemann*	*Mary Kay Schmidt*	*Donna Wieland*
Eileen E. Gardner	*Mary Lipnicke*	*Robby Schmidt*	*Olga Wilke*
Sally Levis Gerlinger	*Mrs. Fred Lipscomb*	*Teddy Schmidt*	*June Zinkgraf*

Production Credits

Typesetting
Zahn-Klicka-Hill

Color Separations
Mandel Company

Keyliners
Barb Adams & Jerry Adams

Printing
HM Graphics, Inc.

Binding
Ringier America, Inc.

Photographic Properties

Dave Boyles
Kathleen Hibscher
Scott Lanza
Sharon K. Lundgren
Carol Manegold
Lorene Johnson
Effie Meyer
F. Lynn Nelson
Steven Plater
Kathryn Sherwood
Rachel J. Stephens
Hans J. Ziegler

Acknowledgements

Patricia R. Connors
Dennis Frankenberry
Diane Germanotta
Glenn Gilchrist
Don Hill
Rick Mandel
Kathleen Marquardt
Effie Meyer
Robert L. Meyer
Ellen Rolfes
James S. Sandstrom

Index

INDEX

Please send me _____ copies of GATHERINGS @ $21.95 per copy plus $2.50 shipping/handling charge for each book. Wisconsin residents please add 5½% sales tax.

Make checks payable to Junior League of Milwaukee or charge to VISA or MasterCard.

Account # _____

Signature _____ Exp. Date _____

Name _____

Address _____

City _____

State _____ Zip _____

GATHERINGS

A collection of highly entertaining menus by The Junior League of Milwaukee.

Junior League of Milwaukee, Inc.
626 N. Broadway
Milwaukee, WI 53202
Tel: 800-365-6613   (276-6613 in Milwaukee)

To:
Name _____

Address _____

City _____

State _____ Zip _____

Mailing Label – Please Print

The Nation's Best Community Cookbook
1987 IACP/Seagram Award

— —

Please send me _____ copies of GATHERINGS @ $21.95 per copy plus $2.50 shipping/handling charge for each book. Wisconsin residents please add 5½% sales tax.

Make checks payable to Junior League of Milwaukee or charge to VISA or MasterCard.

Account # _____

Signature _____ Exp. Date _____

Name _____

Address _____

City _____

State _____ Zip _____

GATHERINGS

A collection of highly entertaining menus by The Junior League of Milwaukee.

Junior League of Milwaukee, Inc.
626 N. Broadway
Milwaukee, WI 53202
Tel: 800-365-6613   (276-6613 in Milwaukee)

To:
Name _____

Address _____

City _____

State _____ Zip _____

Mailing Label – Please Print

The Nation's Best Community Cookbook
1987 IACP/Seagram Award

6/19